GUIDE

to

MANUSCRIPTS COLLECTIONS

of

The Norwegian-American
Historical Association

Compiled and Edited
by
LLOYD HUSTVEDT

Collection groups processed and catalogued
by
Beulah Folkedahl and Charlotte Jacobson

NORTHFIELD, MINNESOTA 1979
Norwegian-American Historical Association

Introduction

The collecting of books, periodicals, newspapers, manuscripts, and other documents relevant to Norwegian migration and to the Norwegian immigrant's subsequent life in the New World began with the founding of the Norwegian-American Historical Association (NAHA) in 1925, one hundred years after the first shipload of emigrants left Norway for New York. Ole E. Rølvaag, the Association's first secretary (1925–1931) was an energetic collector. J. Jørgen Thompson, his successor, gave sustained attention to new acquisitions during his long tenure as secretary (1931–1958). Carlton C. Qualey served the NAHA for a time as a field agent and collected valuable material that otherwise might have been lost. Theodore C. Blegen, Kenneth O. Bjork, more recently Odd S. Lovoll, and others have turned in papers they have uncovered while researching various aspects of Norwegian-American history. Rolf Erickson in Evanston, Illinois, is responsible for securing many collections from the Chicago area. A large portion of the existing collection has, however, come as voluntary donations from friends and members of the NAHA.

Proper organization of the manuscripts collection began in 1960, when Beulah Folkedahl became the Association's first curator of manuscripts. Approximately eighty percent of the collection groups described in this *Guide* were organized and catalogued by her before she died in 1971. The remaining groups have been processed and catalogued by Charlotte Jacobson, a former librarian at St. Olaf College who replaced Miss Folkedahl as curator in 1974.

The descriptions prepared for the *Guide* are edited and reduced — often drastically — versions of the basic descriptions prepared earlier by Miss Folkedahl and Miss Jacobson. The original description catalogue (5×8 cards) should be examined by researchers who visit our archives. It contains a more complete inventory than does the *Guide* and gives more attention to detail, such as names of donors and lists of correspondents.

For interested researchers and future donors, brief mention should be made about other segments of the NAHA archival collection that fall outside the scope of this *Guide*, namely, books, periodicals, and newspapers.

The Association has collected and continues to collect all American imprints (books, pamphlets, tracts, etc.) in the Norwegian language, regardless of quality or topic; all books published for or about Norwegian Americans, regardless of language used or where published; to a controlled degree, books written by Norwegian immigrants or their descendants; and books brought to this country by the immigrants themselves or those which proved to be popular reading in their homes. No master list is available for publications falling into the categories mentioned above; thus no firm estimate can be made as to how complete our collection might be. Some 8,000 volumes, however, fall into one category or another. Some years ago the Association's books were integrated with the St. Olaf College Library holdings, but ownership identity has been retained.

The periodical collection is located in the archives and can be rated as quite complete. It includes a number of journals published in Norway. These may have only incidental value to migration research.

The newspaper collection falls short of what might be wished. This is explained in part by the fact that the NAHA was established seventy-eight years after the first Norwegian-American newspaper appeared on the scene in the Middle West. There are complete bound files of *Amerika* (1884–1922), Madison, Wisconsin; *Reform* (1891–1941), Eau Claire, Wisconsin; and *Washington Posten* (1889–1964), Seattle, Washington. The remaining thirty titles range from fairly complete to fragmentary. Fortunately the Koren Library at Luther College, Decorah, Iowa, has an excellent collection of Norwegian-American newspapers, and a large portion of it has been microfilmed. If one considers collectively the newspaper holdings of the Koren Library, the NAHA, the state historical societies of Minnesota, North Dakota, and Wisconsin, and several other repositories, the composite picture is good.

Some acknowledgments are in order. The contributions made by Charlotte Jacobson and the late Beulah Folkedahl have been alluded to, but their significance merits emphasis by repetition. Elaine Kringen has typed the manuscript. Siri Hustvedt assisted in checking the collections for missing or needed additional information. Two St. Olaf College students, Joy Buikema Fjærtoft and Elisabeth Stitt, helped to prepare the index. Most of all, we are indebted to the National Historical Publications and Records Commission, Washington, D.C., for a grant of $4,000. Without this assistance, the publication of this *Guide* would not have been possible.

Lloyd Hustvedt, Secretary
Norwegian-American
Historical Association

Explanation

Most of the NAHA manuscripts are stored in document boxes measuring five inches in width, ten inches in height, and slightly more than twelve or fifteen and one-half inches in length. Such a box will hold approximately 500 single manuscript pages. The current collection requires 1,268 such boxes. Bulkier material such as ledgers and scrapbooks are stored in cases measuring twenty inches in length and twelve inches in height and width (current inventory, 27). Items that will not fit into either boxes or cases are wrapped or rolled. The *Guide* does not indicate when a collection group may have two or more storage locations, but this information appears in the card catalogue.

When they are known, the pertinent dates for the creator of a collection are entered. When the origin of the collection is a person (as opposed to organization or institution) and when only the year of his birth or death is known, the letter "b" or "d" precedes the date. The letter "b" also applies to persons known or assumed to be living at the time the *Guide* was published. The dates that follow the title circumscribe the collection in time. For example, if the title is "Diary," the dates indicate when the first and last entries were made. If the collection contains multiple items, the dates of the earliest and latest documents are recorded. When no dates can be established, the abbreviation "n.d." is used. Save for a few cases where misunderstanding is possible, no indication is given that a document is in handwritten (manuscript) form. The term "typescript" is used for both reproduced and original typewritten documents. Each collection group has a sequence number and a P (abbreviation for papers) number. The index refers to the first; the second indicates shelf location.

When references are made to the Norwegian-American Historical Association, the initials NAHA are used. From time to time references are made to *Norwegian-American Studies and Records*, a series published by the NAHA. The shorter term *Studies and Records* is used in the *Guide*.

As users of the *Guide* will note, some items not normally classified as manuscripts or personal papers have been included. For example, photographs, pamphlets, and reprints have not been culled out when they were found to have a close relationship with the creator of the collection. In other instances the rareness, physical condition, or the diminutive size of some commercially printed materials have been included for security reasons.

A number of descriptions include some biographical information about the creator of the collection. The purpose is not to honor the individual but to add a descriptive dimension to the collection itself. When a person is assumed to be well-known, little biographical data is included. The size of the collection also enters as a factor. For example, if the collection is small, little information is provided even if the person in question holds a prominent position in Norwegian-American history. When the collection is large, the opposite is generally true.

Attention is called to the fact that collections which fall outside the category "manuscripts" are described at the end of the *Guide* under the heading "Special Collections."

Dedicated
to
CHARLOTTE JACOBSON

COLLECTIONS

Collections

1. AABERG ACADEMY. PAPERS, 1914–1921. 4 items. P 470.
Correspondence and reports concerning a Devils Lake, North Dakota, school held by Pastor Ole H. Aaberg for his parishioners during the winter months from 1888 to 1903.

2. AAKER FAMILY. PAPERS, 1845–1969. 3 boxes. P 1.
Papers of Knud Saavesen Aaker (1797–1873) and his descendants: articles, correspondence, Civil War letters, notebooks, scrapbooks, albums, clippings, family histories, charts, and a diary. Includes letters from B. J. Muus, G. Hoyme, and Knute Finseth.

3. AAKER'S BUSINESS COLLEGE. REPORT, n.d. 1 item. P 469.
Report about a business school founded at Fargo, North Dakota, in 1902 by Hans H. Aaker and continued by Oscar J. Hanson.

4. AANAAS, LEIF TORGRIMSON. EMIGRATION PAPER, 1848. 1 item. P 2.
Release document issued to Aanaas and his family upon their departure for America from Telemark, Norway.

5. AASE HAUGEN HOME. PAPERS, 1915–1974. 6 items. P 627.
Constitution, brochure, and history of a Decorah, Iowa, retirement home founded in 1914 by the Norwegian Lutheran Church of America.

6. AASEN, JOHANNES JOHNSEN (b. 1860). PAPERS, 1862–1881. 8 items and 1 volume. P 3.
A vaccination certificate and daily account of a Norwegian-trained businessman's journey (1881) from Bergen to Morris, Illinois.

7. AASEN, NIELS W. (1878–1925). PAPERS, 1925. 2 items. P 4.
A clipping and a pamphlet concerning the Aasen Corporation of America, Stoughton, Wisconsin, and its Norwegian founder. Aasen invented several military devices including the hand grenade, deep water bomb, modern trench mortar, and the air bomb. Aasen lived in the United States less than two years.

8. AASGAARD, JOHAN A. (1876–1966). PAPERS, 1934–1957. 7 items.
    P 5.
Biographical data about a Lutheran clergyman who was president of
Concordia College, Moorhead, Minnesota, and later president of the
Evangelical Lutheran Church.

9. AASLAND, OLE HERBRANDSEN (1795–1864). PAPERS, 1831–1846,
    1934. 19 items. P 6.
Emigration papers, receipts, promissory notes, and recipes of a
Norwegian-born farmer at Kendall, New York.

10. ABRAHAMSEN, CHRISTIAN (b. 1887). PAPERS. 17 items. P 891.
Biographical information about a Norwegian-born artist who came to
the United States in 1918. He established himself in Chicago and became widely known as a portrait artist.

11. ADER, SVERRE H. PAPERS, ca. 1931. Typescript, 408 pages. P 7.
"Amerika feberen begynner: Av norsk utvandrings historie 1839"
dealing with the 1839 Norwegian immigrants and the causes and results
of their migration. A letter (1839) by Ansten Nattestad, Jefferson
Prairie, Wisconsin, is included.

12. AGER, WALDEMAR THEODOR (1869–1941). PAPERS, 1874–1943.
    7 boxes. P 601.
Papers of a Norwegian-born journalist, author, and lecturer: clip-
pings, articles, correspondence, manuscripts of books, periodicals,
poems, programs, records, sketches, and stories dealing with subjects
such as Norwegian culture and heritage, Americanism, memorials to
Norwegians in America, Norwegians in Eau Claire, Wisconsin, and
temperance.
    Among the correspondents are Carl F. Berg, Arne K. Berger, L. W.
Boe, H. A. Ecker, John O. Evjen, Ruth Fjeldsaa, Sigurd Folkestad,
Einar Haugen, John Heitman, H. R. Holand, Simon Johnson, Arne
Kildal, Lars Lillehei, E. L. Mengshoel, Jon Norstog, Torkel Oftelie, K.
Prestgard, D. G. Ristad, Mrs. O. E. Rølvaag, Johan Selnes, T. A.
Siqueland, Edvard Skille, Charles C. W. Storck, J. L. Urheim, and
Alexander Wiley.
    Ager was editor of *Reform*, Eau Claire, Wisconsin. Among his best
known books are *Paa drikkeondets konto* (1894), *Kristus for Pilatus*
(1910), *Oberst Heg og hans gutter* (1916), *På veien til smeltepotten*
(1917), *Gamlelandets sønner* (1926), and *Hundeøine* (1929).

13. ALBERTSON, HANS (1846–1931). PAPERS, 1847–1890. 9 items.
    P 8.
Papers of a Norwegian-born farmer in Green County, Wisconsin: a
land indenture, tax receipts, marriage certificate, and baptismal records.

14. ALBION ACADEMY. PAPERS, 1916–1966. 40 items. P 471.
Articles, correspondence, and reports of a secondary school at Al-

bion, Wisconsin, founded in 1854 by the Seventh Day Baptist Church and operated by Norwegian Lutheran congregations in the area from 1901 to 1918.

15. AMDAL, MARIE ODLAND. LETTER, 1915. 1 item. P 846.
Copy of a letter entitled "My Trip Across the Ocean." The letter relates the author's experiences leaving Norway, crossing England, and during the journey across the Atlantic on the ship *Northland*.

16. AMERICA LETTERS. PAPERS, 1807–1956. 7 boxes. P 435.
Original, typescript and photocopies of letters written by Norwegian immigrants to relatives, friends, and newspapers in Norway, including letters and articles treating emigration to Australia, Canada, New Zealand and Queensland. A representative selection of these letters are independently described. See Nos. 160, 196, 228, 243, 246, 285, 286, 317, 413, 433, 443, 476, 485, 498, 530, 547, 772, 874, 903, 920, 925.
A large portion of the letters were collected by Theodore C. Blegen. Some 300 letters have been collected by Norsk Historisk Kjeldeskrift Institutt in Oslo, Norway. The collection contains an index.

17. AMERICAN RELIEF FOR NORWAY, INC. PAPERS, 1940–1952. 42 boxes and 5 volumes. P 646.
Papers of the association incorporated as Norwegian Relief, Inc. (changed to American Relief for Norway, Inc. in 1944) under the laws of Illinois, April 19, 1940, ten days after the invasion of Norway during World War II. Founded to "relieve distress" among the people of Norway, it was officially dissolved December 31, 1946.
Correspondence, reports, and publicity materials, fall into five categories: clothing drive files, executive secretary's files, president's files, treasurer's files, and corporate records.
Topics treated include clothing drives; collection of funds; purchase and distribution of food, clothing, shoes, drugs; publicity; problems of storage and transportation; relations with governments; merging of relief agencies; affiliation with the National War Fund; women's activities; tools for Finmark; and the Anfin O. Sather trust fund for the National Association of Norwegian Agricultural Clubs.

18. AMUNDSEN, ROALD (1872–1928). PAPERS, 1907–1928. 22 items. P 10.
Clippings, programs, and speeches concerning Amundsen's explorations.

19. ANDERS, J. OLSON. BIOGRAPHY, n.d. Booklet, 22 pages. P 437.
"From Selbu to the Dakota Prairie," an account of the life of Andrew Olson (Størset) and his frontier experiences at Andover, South Dakota, as related by his son.

20. ANDERSEN, ARLOW W. (b. 1906). MANUSCRIPT, 1962. Typescript, 398 pages. P 11.

Manuscript of *The Salt of the Earth* (1962), a history of Norwegian-Danish Methodism in America.

21. ANDERSEN, ARTHUR (1885–1947). PAPERS, 1925–1947. 33 items. P 13.

Information on, and articles and speeches by Andersen dealing with financial and economic problems. He was the founder and senior partner of the internationally known accounting firm, Arthur Andersen and Company, and president of NAHA (1936–1942).

22. ANDERSEN, LEWIS O. ESSAY, n.d. Typescript, 3 pages. P 14.

"People's ' Revolution," written during World War II, discusses nationalism vs. internationalism.

23. ANDERSON, ANDREW RUNNI (b. 1876). ARTICLES, 1925. 2 items. P 15.

Articles by a Norwegian-born professor of classical languages at the University of Utah, dealing with John Owen, Henrik Harder, and Ludvig Holberg.

24. ANDERSON, CHRISTIAN (b. 1874). ADDRESS, 1927. Pamphlet, 19 pages. P 556.

Excerpts from an address entitled "Hvad var den gamle norske synodens stilling i lære og praksis?" by the president of the Norwegian Synod of the American Evangelical Lutheran Church ("Little Synod") concerning the old Norwegian Synod's doctrinal position and practice.

25. ANDERSON, HARRY H. LOCAL HISTORY, 1939. 22 pages. P 722.

"Early Scandinavian Settlement in Milwaukee County." Published in *Historical Messenger of the Milwaukee County Historical Society*, March, 1969.

ANDERSON, JOHN. See John Anderson Publishing Company, No. 412.

26. ANDERSON (NORLAND), PAUL (1821–1891). BIOGRAPHY, 1948. I item. Typescript, 4 pages. P 16.

A biography of a Norwegian-born Lutheran clergyman in Chicago (1848–1861; 1876–1884), by Arthur E. Alfsen. Anderson introduced English services and Sunday school, and helped organize Northern Illinois Synod, Scandinavian Augustana Synod, and Norwegian Augustana Synod.

27. ANDERSON, RASMUS BJØRN (1846–1936). PAPERS, 1869–1965. 126 items. P 717.

Clippings, correspondence, genealogy, music, pamphlets, and photographs of a Wisconsin-born author, diplomat, editor, and educator. The clippings deal largely with Anderson controversies as do letters by Laur. Larsen and Johs. B. Wist.

Anderson was professor of Norwegian at the University of Wisconsin, United States minister to Denmark, and editor of *Amerika* (1898–1922), Madison, Wisconsin.

28. ANDERSON, SIGURD. LECTURES, 1961–1963. 2 items, 23 pages. P 17.

A lecture entitled "Lawyers in the Civil War" delivered before the Bar Association of the District of Columbia, and an outline of an address, "Whatever happened to Ole," delivered before Det Norske Nationalforbund, Minneapolis, Minnesota.

29. ANDREASSEN, A. B. CATALOGUE, n.d. 1 item. P 18.

Norwegian-born artist and manager of a Norwegian art shop in Minneapolis, who dealt in reproductions of Norwegian art.

30. ANDRESEN, ALFRED. ADVERTISEMENTS, 1897. 3 items. P 19.

Advertisements from the firm, Alfred Andresen, the Western Importer, Minneapolis, established in 1893, regarding such items as Sal-Sanitatis and other medications, spinning wheels, and *kromkagejern*.

31. ANDRESEN, NICOLAI (1889–1963). MEMOIRS, 1960 (?). Typescript, 41 pages. P 847.

Reminiscences from the author's home in Oslo and from his visits to other parts of Norway at the turn of the century, written during the last twenty-five years of Mr. Andresen's life in the United States.

32. ANDRESON, (ANDERSON) OLE (ca. 1822–1864). CORRESPONDENCE, 1864. 20 items. P 20.

Letters from a Norwegian-born farmer to his wife at Wiota, LaFayette County, Wisconsin, who enlisted February 2, 1864, with Company H of the Third Wisconsin Regiment of Infantry and was killed May 25, 1864, at Dallas, Georgia. Andreson gives instructions to his wife regarding farm operations, purchase of land, and collection of his pay. He describes the health and living conditions of his company, the slaves he meets, destruction of property, and the battle engagement north of Atlanta. Two letters from Rice Lake, Wisconsin, are descriptive of logging days.

33. ANFINSEN, TØRRES (b. 1816). PAPERS, 1819–1854. 6 items. P 797.

Immigration papers, citizenship papers, and a letter written from Ottawa, Illinois, 1851.

ANNIVERSARIES. See Special Collections, No. 936.

34. ANSTENSEN, ANSTEN (b. 1899). PAPERS, 1916. 2 items. P 892.

A *Sjøfartsbok*, with notations for 1916–1918, and a notebook entitled "Norske Stiler."

35. ANTHONISEN, GEORG B. PAPERS, 1934–1940. 8 items. P 22.

Papers of a Norwegian-born inventor and engineer: correspondence and blueprints of his spring spikes and variable twisted track spikes.

36. ANUNDSEN PUBLISHING COMPANY. PAPERS, 1922–1934. 11 items and 1 volume. P 23.
Papers concerning the history of *Decorah-Posten* and a volume of its comic strip, "Han Ola og Han Per."

37. ARNE GARBORG KLUBB, CHICAGO. RECORD BOOKS, 1891–1895. 2 volumes. P 430.
Minutes of business meetings, lectures, and discussions, together with financial records of a Chicago literary society.

38. ARNESON, AXEL (1862–1941). LOCAL HISTORY, n.d. Typescript, 14 pages. P 25.
"Notes on Norwegian Settlements in Texas," telling of pioneer life, frontier hospitality, relations with Indians, church and school life.

39. ARNOLD, MAGNUS A. PAPERS, 1945–1955. 37 items. P 26.
Letters and clippings from Arnold's column, "Notes by the Observer," which appeared in *The Bee*, Phillips, Wisconsin, dealing with such subjects as books, education, and national politics.

40. ARNTZEN, ARNT (b. 1890). BIOGRAPHY, 1975. Typescript, 52 pages. P 912.
An account of a Norwegian immigrant fisherman and sailor from Narvik who came to New Orleans in 1908. After trying various kinds of work and living in different places in the U.S. and Canada, he settled in British Columbia. Included is "A Tribute to Einar on his 80th Birthday from Johann" (5 typewritten pages).

ARTICLES. See Special Collections, No. 937.

ARTIFACTS. See Special Collections, No. 938.

41. ASSERSON, PETER CHRISTIAN (1839–1906). PAPERS, 1902–1935. 3 items. P 27.
Biographical information on a Norwegian-born rear admiral and civil engineer in the United States Navy. Asserson was an ensign in the U.S. Navy during the Civil War.

42. ATTERDAG COLLEGE. CATALOGUES, 1915–1921. 2 items. P 472.
Two catalogues of a Danish-American secondary school established in Santa Barbara, California, in 1911.

43. AUGSBURG COLLEGE AND SEMINARY. PAPERS, 1874–1953. 2 boxes. P 483.
Papers of a Lutheran institution founded at Marshall, Wisconsin, in 1869 and moved to Minneapolis in 1872: journals, pamphlets, catalogues, yearbooks, pictures, and a court record.

44. AUGSBURG PUBLISHING HOUSE. PAPERS, 1915–1944. 6 items. P 28.

A historical sketch of the company and pamphlets dealing with church conventions, equipment, personnel, sales, sites, and stock.

45. AUGUSTANA ACADEMY. PAPERS, ca. 1870–1959. 2 boxes. P 481.
Brochures, bulletins, catalogues, clippings, journals, and reports of a school founded in Chicago in 1860. Located in Canton, South Dakota, since 1881.

46. AUGUSTANA COLLEGE. PAPERS, 1918–1964. 2 boxes. P 482.
Brochures, bulletins, clippings, journals, programs, a typescript copy of a fragment of Emil Erpestad's history of the college, and a history of the Marshall, Wisconsin, era of the institution. Augustana, located in Sioux Falls, South Dakota, was founded in Chicago in 1860.

47. BACON, ASTRID IHME (b. 1903). LOCAL HISTORY. Typescript, 29 pages. P 832.
"Bridges of Brotherhood " relates experiences and life of the Norwegian colony at San Pedro, California. The author, born in Tvedestrand, Norway, emigrated to the U.S. in 1914.

48. BAKER, MONS SAMUEL (MONSSINI) (1849–1927). PAPERS, n.d. 4 items. P 252.
Papers of a Norwegian-born poet, teacher, and machinist: a collection of songs entitled "Truth and Justice," and copies of other poems: "The Wanderer's Return to Minneapolis," "A Hymn to the Virgin Mother," and "The Klondike Song." Baker, who emigrated in 1870, was a socialist.

49. BARTH, C. H. EXPOSITION, n.d. 1 volume. P 662.
Treats the origin of Norway's oldest national song. "Den Kronede Norske Nationalsang" was written by Henrik Anker Bjerregaard and the melody was composed by Chr. Blom in 1820.

50. BAUMANN, JULIUS B. (1870–1923). PAPERS, 1909–1923. 100 items, including 3 volumes. P 29.
Papers of a Norwegian-born poet and register of deeds in Carlton County, Minnesota: poems, letters, clippings, and three scrapbooks containing newspaper articles by Baumann, responses to his articles, and discussions on Norwegian-American literature by a variety of authors. Baumann published three volumes of poems: *Digte* (1909), *Fra Vidderne* (1915), and *Samlede Digte* (1924).

51. BECK, RICHARD (b. 1897). PAPERS, 1938–1951. 18 items. P 31.
Correspondence, clippings, and pamphlets of an Icelandic-born professor of Scandinavian languages and literature at the University of North Dakota.

52. BEKKER, JOHN A. ESSAY, 1940. Typescript, 8 pages. P 32.
"Norway's Final Bulwark" deals with the durability of a democracy in Norway.

53. BENGSTON, JOHN D. ARTICLES, 1975, 1977. 2 items, typescript, 57 and 27 pages. P 826.

"A Study of Lexical Interference in the English of Norwegian-Americans" surveys English as spoken by Minnesotans of Norwegian descent, pointing out influences in vocabulary from Norwegian. The second, "Han Ola og Han Per," treats the language and literature in the comic strips of Peter Julius Rosendahl which ran for many years in *Decorah-Posten*, Decorah, Iowa.

54. BENSON, THOMAS I. (b. 1934). THESIS, 1868. Typescript, 193 pages. P 694.

"The Norwegians in California, 1850–1900: A Preliminary Survey," MA degree in history at the College of the Holy Names, Oakland, California.

55. BERG, ANDERS T. (ca. 1857–1893). CORRESPONDENCE, 1888–1894. 15 items. P 33.

Letters to a Norwegian-born farmer at Sunburgh, Minnesota. Correspondents include Johannes Halvorson, Bjug A. Harstad, and Johannes Tingelstad.

56. BERG, GEORGE O. (1875–1935). NOTEBOOK, 1900. 1 volume. P 421.

Notes on Greek and Latin studies by a member of the St. Olaf College faculty for 29 years.

57. BERGE, GULBRAND (1827–1886). AUTOBIOGRAPHY. Typescript, 19 pages. P 749.

Copy of "The Autobiography of Gulbrand O. Berge, 1827–1886." Born in Valdres, Norway, Berge settled near Manitowoc, Wisconsin. He served in the 37th Wisconsin Regiment during the Civil War.

58. BERGE (BERGH), KNUT EILEVSON (1838–1875). POEMS, 1857. 4 items. P 34.

Manuscript volume of four poems about emigration to America. Bergh was a teacher at Luther College.

59. BERGE, OLE OLSEN. PAPERS, 1853–1865. 12 items. P 35.

Papers of a Norwegian-born farmer at Manitowoc, Wisconsin: Civil War letters by Berge, other correspondence, and a poem. Berge's wife was Berit Veblen Nygard.

60. BERGE, OTTO G. LOCAL HISTORY, 1930. Typescript, 3 pages. P 798.

Copy (1947) of "A History of Valders." Valders is a town near Manitowoc, Wisconsin.

61. BERGER, ARNE K. (1872–1951). PAPERS, 1931. 3 items. P 36.

Papers of a Norwegian-born artist: catalogue, list of paintings, and a critique.

62.　BERGESON, BERGES JULIUS (1867–1942). PAPERS, 1929–1942. 14 items. P 37.
Pamphlets written by the founder of Mid-west Livestock Commission Company, Sioux City, Iowa.

63.　BERGH, BOLETTE STUB (1852–1940). CLIPPINGS, 1944. 3 items. P 38.
Memoirs of a Lutheran minister's wife, Mrs. Johannes E. Bergh, who lived at Sacred Heart, Minnesota (1872–1905).

64.　BERGH, JOHAN ARNDT (1847–1927). ADDRESSES, 1884, 1906. 2 items. P 556.
A lecture given at the convention of the Norwegian-Danish Conference, aimed at clarifying issues within that Synod, and later published (pamphlet), *Den gamle og nye retning*. "A history of the United Church," presented at the annual convention of the United Norwegian Lutheran Church in 1906 and translated by L. A. Mathre in 1965 (typescript, 14 pages).

65.　BERGH, OLAI O. (1852–1930). AUTOBIOGRAPHY, 1929. Typescript, 81 pages. P 738.
Autobiography of a Norwegian-born Lutheran minister and farmer, Volga, South Dakota (1884–1919). Translated by his son, John E. Bergh in 1954.

66.　BERGLAND, BOB SELMER (b. 1928). PAMPHLET, 1978. 10 pages. P 938.
A brochure, prepared by Halvor Nordbø, welcoming the Berglands to Telemark, Norway. Includes information about Bergland's Norwegian ancestry and about the Bergland farmstead in Telemark. Bergland, a former Minnesota Congressman, was Secretary of Agriculture at this time.

67.　BERNTS, OLAF (1870–1936). PAPERS, 1870–1936. 152 items and 1 volume. P 889.
Documents, correspondence, clippings, photographs and a scrapbook of a Norwegian-born attorney who came to the United States in 1907 and began service with the Norwegian Consulate in Chicago in 1909. He was appointed Consul General in 1920 and held that post until his death in 1936.

68.　BETHANIA COLLEGE. PAPERS, 1910–1921. 8 items. P 473.
A catalogue, correspondence, and reports concerning a Lutheran secondary school located in Poulsbo (1894–1896), and Everett (1904–1917), Washington.

69.　BETHANY LUTHERAN COLLEGE. PAPERS, 1925–1938. 16 items. P 474.
Bulletins and catalogues of a school at Mankato, Minnesota, founded in 1911.

70. BETHESDA HOMES. PAPERS, ca. 1924–1953. 5 items. P 628.
History and journal of a children's home and a home for the aged at Beresford, South Dakota and at Eagle Lake, Minnesota.

71. BIBLE INSTITUTE AND ACADEMY. CATALOGUE, 1918. 1 item. P 475.
Catalogue of an institution founded by the Norwegian Evangelical Free Church in 1909 in Rushford, Minnesota, and moved to Minneapolis in 1916.

72. BIBLE SCHOOLS. REPORTS, 1923. 7 items. P 476.
Reports regarding several Bible schools in Minnesota and North Dakota.

73. BIØRN, EMIL (1864–1935). SCRAPBOOK. 1 volume. P 776.
Scrapbook of clippings, programs of musical, dramatic and other entertainment activities in Chicago (1890–1900). Biørn, a versatile musician and artist, was a cultural leader among Scandinavians in Chicago.

BIOGRAPHICAL FILE. See Special Collections, No. 939.

74. BIORNSTAD, GISLE (1867–1940). PAPERS, ca. 1910–1917. 5 items. P 39.
Papers of a Norwegian-born physician, who established a clinic and sanitorium in Minneapolis.

75. BIRKHAUG, KONRAD (b. 1892). WORLD WAR II. Typescript, 364 pages. P 742.
Birkhaug's translation of his book, *Televåg: Fiskeværet som tyskerne slettet ut i 1942*, Oslo, 1946. 297 p. Title of translation is "Tela Bay: The Norwegian Fishing Village Destroyed by the Germans." Televåg, located on an island near Bergen, was an important center of traffic with England during World War II.

76. BJØRNSON, BJØRNSTJERNE (1832–1910). PAPERS, 1882–1939. 8 items. P 40.
Correspondence, clippings, and a copy of *Vis-Knut*. One of the letters is by Bjørnson to Thoralv Klaveness concerning the latter's book, *Det Norske Amerika* (1904).

77. BJØRNSON, HALVOR (1868–1943). ADDRESS, 1922. Pamphlet, 32 pages. P 556.
Tidens særlige krav til den lutherske kirke, a lecture delivered at the Northern Minnesota District Convention in 1919 by Pastor Bjørnson, is a discussion of the era's special demands on the Lutheran Church.

78. BJØRNSON, VALDIMAR (b. 1906). LECTURES, 1949. 3 items, 7 pages. P 41.
Printed reproductions of three lectures delivered over WCAL, St.

Olaf College radio station (October, 1948). Titles are "The Viking Voyagers," "Modern Migrations Begin," and "Evaluating the Contribution."

79. BJORK, KENNETH O. (b. 1909). ADDRESSES, 1949–1963. 4 items. Typescript, 14 pages. P 42.

Addresses by a professor of history at St. Olaf College. One given before the Norwegian-American Technical Society, the other given on Founders Day (November 6, 1963) at St. Olaf College.

80. BJORNDAL, MAGNUS (1899–1971). PAPERS, 1946–1971. 2 boxes. P 765.

Manuscripts, correspondence, research notes, and articles of a Norwegian-born American engineer, who came to the United States in 1922 and who founded and was president of Technical Laboratories in Weehawken, New Jersey. A leader in many Norwegian-American activities, he also did considerable research on the Norwegian discovery of America. He was President of NAHA (1969–1971).

81. BLEGEN, HANS O. (1853–1921). PAPERS, 1914. 2 items, P 729.

Copy of Governor L. B. Hanna's appointment of Blegen as member of the committee to present a bust of Lincoln from North Dakota to Norway.

82. BLEGEN, HELMER M. (b. 1898). COLLEGE HISTORY, 1970. 1 volume, 349 pages. P 730.

Articles, notes, and statistics on the history of Augustana College, Sioux Falls, South Dakota, by a professor of Romance languages at Augustana College.

83. BLEGEN, THEODORE C. (1891–1969). PAPERS, 1944–1968. 158 items. P 819.

Letters, speeches, and a typescript copy of a family memoir, "Minnetonka Family, the Story of Saga Hill," by Theodore C. Blegen, historian, educator, and editor of the Norwegian-American Historical Association publications (1925–1960). The letters are written to Mrs. Helen Katz, his editorial assistant. For additional Blegen correspondence, see NAHA, No. 609.

84. BODE LUTHERAN ACADEMY. PAPERS, 1891–1921. 5 items. P 477.

A catalogue and reports of a secondary school in Bode, Iowa, established in 1887 by the local congregation, and in 1895 continued by interested individuals until 1902.

85. BOE, A. SOPHIE (1879–1937). PAPERS, 1814–1936. 62 items, including 1 volume. P 663.

Correspondence, articles, pamphlets, and clippings. The papers include letters by Lars Davidson Reque, Miss Boe's grandfather; a history of the Liberty Prairie church, Deerfield, Wisconsin, of which many of her relatives were members; materials concerning Augsburg Seminary; information about Svein Nilssen, editor of *Billed-magazin*; family history and a manuscript volume of a biography of her father, the Reverend N. E. Bøe.

86. BOE, LARS WILHELM (1875–1942). PAPERS, 1900–1953. 2 boxes. P 460.

Articles, pamphlets, clippings, scrapbooks, and pictures dealing largely with biography. L. W. Boe was the fourth president of St. Olaf College. The two scrapbooks were compiled by his sister, A. Sophie Boe.

87. BOE, VIGLEIK E. (1872–1953). LOCAL HISTORY, 1933. Typescript, 5 pages. P 43.

History of Østervold congregation (1883–1933), Finley, North Dakota, by a Norwegian-born Lutheran clergyman, containing information on pastors, church construction, congregational policies, and societies. Boe was minister in Finley for 30 years.

88. BØE (ANDERSON), NILS ENDRESON (1846–1925). PAPERS, 1864–1927. 2 boxes. P 461.

Papers of a Norwegian-born Lutheran clergyman who attended Albion Academy, Augustana College (Paxton, Illinois), and Augsburg Seminary (Marshall, Wisconsin) and who served pastorates in Kansas, Michigan, Illinois, Iowa, and Wisconsin. Bøe was the father of L. W. Boe.

The correspondence, consisting largely of letters to Bøe written by clergy, laity, and relatives, describes economic, social, and church conditions especially in Iowa, Kansas, Michigan and Wisconsin; provides information regarding problems connected with Marshall Academy and Augsburg Seminary; and discusses topics such as the professor fund, proselytism, *den nye retning, erklæringer, Wisconsinisme*, and *Augustanaisme*.

The papers include three articles by Bøe, entitled "Protest" (1885), "Om Augsburgernes Principer" (1898), and "Det engelske Sprog indenfor vort Samfund" (ca. 1920). For a list of correspondents, see description catalogue in the NAHA Archives.

89. BOECKMANN, CARL L. (1868–1923). PAPERS. 29 items. P 856.

Clippings, photos and exhibition descriptions of a Norwegian-born artist who came to the United States in 1887. He painted portraits, landscapes and religious subjects. The papers were collected in connection with an exhibition of Boeckmann paintings at the Hennepin County Government Center (October 4–6, 1976) under the sponsorship of the Richfield, Minnesota, Bicentennial Commission.

90. BOOMER, JØRGINE SLETTEDE. CLIPPINGS, (1932–1968). 3 items. P 873.

Clippings concerning the Norwegian-born wife of Lucius Boomer, for a time the owner of the Waldorf Astoria Hotel in New York City.

91. BORAAS, JULIUS (1871–1952). PAPERS, 1908–1952. 105 items. P 823.
Papers of a professor of education at St. Olaf College: articles on educational subjects, a history of the Boraas family, correspondence, biographical data, clippings, and a record of Boraas's public addresses.

92. BORGE, MICHAEL O. (1846–1928). PAPERS, 1870–1950. 28 items. P 704.
Papers of a Norwegian-born Lutheran clergyman. Correspondence includes letters from Morrisonville, Wisconsin, area in the 1870s and Norway letters (1902). Clippings consist of articles about pioneer life in the Volga, South Dakota, area in the 1880s. References are made to H. A. Preus and U. V. Koren.

93. BORLAUG, NORMAN (b. 1914). PAPERS. 65 items. P 766.
Clippings, programs, and speeches regarding the Norwegian-American agricultural scientist who was awarded the Nobel Peace Prize in 1970. Dr. Borlaug was born on a farm near Cresco, Iowa, and was educated at the University of Minnesota. He was honored for his work in developing high-yielding dwarf wheat which held great promise for alleviating world hunger and was hailed as a leader in the "Green Revolution."

94. BOYESEN, HJALMAR HJORTH (1848–1895). PAPERS, 1871–1966. 125 items. P 462.
Biographical miscellany, articles, poems, and stories of a Norwegian-born novelist, poet, essayist, and teacher. Boyesen was on the faculty at Ohio State University, Cornell University, and Columbia College. He wrote extensively for the leading journals and his first and perhaps best-known novel was *Gunnar*.

95. BRAATEN, SVEN O. (1852–1926). POEMS, 1883–1904. 18 items. P 316.
Poems by a Norwegian-born Lutheran clergyman, Thompson, North Dakota.

96. BRACK, JOSEPHINE (1884–1973). PAPERS, 1908–1973. 6 boxes. P 921.
Correspondence, clippings, pamphlets, minutes, records of a St. Paul woman who was a leader in Norwegian-American organizations, especially in the Norse-American Centennial celebration in 1925, the Norse American Centennial Daughters of St. Paul, and the Minnesota Leif Erikson Monument Association. She was also an officer in the group which administered Lyngblomsten Home for the Aged in St. Paul. The papers include some of these records.

97. BRANDT, NILS (1824–1921). MEMOIRS, ca. 1907. Clippings.
   P 739.
Abridged memoirs of a Norwegian-born Lutheran clergyman who emigrated in 1851 to a parish at Oconomowoc, Wisconsin. The memoirs deal largely with his travels as a home missionary in Iowa, Minnesota, and Wisconsin. Brandt was the first Norwegian minister to preach west of the Mississippi River.
Translated by Olaf O. Brandt, Decorah, a grandson, these memoirs were published in six installments in the Decorah *Journal* (July 31–August 25, 1970).

98. BREDESEN, ADOLF (1850–1913). PAPERS, 1920–1923. 5 items.
   P 46.
"Af vore indvandreres liv" (clippings), by a Norwegian-born Lutheran clergyman, contain biographical sketches of H. A. Preus, president of the Norwegian Synod (1862–1894) and of Nils Brandt, Luther College (1865–1881). Reprint of "Mod Bennettloven." The Bennet Law (Wisconsin) provided for compulsory school attendance of children from 7 to 14 years of age. The requirements that instruction be in English was opposed by the supporters of parochial schools.

99. BREKKE, SJUR J. (1876–1932). NOTES, 1905–1908. 1 volume.
   P 422.
Book of sermon notes by a Norwegian-born Lutheran clergyman.

100. BREVIK, KRISTINE. CLIPPINGS, 1968. 2 items. P 913.
"Silver Mountain," a fairy tale by Kristine Brevik, illustrated by Odd Nesse, published as a supplement to the *Chicago Tribune* (January 14, 1968) and a clipping from *Vinland*, Chicago, describing the work.

101. BRØGGER, ANTON W. (b. 1884). LECTURE, 1936. 2 items. P 47.
Reprint (20 pages), "Vinlandsferdene" (Voyages to Vinland), delivered before Det norske geografiske selskab (1936) and then printed in *Norsk geografisk tidsskrift*, and a clipping reporting a similar lecture held in Minneapolis.

102. BROSTE, OLE K. REMINISCENCES. 1 item, typescript, 12 pages.
   P 755.
"Coming to America, 1868," as told to Petra M. Lien, Hanska, Minnesota.

103. BRUCE, GUSTAV MARIUS (1879–1963). PAPERS, 1860–1957. 3 boxes, including 3 volumes. P 463.
Correspondence, reports, clippings, pictures, and record books of a Norwegian-born Lutheran clergyman, theological professor, author, editor, and lecturer.
Bruce immigrated to Yankton County, Dakota Territory, in 1884; attended Fremont College, Red Wing Seminary, University of South Dakota, Temple University (Ph.D.), and Hartford Seminary (D.D.).

He was a minister in South Dakota, Illinois, Minnesota, and Nebraska parishes; teacher in the public schools of Yankton County, Jewell College, and Red Wing Seminary; professor at Luther Theological Seminary (1917–1949); vice-president of the NELCA; member of the Committee on Social Trends in the National Lutheran Council; delegate to the Lutheran World Convention in Copenhagen (1929); a founder of Lutheran Brotherhood; and vice-president of the National Temperance Movement.

He was publicity chairman of the Norse-American Centennial, president of Østfoldlaget for 16 years, and of Bygdelagenes Fellesraad for 5 years. He was editor of several religious periodicals, a contributor to newspapers and magazines, and the author of several books on social and educational subjects.

Correspondence and reports in this collection deal with Knut Gjerset's proposed encyclopedia on Norwegian Americans, disputes and realignments among Norwegian Lutheran congregations, organization of the Luther League after the 1917 church union, Norwegian pioneers in Canada, and bilingualism in the church. An article, "Lidt pionærhistorie," is an account of the snow-storm of January 12, 1888, as it affected the Bruce family. Another article is a biography of Lars O. Haug, prominent in *bygdelag* affairs.

104. BRUFLAT ACADEMY AND BUSINESS INSTITUTE. PAPERS, 1890–1966. 18 items. P 478.

Catalogues, constitution, correspondence, and reports of a Lutheran school located at Portland, North Dakota (1889–1918), and a history of the school by Theodore Gilbertson, one of its graduates.

105. BRUFLOT, ARNFINN (b. 1904). PAPERS, 1968–1974. P 795.

Clippings of reviews and other papers concerning a poet born in Naustdal, Sunnfjord, Norway. He emigrated in 1928 and arrived in Tacoma, Washington, where he engaged in various kinds of work, some of the time as a house-painter.

His volumes of poetry, *Juni-båten* (1969), *Det storkna havet* (1970), and *Præriekveld* (1973), published in Oslo by Det Norske Samlaget, written in *ny norsk*, have been well received.

106. BRUSTUEN, ANNIE OLSON. REMINISCENCES, 1960. Typescript, 16 pages. P 48.

"Pioneer Incidents as told by My Mother." Hegbert Township, Swift County, Minnesota.

107. BRYE, MARTHA M. (1864–1946). SCRAPBOOK, 1880. 1 volume. P 423.

Scrapbook of clippings compiled by a school teacher and nurse from Coon Valley and La Crosse, Wisconsin. Among the items are a poem by Kristofer Janson, O. J. Breda's address at the Kristofer Janson festival in Decorah, and Laur. Larsen's address at the President Garfield memorial program in Decorah.

108. BRYNESTAD, LAWRENCE. REPORT. Typescript, 9 pages. P 754.
"Norwegian Lutheran Periodicals, 1860–1880, and Their Reference to the Darwinian Theory of Evolution."

109. BU, OLAF A. (1842–1931). PAPERS, 1845–1924. 54 items. P 49.
Correspondence, clippings, and speeches. Most of the letters are by Bu and his wife to his parents in Gudbrandsdalen, Norway, dealing with his student days in Christiania, their emigration in 1875, and life in Ostrander, Minnesota, where Bu was a Lutheran minister (1875–1908). The clippings contain reminiscences. The speeches deal with Norwegian heritage.

110. BUDDE, JAN ADOLF. LETTER, 1850. Typescript, 13 pages. P 50.
Typewritten copy of "Af et brev om Amerika" by the head of the Stavanger agricultural school containing arguments against emigration. The original is in the University of Oslo Library.

111. BUE, HAGBARTH (b. 1887). PAPERS, 1908–1913. 2 items.
A roster of gifts by Norwegian Americans to Norway (Independence Centennial) and pages from a scrapbook dealing with World War I.

112. BUFFALO COUNTY, WISCONSIN. CLIPPING, 1975. I item. P 893.
"Norwegians Observe Emigration to States" by Lee Grippen. Article consists of translated excerpts from H. R. Holand's *De Norske Settlementers Historie* and covers early immigration to Buffalo County.

113. BULL, OLE (1810–1880). PAPERS, 1882–1966. 27 items. P 52.
Reprinted articles, clippings, and photographs concerning the Norwegian violinist, and "The Saga of Ole Bull" by Harmon M. Gehr.

114. BULL, STORM (1856–1907). LETTERS, 1894–1907. I volume. P 774.
A copybook of letters written by Storm Bull, a Norwegian-born, Swiss-trained engineer, who came to Madison, Wisconsin, in 1879, where his uncle, the violinist Ole Bull, had lived earlier.
Storm Bull, a member of the engineering faculty at the University of Wisconsin, served on the city council and was for a time mayor of Madison. The letters deal with affairs at the University.

115. BUSLETT, OLE AMUNDSON (1855–1924). PAPERS, 1873–1925. 6 boxes. P 464.
Letters, notes, poems, manuscripts, reports, speeches, reviews, clippings, and biographical miscellany of a Norwegian-born author, poet, journalist, legislator, and merchant in Northland, Wisconsin.
The letters received by Buslett, deal with local church problems, bilingualism in the church, criticism of current Norwegian-American literature, materialism among Norwegian Americans, the Wisconsin exhibit at Norway's Independence Centennial in 1914, a State Park in Door County, Wisconsin. The letters by Buslett are to his wife.

Among the papers are a review of O. E. Rølvaag's *Paa Glemte Veie*, a copy of *Wergelands Talsmand* (Stevens Point, 1886), a roster of small towns in the United States with Scandinavian names arranged by states, articles on woman suffrage and socialism, reports from the Wisconsin Good Roads Committee of 1909, and a bibliography of Buslett's works.

The collection contains letters from significant Norwegian-American authors and journalists of the day, among them R. B. Anderson, B. Anundsen, Julius Baumann, John Benson, Sigurd Folkestad, O. S. Hervin, H. R. Holand, P. P. Iverslie, Simon Johnson, Jon Norstog, Torkel Oftelie, O. E. Rølvaag, Peer Strømme and Johs. B. Wist.

116. BUU, JOHN GULLECKSON. REMINISCENCES, 1857. 10 pages. P 51.
"Beskrivelse av vor reise fra Norge til Amerika, aar 1857" is a description of Gulleckson's journey to America together with his wife and five children, beginning May 8 at Bergen and ending July 7 at Liberty Prairie, Wisconsin. Copy made in 1888 by Iver J. Jaastad.

117. BYGDELAGENE. PAPERS, 1900–1970. 7 boxes. P. 465.
Papers of *bygd* societies and their Common Council (Bygdelagenes Fellesraad), clippings, constitutions, correspondence, minutes and financial records, pamphlets, pictures, programs, and reports, dealing with conventions, officers, special projects, and the Norse-American Centennial of 1925. The *bygdelag*, organized around the turn of the century, were societies based on regional origins in Norway.

CALENDARS, See Special Collections, No. 940.

118. CALIFORNIA GOLD RUSH. CLIPPINGS, 1941. 3 items. P 54.
Fjell-Ljom, Nord-Trøndelag and *Inntrøndelagen* (newspapers) articles on Norwegians emigrating to California in the 1850's. One includes a letter from San Francisco.

119. CAMP LITTLE NORWAY ASSOCIATION. PAPERS, 1941–1947. 6 boxes. P 466.
Correspondence, pamphlets, publications, pictures, reports, minutes, albums, ledgers, journals, publicity, lectures, and clippings of a nation-wide association organized in Minneapolis (September, 1941) to raise funds for Norway and Norwegian nationals in Canada and the U.S. for medical care, food, housing, clothing and for recreation in hospitals and rest homes. Camp Little Norway in Toronto, Canada, was a training base for the Royal Norwegian Air Force. The association was co-ordinated with American Relief for Norway in 1944.

120. CAMP NIDAROS, OTTERTAIL LAKE, OTTERTAIL COUNTY, MINNESOTA. PAPERS, 1923–1971. 10 items. P 785.
Constitution, minutes, and historical sketches of a camp made up of summer cottages owned mainly by ministers. The original site, pur-

chased in 1909, was expanded later. Camp Nidaros, together with three other similar camps, organized the Lutheran Camp Service Association.

121. CAMROSE LUTHERAN COLLEGE. PAPERS, 1914–1956. 24 items. P 479.
Catalogues and reports of an academy founded at Camrose, Alberta, in 1911.

122. CANUTESON, RICHARD. PAPERS, 1974. 5 items. P 775.
Letter, photograph, and clippings concerning the erection of a marker at Kendall, New York, commemorating the "Slooper Settlement" there following the arrival of Norwegian immigrants on the sloop "Restauration."

123. CARLSEN, CLARENCE J. (1894–1959). THESIS, 1932. Typescript, 198 pages. P 605.
"Elling Eielsen, Pioneer Lay Preacher and First Norwegian Lutheran Pastor in America," MA degree, University of Minnesota.

124. CARMEL HIGHLANDS NORWEGIAN LODGE, 1956–1963. PAPERS. 4 items. P 55.
Article and correspondence concerning a Norwegian estate at Carmel, California.

125. CASBERG, SELMA S. GENEALOGY, 1976. 1 item. P 922.
A documented paper, "Importance of Genealogy," describing the process of searching for family history by a retired teacher of history.

CATALOGUES. See Special Collections, No. 941.

126. CENTRAL WISCONSIN COLLEGE. PAPERS, 1893–1962. 40 items and 3 volumes. P 649.
Financial records, minutes of the board of trustees, historical sketch, student year books and journals, pictures, programs, and catalogues of a Lutheran academy founded in 1893, and a junior college in 1921.

127. CERTIFICATES, 1829–1927. 16 items. P 56.
Emigration papers, a Norwegian-American Steamship Line passenger contract, marriage and confirmation certificates, and a bounty land deed.

128. CHARNEY, SETH D. BIOGRAPHY, n.d. Typescript, 3 pages. P 606.
Biographical sketch of Minnesota-born Vilhelm Magnus (1871–1929) and his discoveries in the field of medicine.

129. CHICAGO LUTHERAN BIBLE SCHOOL. PAPERS, 1922–1923. 25 items. P 480.
Brochures, correspondence, and reports of a school founded in 1917.

130. CHICAGO NORWEGIAN TECHNICAL SOCIETY (1922–) PAPERS. 10 items. P 882.

Minutes, yearbook, membership lists, and correspondence of a technical society organized in Chicago in 1922. Similar societies were later organized: Norwegian Engineering Society of New York (1925); Norwegian-American Technical Society (1927).

131. CHRISTIAN THE SEVENTH, KING OF DENMARK AND NORWAY (1749–1808). LEGAL DOCUMENTS, 1789–1807. 2 items. P 58.
Proclamations by the King concerning disease and minerals.

132. CHRISTIANSEN, F. MELIUS (1871–1955). PAPERS, 1896–1955. 108 items. P 467.
Musical compositions, arrangements, bulletins and clippings of a Norwegian-born choir director, composer, organist, and teacher. Christiansen was director of the St. Olaf choir (1903–1944).

133. CHRISTOPHER, OLE C. PAPERS. BIOGRAPHY, 1974. Typescript, 418 pages. P 779.
"The Norse American Adventure." The author's stated purpose is ". . . to bring to the front the accomplishments of our leading personalities in the many and various fields of endeavors." A two-page index at the beginning notes the fields he has covered. The information includes known and lesser-known personages.

134. CHURCH SCHOOLS. RECORDS. 1 volume, 1891–1900. P 426.
Records of schools and confirmation classes in Fillmore County, and at Kenyon, Cottonwood, and Hanley Falls, Minnesota.

135. CIVIL WAR. PAPERS, 1861–1966. 123 items. P 468.
Articles, certificates, Confederate money, correspondence, diary, maps, pictures, and rosters.
The rosters of Norwegians in the Confederate Army were compiled from muster rolls in National Archives and Texas State Archives by Derwood Johnson, Waco, Texas. Among the articles are "Femtende Wisconsin" by O. K. Flaaten and "I Andersonville Prison 6 Maaneder."

136. CLAUSEN, CLAUS L. (1820–1892). PAPERS, 1841–1900. 9 items. P 59.
A diary, letters, and photographs of a Danish-born Lutheran clergyman, and articles on the history of the Norwegian settlements in Mitchell County, Iowa. Clausen served congregations in Racine and Rock counties, Wisconsin, before moving to Iowa.

137. CLAUSEN, MARVIN. SPEECH, 1939. Typescript, 7 pages. P 60.
Manuscript of a speech on the futility of war.

138. CLENG PEERSON MEMORIAL INSTITUTE. ARCHIVES, 1977. P 923.
A pamphlet describing the activities and collections of Norsemen's

World-Wide Archives, Stavanger, Norway. The institute was established in 1970.

139. CLIFTON JUNIOR COLLEGE. CATALOGUES, 1924–1953. 23 volumes. P 484.
Catalogues of a Lutheran school founded at Clifton, Texas, in 1897.

CLIPPING FILE. See Special Collections, No. 942.

140. THE COEUR D'ALENE HOMES. JOURNALS, 1933–1935. 11 items. P 629.
Journals of a home for the aged at Coeur d'Alene, Idaho.

141. COLLOQUIUM AT MADISON (WISCONSIN), 1882. Pamphlet, n.d. 12 pages. P 556.
Treats the "election controversy" in the Norwegian Synod.

142. COLUMBIA LUTHERAN COLLEGE. PAPERS, 1914–1920. 6 items. P 485.
Bulletins and reports of an Everett, Washington, academy founded in 1909.

143. CONCORDIA COLLEGE. PAPERS, 1897–1957. 186 items. P 490.
Brochures, catalogues, clippings, journals, programs, reports, and history of a Lutheran College, Moorhead, Minnesota, founded in 1891.

144. CONCORDIA COLLEGE LANGUAGE CAMPS, MOORHEAD, MINNESOTA. SONGS. 1 item. P 924.
"Skogfjorden sangbog," a collection of thirty-three songs with music designed to be used in the summer language camps.

145. CONGREGATIONS. 26 boxes. P 537.
Printed and typescript histories, constitutions, programs, yearbooks and records of some 400 Norwegian-American churches, filed alphabetically by state and city (or county).

146. CROOKSTON COLLEGE. CATALOGUES, 1896–1925. 21 items. P 486.
Catalogues of a private business and teachers' training school founded in Crookston, Minnesota, in 1895.

CUTS COLLECTION. See Special Collections, No. 943.

147. DAAE, AUSTEN (1905–1978). CLIPPINGS, 1936–1970. 1 box. P 736.
Clippings of articles by Daae as they appeared in the Chicago press. Daae was editor of *Scandia*, Chicago. His name appears as Doe in many of the clippings, an earlier spelling.

148. DAHL, BORGHILD (b. 1891). PAPERS, 1944–1964. 9 items. P 61.
Articles, brochures, and correspondence of a writer, lecturer, and teacher.

149.   DAHL, DORTHEA (1883–1958). PAPERS. 8 items. P 820.
Copies of miscellaneous information about Dahl, a Norwegian-born author who came to America at the age of two. She wrote several books and a number of short stories published in the Norwegian American press.

150.   DAHL (ØKSENDAHL), NELS TOBIAS (1863–1940). AUTOBIOG-
RAPHY, 1925. Typescript, 25 pages. P 939.
Covers ancestry and childhood in Norway, emigration to Wisconsin in 1867, and subsequent events in the life of a farmer and business man who lived in Wisconsin, Minnesota, and North Dakota. Appended notes are dated March 30, 1939. The reminiscences were recorded by Valborg Dahl, a daughter.

151.   DAHLBY, ANNE (MRS. OLE) (b. 1863). PAPERS, 1850–1918. 13
items. P 62.
An emigration document and letters to Mrs. Dahlby, a Norwegian-born farmer's wife at Mount Horeb, Wisconsin.

152.   DAHLE, JOHN (1853–1931). JOURNALS, 1890–1905. 34 items.
P 63.
Magazines edited and published by a Norwegian-born organist, composer, choir director, writer, and teacher.
Dahle published in 1884 *Sangbog for kirkekor*, the first collection of songs for church choirs among Norwegian Americans. He was the composer of two cantatas, *The Twenty-Third Psalm* and *Poor and Forsaken*, taught in the Norwegian department at St. Olaf College and Concordia College, and was professor of hymnology at Luther Theological Seminary in St. Paul.

153.   DAKOTA LUTHERAN HIGH SCHOOL. PAPERS, 1948–1957. 27
items. P 487.
Correspondence, brochures, journals, and reports of a Minot, North Dakota, school (1948–1964).

154.   DALLAS NORSK EVANGELISK LUTHERSK KIRKEGAARD. RECORDS,
ca. 1885. 3 items. P 64.
Fragments of by-laws, minutes, and roster of burials of a Barron County, Wisconsin, cemetery association.

155.   DAUGHTERS OF NORWAY LODGE. PAPERS. 3 items. P 857.
Brochures and clippings relating to anniversaries and history of Freya Lodge (the original lodge), and a comprehensive history of the national organization. Daughters of Norway merged with Sons of Norway in 1951.

156.   DECORAH INSTITUTE. JOURNALS, 1901–1905. 5 items. P 488.
A journal published by a secondary school, founded by John Brecken-ridge in 1874 in Decorah, Iowa. The school also offered teacher training and business courses.

157. DEED, 1541. 2 items. P 65.
A legal document on sheep skin and a transcript of same, regarding conveyance of property in Norway.

158. DEEN, TILLA R. DAHL (b. 1868). REMINISCENCES, 1949. Type-
      script, 16 pages. P 711.
"Chronicles of a Minnesota Pioneer" covers approximately the period 1870 to 1890 in the Minnesota counties of Blue Earth, Cotton-wood, and Minneota.

159. DEWITT, RUTH. LOCAL HISTORY, 1976. 1 volume, 41 pages.
      P 841.
"Rural America Revisited, Town of Dunn Bicentennial Tour," a record of the landmarks and history of Dunn Township, Dane County, Wisconsin, prepared for the United States Bicentennial celebration.

160. DIARY, 1901. 1 item. P 71.
An unidentified diary dealing largely with search for work in Brooklyn, New York, Philadelphia, and Pittsburgh.

161. DIETRICHSON, GUSTAV FREDRIK (1813–1886). LETTERS, 1851–
      1854. P 435.
Copies of two letters by a Lutheran clergyman in Luther Valley, Wisconsin. The first expresses gratitude for a comfortable and safe passage to America and the second announces a new parish at Wiota, Wisconsin, and includes a historical sketch of the congregation.

162. DIETRICHSON, JOHANNES WILHELM CHRISTIAN (1815–1883).
      PAPERS, 1844–1896. 16 items. P 66.
Typescript copies of letters by a Norwegian-Lutheran clergyman describing his journey in 1844 to Wisconsin, his trips as itinerant pastor to various Norwegian settlements, establishment of the Koshkonong congregations, doctrinal differences, plans for a seminary, and relations with the Mormons. There are references to Søren Bache, Claus L. Clausen, Elling Eielsen, Lauritz J. Fribert, Hans Gasmann, Cleng Peerson, J. D. Reymert, John G. Smith, and Gustaf Unonius. After founding many congregations in Wisconsin, Dietrichson returned to Norway in 1850. He was opposed to emigration.

163. DØVING, CARL (1867–1937). PAPERS. 2 items. P 67.
Research notes on the hymn, "Praise to the Lord the Almighty, the King of Creation." Døving, a Lutheran clergyman, was a translator and student of hymns.

164. DOVRE MENIGHED, OSNABROCK, NORTH DAKOTA. RECORD
      BOOK, 1882–1932. P 427.
The minutes of Dovre congregation, including a history of its first fifty years, a constitution, names of members, and a list of persons owning lots in the cemetery.

165. DREWSEN, VIGGO (1858–1930). BIOGRAPHY, 1930. 2 items, typescript, 18 pages. P 68.
A biography and a memorial address concerning a Norwegian-American chemist who emigrated in 1894, became chief of the technical research department of West Virginia Pulp and Paper Company in New York, and held many patents in the cellulose industry.

166. DUCKSTAD, PAUL A. (b. 1913). ARTICLE, 1936. Typescript, 5 pages. P 69.
"We are Norwegian-Americans" summarizes the contributions to American culture made by the Norwegian immigrants.

167. DUFFNER, RUSSELL. ARTICLE, 1961. 1 item. Typescript, 14 pages. P 70.
A paper which seeks to disprove the existence of Norumbega, a Norwegian colony believed by some to have existed in the area of Boston about the year 1000.

168. ECKHOLTH, TORGEIR T. ARTICLE, ca. 1906. 13 pages. P 72.
"Lidt Wisconsin politik," written for *Fremtiden*, Drammen, Norway, by a resident of Wheeler, Wisconsin. The article deals with Wisconsin politics during the time of LaFollette and James O. Davidson.

169. EGEBERG, HANS O. (1875–1933). PAPERS, 1933–1952. 3 items. P 73.
A biography, tributes, and a letter concerning a Norwegian-born engineer and Gary Steel Works employment manager.

170. EIDE, ARTHUR H. (b. 1886). PAPERS, 1915–1972. 207 items. P 743.
Articles, correspondence, and clippings of a Norwegian-born teacher, missionary, author, and lecturer. Eide taught among the Eskimos on Little Diomede Island; was a missionary at Point Barrow, Alaska; promoted the establishment of industrial schools for Eskimos; donated his collection of Alaskan artifacts to the museum at Anchorage; and wrote three books on Alaska: *New Stories from Eskimo Land*, *Blandt byttekonefolket*, and *Drums of Diomede*.

171. EIDE, LARS BASTIANSEN. LETTER, n.d. P 75.
Letter written in Norway by Lars Eide to his children, Lars, Britha, and Margrethe in America. Britha, married to Ole Berhow, immigrated first to Illinois and then to Iowa in 1858.

172. EIDE, RANDOLPH (b. 1888). PAPERS, 1944. 3 items. P 76.
Biographical sketch (3 typescript pages) of the president of the Ohio Bell Telephone Company (1930–1953) and two issues of *The Ohio Bell*.

173. EIELSEN, ELLING (1804–1883). PAPERS, 1804–1943. 5 items and 1 volume. P 74.
Papers concerning a Norwegian-born Lutheran clergyman: copies of

Eielsen's certificate of ordination and of letters by him; transcripts of his baptism and confirmation records; typescript article (15 pages) entitled "Haugianarfolket paa Sundve Fraasegnuppskrifter" (1931) by Knut Bjorgaas; a thesis entitled "Elling Eielsen: Pioneer Lay Preacher and First Norwegian Lutheran Pastor in America" by Clarence J. Carlsen; an Eielsen bibliography by Olaf M. Norlie; a copy of an Eielsen letter to friends in Bergen; and some articles, clippings and pamphlets.

174. EIKELAND, PETER J. (1852–1927). PAPERS, 1880–1934. 4 boxes. P 538.
Articles, sermons, speeches, notebooks and manuscripts of a Norwegian-born educator and theologian. Topics include child training, Norwegian language, Norway's literature and history, church schools, Ibsen, and reminiscences.

175. EINERSON (TJØN), JOHN (1820–1900). PAPERS, 1823–1889. 8 items. P 77.
Immigration documents, and a bill of sale issued to a Norwegian-born Green County, Wisconsin, farmer.

176. EITTREIM, KNUD GUNDERSON. PAPERS, 1818–1872. 6 items. P 78.
Military discharge, probate settlement, and other Norwegian legal documents.

177. EKROLL, ØYSTEIN. FAMILY HISTORY, 1978. Typescript, 81 pages. P 940.
Paper written by a St. Olaf College student from Norway concerning his Norwegian-American relatives in the Thorstensen, Ekrem, Larson, Ellingson, and Nygaard families.

178. ELHOLM, AUGUSTUS CHRISTIAN GEORGE (Hans Abramson) (1731–1799). PAPERS, 1932. 4 items. P 79.
Correspondence and an article regarding Elholm, an army major in the American Revolutionary War, a companion of Pulaski, and a co-founder of the state of Franklin (later Tennessee). This essay by Miecislau Haiman is included in his book, *Poland and the American Revolution* (1932).

179. ELLEFSEN, EDWARD MARIUS (1883–1917). CHURCH HISTORY, ca. 1911. Typescript, 26 pages. P 80.
Historical sketch of a Norwegian Lutheran church in Chicago (1839–1900). Ellefsen was the pastor in Our Savior's Church (1915–1917).

180. ELLESTAD, GILBERT B. (1860–1938). PAPERS. 16 items. P 756.
A biographical sketch, farm contract, invoices, an account book, and photographs of a watchmaker, jeweler, and optician who lived at Lanesboro, Minnesota.

181. ELLINGSEN, JOHN (1855–1939). PAPERS, 1891–1947. 33 items. P 81.

Correspondence and articles of a Norwegian-born farmer and mason, Platte, South Dakota, which discuss local church life, the snowstorm of 1888, the depression in the 1890's, and World War I. References are made to Sven Oftedal, Theodor S. Reimestad, and Georg Sverdrup.

182. *EMIGRANTEN* (1852–1868). ARTICLE, 1972. 5 pages. P 800.

An issue of *The Journal of the Civil War Token Society* (Summer, 1972) containing an article by David D. Gladfelter, discussing *Emigranten*, an early Norwegian-American newspaper.

183. ENESTVEDT, OLE O. (1865–1958). PAPERS, 1932–1948. 17 items. P 82.

Articles and clippings of a Norwegian-born Minnesota farmer. The clippings are a series on local history that appeared in *Sacred Heart News* in 1944. "De Forenede Staters Værste Indianerkrig" (typewritten, 39 pages) deals with the Sioux uprising in 1862 as does "Intervju med Guri Endressen" by Gabriel Stene. The latter appeared in revised form in *Minneapolis Tidende* (January 19, 1933). The third article, which appeared in *Skandinaven* (January 1, 1937), concerns the snowstorm of January 7, 1873. Enestvedt wrote a column for *Decorah-Posten*, "Norske Pionerslegter," and was editor of Numedalslag yearbook for many years.

184. ENGER, RALPH. PAPERS, 1947–1949. 9 items including 1 typescript volume, 92 pages. P 664.

"The History of the Norwegian Club of San Francisco, 1898–1946," compiled and edited by Enger, editor of *The Pacific Coast Scandinavian*, treats the main events in the club's history: guests like Roald Amundsen after his discovery of the Northwest Passage, the purchase of Amundsen's ship *Gjøa* as a gift to San Francisco, the club's constitution, by-laws, and lists of officers from 1906 to 1946. The other documents also concern the activities of the club.

185. ENOCHSON, MARIE JOHNSON (1864–1953). REMINISCENCES. Typescript, 15 pages. P 840.

"The Story of Marie Johnson Enochson" recounts the author's memories of Norway, the journey to America, and life in the Wild Rice Community, North Dakota, located in the Red River Valley.

186. EPHPHATHA MISSIONS. PAPERS, 1925–1962. 10 items. P. 630.

An article, letter, and pictures relating to the Lutheran church for the deaf and the blind at Faribault, Minnesota. The article entitled "The Scandinavian Influence in Minnesota" by Wesley Lauritsen, a teacher for forty years at the Minnesota School for the Deaf, stresses the contributions of the Norwegians.

187. ERICKSON, JOHN T. PAPERS, 1975–1976. 21 items. P 830.

Papers collected and compiled by John Erickson: an account book

(1882) of Sorenson and Storaasli, merchants, Glyndon, Minnesota (Clay County); fliers from American Line, Chicago, and letters (some in German) dated 1869 and into 1870's; "Heritage, Peterson, Mn." compiled and edited by Erickson (1976); and Anton C. Tommeraasen papers, including correspondence and Norwegian military documents.

188. ERICKSON, THOMAS. COPYBOOK, 1877–1883. 1 volume. P 887.
Copybook of accounts and letters addressed to G. Gundersen, Stavanger, from Thomas Erickson from various ports in Europe. Transferred from Newberry Library, Chicago, (1977).

189. ERIKSEN, INGEBRET (1819–1896). PAPERS, 1846–1848. 41 items and 1 typescript volume, 96 pages. P 83.
Letters to Eriksen, farmer and merchant at Scandinavia, Wisconsin, from Lutheran clergymen regarding theological disputes; from friends and relatives concerning agricultural profits and losses; and from Civil War soldiers. The volume contains typewritten copies of these letters, copies of documents, and a family history. Correspondents include O. F. Duus, N. J. Ellestad, W. J. L. Frich, J. Krohn, A. Mikkelsen, and H. A. Preus. Alfred O. Erikson's article, "Scandinavia, Wisconsin," in *Studies and Records*, 15:185–209 (1949), is based partly on these papers.

190. LEIF ERIKSON. PAPERS, ca. 1889–1966. 5 boxes. P 552.
Correspondence, pamphlets, programs, clippings, minutes, financial reports, and scrapbooks concerned with promoting Leif Erikson as a discoverer of America. Among the papers are those of the Minnesota Leif Erikson Monument Association, incorporated in 1931 and dissolved in 1952, after erecting a bronze statue at the state capital grounds in St. Paul (October 9, 1949).

191. ERNSTSEN, OLINE (MRS. DANIEL) (b. 1882). REMINISCENCES, 1939, 1956. 2 items. P 84.
Recollections by a Norwegian-born pioneer housewife at Bear River, Minnesota, of her passage to America and of early pioneer days. Deals largely with religious life, transportation, and communication. Also, a historical sketch of the origin (1906) of the ladies aid at Bear River, Minnesota, Lutheran congregation.

192. ETHNIC STUDIES. PAPERS. P 813.
The Balch Institute reading lists, Minneapolis Multiethnic Curriculum Project, National Ethnic Studies Assembly Newsletter, University of Wisconsin Ethnic and Minority Studies Review, and ethnic conference announcements.

193. EVANGELICAL FREE CHURCH. REPORTS, 1913–1914. 2 items. P 85.
Yearly reports entitled *Aarsrapport for De evangeliske frikirkeforeningers aarsmøde*.

194. EVANSON, EVAN I. (1846–1902). PAPERS, 1879–1965. 9 items. P 86.
Correspondence and articles of a Norwegian-born farmer of Portland, North Dakota, and Stanwood, Washington, dealing with church, farm, family, health, and patriotism. Correspondents include Bjug Harstad and John Tingelstad.

195. EVANSTON BIBLE SCHOOL. CATALOGUES, 1933. 2 items. P 489.
Catalogues of an institution of the Norwegian-Danish Educational Society of the Methodist Episcopal Church in Evanston, Illinois.

196. EVENSEN, ANDERS. LETTER, 1861. 1 item. P 87.
Letter from a Freeborn County, Minnesota, farmer dealing with farm crops, the war and church conditions. Published in *Drammens Tidende* (December 3, 1949).

197. EVENSEN, LARS. REPORT, 1845. 1 item. P 435.
"Udvandringen til Amerika angaaende" appeared in *Morgenbladet* (February 16, 1845). The author reports on his trip to America to investigate living conditions among Norwegians. He supports J. W. C. Dietrichson in his opposition to emigration.

198. EVENSON (EVANS), BENEDICK (d. 1910). ARTICLE, 1911. Pamphlet, 16 pages. P 556.
"Nogle bemærkninger om ellingianernes og hauges synodes forhold til læren om den rosianske og den haugianske aandsretning," by a South Dakota farmer.

199. EVINRUDE, OLE (1877–1934). BIOGRAPHY. 4 items. P 88.
"Ole Evinrude and the Old Fellows," a 41-page biography of the Norwegian-born inventor of the outboard motor, by Gordon MacQuarrie, and circulars.

200. FAEREVAAG, LARS. AUTOGRAPH ALBUM, 1900. 1 item. P 415.
Autographs written by students at Fitjar amtskole, Norway.

201. FAIRVIEW HOSPITAL. THOMAS HOSPITAL. PAPERS, 1910–1942. 22 items. P 620.
Pamphlets, programs, and reports of two Minneapolis hospitals founded in 1906 and 1915 by members of the United Norwegian Lutheran Church of America.

202. FALKBERGET, JOHAN (1879–1967). JOURNAL, 1949. 1 item, 4 pages. P 89.
A statement, published and edited by Falkberget in response to the recognition given him on his seventieth birthday.

203. FAMILY HISTORIES AND GENEALOGIES. 9 boxes. P 539.
Manuscript, typescript, and printed accounts of Norwegian-American

families. For specific names, see description catalogue in NAHA archives.

204. FARSETH, OLAUS CHRISTIANSEN (1852–1913). NOTEBOOK, 1886. 1 item. P 925.
Notebook used by O. C. Farseth when he was a student at St. Olaf's School in 1886.

205. FARSETH, PAULINE (1889–1972). CLIPPINGS, 1972. 3 items. P 926.
Tributes to Pauline Farseth published in *Minnesota Posten* by Nina Draxten and Audrey Lawrence. Both writers had been students of Miss Farseth, who taught at North High School, Minneapolis, and was active in cultural activities in the Twin City area.

206. FEDDE, ELIZABETH (1850–1921). MEMOIRS. Typescript, 40 pages. P 801.
"Memoirs of Sister Elizabeth" (translated by P. J. Hertsgaard), an account of a Norwegian-born deaconess who began her career at the Deaconess Home in Christiania (now Oslo) in 1873, and who came to New York in 1883, where she organized a deaconess program in connection with the Seaman's Mission Church in Brooklyn. Eventually she established deaconess hospitals in Brooklyn and in Minneapolis. This account covers briefly her career in Norway and only the first two years in the United States. An account of her career is in *Studies and Records*, v. 20.

207. FEDERATION OF NORWEGIAN WOMEN'S SOCIETIES, CHICAGO. RECORDS, 1915–1964. 1 box. P 907.
Minute books of the Federation of Norwegian Women's Societies, Chicago, covering the years 1915–1924, 1924–1932, 1932–1940, 1948–1954, 1962–1964.
The Federation was organized "to bring women of Norwegian descent into close union for mutual advantage and education, to encourage better civic conditions and to provide scholarships for worthy students of Norwegian descent."

208. FELLAND, OLE G. (1853–1938). PAPERS, 1869–1935. 12 boxes. P 708.
Papers of a Lutheran clergyman (1879–1889), college professor and librarian (1881–1926): articles, clippings, correspondence, photographs, programs, reports, sermons, speeches and a 73-page typescript autobiography.
The correspondence includes letters written from Luther College; Northwestern College; Concordia Seminary; eastern Dane County, Wisconsin; Rothsay, Minnesota; Idaho, and Washington. Among the photographs are several of eastern Dane County, Wisconsin farm scenes and interiors as well as pictures of prominent Norwegian Americans and of St. Olaf College.

209. FETVEDT, ANUND OLSEN (1831?–1911) and SVEINUNG OLSEN FETVEDT (1832–1911). LETTERS, 1868–1885. 45 items. P 768.

Copies of letters written by two immigrant brothers to their family in Norway, beginning with an account of the journey from Norway and later recording their experiences as Minnesota farmers. The later letters are from Ottertail County, Minnesota. A genealogical sketch prepared by a descendant of Anund is included.

The letters were given to F. A. Fedtvedt, Fergus Falls, Minnesota, July, 1970, by Margit Fetvedt, Vinje, Telemark.

210. FINMARK MISJONSFORENING, MINNEAPOLIS. RECORDS, 1924–1960. 5 volumes. P 670.

Minutes and financial records of a society organized to help support mission work in northern Norway.

211. FJELSTAD, ROLF K. (1849–1912). DOCTRINE, 1903. Handwritten, 7 pages. P 556.

"Er det en skjæbnens ironi eller hvad er det? Hvorledes veien synes banet for Missourianismen blandt vort folk" deals with a doctrinal dispute in the Lutheran church. Fjelstad was a Lutheran clergyman.

212. FLADAGER, MONS H. (d. 1905). CORRESPONDENCE, 1859–1867. 5 items. P 91.

Letters received by Fladager at Spring Grove, Minnesota, from his brother, Ole H., in Christiania and Rome, and from an unidentified correspondent at Blue Mounds, Wisconsin. Ole H. was a sculptor.

213. FLEISCHER, FREDERICK (1821–1878). CLIPPING, 1878. 1 item. P 93.

Clipping from *Fædrelandet og Emigranten*, La Crosse, Wisconsin, of which Fleischer was editor, containing his obituary.

214. FLEISCHER, WILHELM. LECTURE, 1919. Typescript, 18 pages. P 94.

Paper entitled "The 400,000 H. P. Hydro-Electric Air-Nitrogen Plant at Notodden, Norway," giving a description and historical development, presented before the Brooklyn Engineers Club. Fleischer was the purchasing engineer for the Norwegian Hydro-Electric Company.

215. FLEKKEFJORDLAGET. RECORDS, 1926–1955. 1 volume. P 95.

Constitution and minutes of Flekkefjordlag in Minneapolis.

216. FLETRE, LARS. (1904–1977). PAPERS, 1977. 2 items. P 943.

Tributes to a sculptor who came from Voss, Norway, to Chicago in 1923, went back to Norway in 1933, but returned to Chicago in 1954.

217. FLOAN, PETER O. (b. 1861). REMINISCENCES, March, 1941. Typescript, 16 pages. P 96.

"Reminiscences from the Pioneer Days in Goodhue County, Minnesota," containing names of early settlers and anecdotes concerning methods of acquiring land, establishment of churches and schools, fear of Indians, and general community life.

218. FLUGUM, OLE NILSEN (1862–1939). PAPERS, 1865–1939. 2 boxes. P 540.
Articles, clippings, poems, records, and scrapbooks of a Norwegian-born farmer and writer.
Scrapbooks of clippings from *Visergutten* and *Decorah-Posten* contain biographies of pioneers in Winnebago County, Iowa, including those of Jens M. Dahl and Niels Chr. Flugum, written by Flugum. A scrapbook of clippings from *Amerika* (1900) contains letters relative to the Boer War and recent Norwegian literature. The Lutheran church record book contains rosters of members and their yearly contributions to the Winnebago, Fertile, West Prairie, North Prairie, Ellington Prairie, and Lake Mills congregations (1865–1887).

219. FOLK ARTS FOUNDATION OF AMERICA. PAPERS, 1943–1955. 209 items. P 97.
Correspondence and reports concerning membership, dues, dinner meetings, recordings of folksongs, and publication of a Midwest folklore journal. The foundation, organized about 1944, flourished for a decade.

220. FOLKEDAHL, BEULAH (1896–1971). PAPERS, 1958–1971. 53 items. P 767.
Correspondence, photographs, tributes and research notes of the curator of the NAHA Archives (1960–1971).

221. FOLKEDAHL, KNUDT OLSEN DAHL (1829–1913). PAPERS, 1836–1884. 10 items. P 98.
Correspondence of a Norwegian-born, Dane County, Wisconsin, farmer. The letters were written from Winona, Minnesota; Grand Forks, North Dakota; Canton, South Dakota; and Auburndale, Wisconsin.

222. FOREIGN LANGUAGE INFORMATION SERVICE. NORWEGIAN BUREAU. REPORTS, 1925–1931. 100 items. P 665.
Reports to Norwegian immigrants concerning United States immigration laws, naturalization process, suffrage, legal and property rights, labor laws, agriculture, education, and languages.

223. FORSHAUG, JENS H. (b. 1911). TRAVEL REPORT, 1951. 1 item. Typescript, 6 pages. P 99.
A manuscript entitled "Alaska" by an Alaskan gold miner, reindeer inspector, and author, with comments on people, climate, geography, and history.

224. FOSS, HANS A. (1851–1929). PAPERS, 1923. 3 items. P 100.
A photograph and clippings of articles which appeared in *Decorah*

Posten dealing with life in the Red River Valley. Foss, journalist and author, emigrated in 1877.

225. FOSSUM, ANDRES (1860–1943). PAPERS, 1875–1941. 2 boxes. P 541.

Correspondence, manuscripts, articles and records of a teacher, author, Greek scholar, and archeologist.

Fossum, born in Allamakee County, Iowa, attended Luther College, Johns Hopkins University (Ph.D.), and the American School of Classical Studies, Athens, Greece. He was author of *The Norse Discovery of America* (1918) and of articles on the theater in ancient Greece.

His correspondents include George O. Berg, Gisle Bothne, Albert E. Egge, O. G. Felland, J. F. Fries, Hjalmar R. Holand, Olaf Huseby, Th. N. Mohn, Anna Mohn (Mrs. Th. N.), Knute Nelson, George A. Torrison, Andrew A. Veblen, and H. T. Ytterboe.

226. FOSTVEIT, KNUT (1900–1974). POEMS. 1 box. P 778.

Norwegian poems by a Norwegian-born amateur poet who lived in New Jersey and New York. He emigrated to the U.S. in 1927, and worked at various trades, but maintained life-long interest in writing poetry. Some of his poems were published.

227. FOX RIVER SETTLEMENT CENTENNIAL. PAPERS, 1933–1940. 1 box. P 542.

Articles, correspondence, clippings, pictures, programs, and reports dealing with the centennial celebration of the first permanent Norwegian settlement in the United States in the Fox River Valley, La Salle County, Illinois.

Among the papers are the addresses by Marshall Solberg and Arthur Andersen and an article, "The Fox River Norwegian Settlement," by Carlton C. Qualey. B. O. Berge, Orlando Ingvoldstad, Joseph M. Johnson, John J. Sonsteby, J. Jørgen Thompson are the chief correspondents.

228. FRANKLIN SCHOOL. REPORT. 1 item. P 491.

Report concerning a school conducted in Bjug A. Harstad's parsonage, Mayville, North Dakota (1878–1880).

229. *FREDERIKSHALDS BUDSTIKKE.* ARTICLE, 1853. 1 item.P 435.

Copy of an article entitled "Nogle ord om udvandringen" published June 16 and 19 and July 7. The article is a rebuttal to the theme of a *Drammens Tidende* article that emigration will not harm Norway. It laments the loss of capital and workers, gives statistics on the number of emigrants at each of several ports of departure, and urges governmental regulation.

230. FREMAD–I MINNEOLA, GOODHUE COUNTY, MINNESOTA. RECORDS, 1889–1894. 2 volumes. P 431.

The constitution and minutes of the meetings of Fremad, a debating society, organized to promote good citizenship. The programs consisted largely of debates on such topics as capital punishment, the power of the press, equitable taxes, restricted immigration, the discovery of America, direct elections, the Farmers Alliance, the preservation of the Norwegian language in America, and the effects of machinery on labor.

231. FREMMEGAARD, ARNE (1883–1946). SCRAPBOOK. 1 volume. P 849.
Scrapbook of clippings and photographs concerning Norwegian Americans and their activities in Minneapolis.

Fremmegaard, a Minneapolis banker, came from Norway in 1924. He was general chairman of the committee in charge of arrangements for the visit of Crown Prince Olav and Crown Princess Märtha in 1939.

232. FRIBERT, LAURITS J. (b. 1808). HANDBOOK, CHRISTIANIA, 1847. Typescript, 96 pages. P 101.
Haandbog for emigranter til Amerikas vest is a typewritten copy of a published work by Fribert, a former Danish official, who farmed near Pine Lake, Wisconsin, from 1843 to about 1847. Although containing comments on Indians, church, and government, it is largely a discussion of methods of agriculture.

233 FRIES, L. A. PAPERS, 1968–1969. 2 items. P 705.
Letters containing data regarding Knud Langeland, Søren Bache, Mons Adland, and Beaver Creek and Muskego settlements.

234. FROHLIN, JOHN (1878–1958). PAPERS. 6 items. P 803.
Bibliographical compilations on the voyages and discoveries of the vikings. Frohlin, an engineer, Bayonne, New Jersey, owned a large library on this subject.

235. FUGLESTAD, TORKEL T. (1856–1954). AUTOBIOGRAPHY. Typescript, 19 pages. P 850.
"Memories from the School of Life, an Autobiographical Account by a Norwegian-born North Dakota Farmer," translated by Charles H. Skalet and R. E. Fuglestad. Born at Bjerkrem, Norway, Torkel Fuglestad emigrated together with his wife in 1883. He lived on a farm near Hannaford, North Dakota, wrote for Norwegian-American newspapers, was a charter member of Oak Grove Seminary, Fargo, North Dakota, and served on its Board of Trustees.

236. FURUSETH, ANDREW (1854–1938). PAPERS, 1895–1954. 52 items. P 102.
Papers of a Norwegian-born labor leader and author. Furuseth's agitation for improved status of seamen resulted in the passage of several laws, including La Follette's Seamen's Act of 1915. He was president of the International Seamen's Union of America (1908–1938).

Among the papers are an Andrew Furuseth bibliography compiled at the Library of Congress; Olaf Ray letters containing information on early experiences of Norwegian sailors in America; an article about Furuseth by A. N. Rygg; and several pamphlets by Furuseth.

237. GALE COLLEGE. PAPERS, 1901–1940. 2 boxes. P 498.
Brochures, bulletins, catalogues, pictures, reports, and a history of a Lutheran academy established in 1901, and a junior college in 1933 at Galesville, Wisconsin. Founded by George Gale in 1854 and consecutively operated by the Methodist and the Presbyterian churches until 1901.

238. GARBORG, ARNE (1851–1924). LETTERS, 1919. 2 items. P 103.
Copies of letters by the Norwegian author to Mrs. Mabel Johnson Leland (1872–1947), Kenyon, Minnesota, wife of Dr. Ragnvald Leland and translator of Garborg's *Den burtkomne faderen*, published in 1920 as *The Lost Father*. The letters discuss practical aspects of publication.

239. GARBORG, HULDA. ARTICLE, 1914–1915. 10 clippings. P 104.
"Et myrdet folk," concerning the American Indian, ran serially in *Morgenposten*, Oslo, after the author's visit to the United States in 1913. Author was the wife of Arne Garborg.

240. GASMANN FAMILY. PAPERS, n.d. 4 items. Typescript, 12 pages. P 105.
Biographical data collected by Alfred Gasmann, Skien, Norway, and J. S. Schneider concerning Hans Jacob and Johan Gotfred Gasmann, their ancestors and descendants. Hans came to Pine Lake, Wisconsin, in 1843 and Johan to Amherst ca. 1847.

241. *GAZETTE WEEKLY*. NEWS SHEET, 1948–1950. 17 items. P 106.
West St. Olaf Avenue (Northfield, Minnesota) neighborhood news, edited by young Robert Fossum.

242. GEIST, WALTER (1893–1951). PAPERS, 1938–1950. 11 items. P 107.
Clippings, letters, and a pamphlet concerning an engineer, inventor, and president of Allis Chalmers Manufacturing Company, Milwaukee, Wisconsin.

243. GIESKE, MILLARD L. BIOGRAPHY. 1 volume, typescript, 186 pages. P 748.
"Heroes, Sagas, Politics: Knute Nelson, 1861–64," is divided into three parts: the Political Genesis of Knute Nelson; Notes and Essays; and Correspondence. The latter consists of 57 letters that Nelson wrote as a Union soldier during the Civil War.

244. GJERDRUM, JØRGEN. LETTERS, 1874–1875. 17 items. P 435.
Copies of letters sent to *Dagbladet* by Gjerdrum while on a trip to Norwegian settlements in America. He discusses life on board ship, the seamen in New York City, the position of the Norwegian servant girl in

American society, the trustworthiness of most immigration agents, comforts of the American hotel, American postal service, social life of La Crosse Norwegians, and confusion among the Lutheran churches.

245. GJERPEN AND VALDRES CONGREGATIONS, MANITOWOC, WISCONSIN. RECORD BOOK, 1864–1868. P 556.
The records of the church schools of the congregations, including the names and ages of pupils and the studies pursued.

246. GJERSET, KNUT (1865–1936). PAPERS, 1920–1937. 5 boxes. P 683.
Papers of a Norwegian-born historian and author: manuscript material of his projected Norwegian-American Encyclopedia, clippings and correspondence about policies and publications of the NAHA and the collecting of artifacts for the Norwegian-American Museum, and a manuscript biography of his father, Ole S. Gjerset. Correspondents include Theodore C. Blegen, Ludvig Hektoen, Laurence M. Larson, Torkel Oftelie, Birger Osland, and Ditlef G. Ristad.

247. GJESTVANG, T. ANDREAS. LETTER, 1852. I item. P 435.
Copy of a letter by the postmaster in Løiten, Hedemark, printed in *Arbeiderforeningernes blad*. The letter is a reply to a series of letters entitled "Billeder fra Nordamerika i 1849 af A. Tolmer." Gjestvang criticized the dark picture the French captain painted of Texas after his trip through parts of the United States. He believed that emigration could be defended on the basis of poverty and unemployment.

248. GLASOE, PAUL M. (1873–1956). LECTURES, 1912–1939. 36 items. P 109.
Lectures given by a member of the faculty over WCAL, St. Olaf College radio station, on various scientific subjects such as pasteurization, national resources, human physiology, master farmers, alcohol, the role of honesty in scientific progress, and six published articles treating chemistry, and influence of Norwegian culture.

249. GLASS, GAINES. TRAVEL REPORT, 1976. Typescript, 65 pages. P 894.
"Summer League Boots," an account of a trip along the Norwegian coast from Bergen to Hammerfest on the ship *Vesteraalen*, and the return to Oslo via ship and train. The account includes historical and legendary details, and is illustrated by photographs taken by the author.

250. GLENWOOD ACADEMY. PAPERS, 1894–1911. 9 items. P 492.
Catalogues, history, and report of a Lutheran institution in Glenwood, Minnesota (1894–1911).

251. GLENWOOD OLD PEOPLE'S HOME. PAPERS, 1915–1924. 3 items. P 631.
Article and pamphlets concerning the history and regulations of an institution founded in 1914 in Glenwood, Minnesota.

252. GLESNE, ELISE TORGRIMSON FJELDE (MRS. OLE) (1869–1946). PAPERS, 1915–1931. 176 items. P 112.
Poems both original and translated, and a story entitled "Da bedstemor var hos os" by the wife of an Iowa Lutheran clergyman.

253. GLESNE, OLE (1869–1955). PAPERS, 1851–1943. 59 items, including 1 volume. P 608.
Correspondence, reports, and a scrapbook of a Lutheran clergyman. The correspondence and reports concern chiefly the activities of the board of publications of the United Norwegian Lutheran Church of America, of which Glesne was a member.
The clippings in the scrapbook are chiefly from *Norden* and *Amerika* and set forth the controversies between them regarding Ragnar M. J. Monrad at Luther College, the anti-Missouri movement within the Norwegian Synod, and politics in Wisconsin. The scrapbook contains letters and articles by Gisle Bothne, John N. Kildahl, Laur. Larsen, Ragnar M. J. Monrad, Herman A. Preus, and L. A. Stenholt.

254. GOODHUE COUNTY LÆRERFORENING. RECORDS, 1885. 3 items. P 110.
Minutes of a meeting of the Goodhue County Teachers' Association held November 30, to discuss co-operation among the Norwegian Synod congregations and the influence of the home, school, and the Bible in child training.

255. GOPLERUD, PER. PAPERS, 1976. 4 items. P 875.
Papers concerning the area of Hedalen, Valdres, the Hedalen Stavkirke, the families of the area, and letters from Per Goplerud.

256. GRAN BOARDING SCHOOL. REPORT, ca. 1920. 1 item. P 493.
Report concerning a school at Mayville, North Dakota, founded in the 1880's by Bjug A. Harstad, local Lutheran clergyman.

257. GRAND FORKS COLLEGE. PAPERS, 1892–1922. 12 items. P 494.
Catalogues and reports of a private Lutheran secondary school founded in Grand Forks in 1891.

258. GRANSKOU, JOHANNES (1859–1938). ARTICLE, ca. 1930. 1 volume, 16 pages. P 556.
A pamphlet entitled *Navneforandringen* by Granskou and others, containing an account of the origin of the name of "Den norsk lutherske kirke i Amerika" and efforts made to change it.

259. GREETING CARDS, 1901–1932. 481 items, 2 boxes. P 615.
An assortment of cards for various seasons and occasions.

260. GREVSTAD, MATHILDE BERG (1862–1952?). REMINISCENCES. 1 volume, typescript, 45 pages. P 746.
"Ole-Iver and Johanne Berg: Pioneers," a translation of Mrs. Grevstad's account of her parents who emigrated from Norway in 1861,

first to Wisconsin, then to Fillmore County, Minnesota, and finally to the Red River Valley. The author presents a vivid picture of the journey to the Red River Valley and of the pioneer community (Lake Park) where her parents settled. Translated by Agnes Grevstad Lee.

261. GREVSTAD, NICOLAY ANDREAS (1851–1940). PAPERS, 1889–1940. 7 boxes. P 553.
Correspondence, articles, reports, and clippings of a Norwegian-born journalist, diplomat, and financier.

Grevstad was a practicing attorney and editor of *Dagbladet* (Oslo) before emigrating in 1883. In America he was editor of *Nordvesten* (St. Paul); leading editorial writer for Minneapolis *Daily Tribune*; editor of *Skandinaven* (Chicago) (1892–1911); United States minister to Uruguay and Paraguay (1911–1915); publicity director of Minnesota Safety Commission; chief of the foreign language press publicity service for the Republican National Committee (1919–1925); agent of a Chicago bank syndicate for Uruguay; and editor of *Skandinaven* (1930–1940). Articles by Grevstad on courts of conciliation in Norway and in America appeared in the *Atlantic Monthly* (September, 1891, and November, 1893).

The correspondence includes dispatches to the United States Department of State and letters concerning American interests in Uruguay and Paraguay; national political problems; Norwegian settlement; and investment opportunities. Among the correspondents are William Jennings Bryan, Gilbert N. Haugen, Nils P. Haugen, E. H. Hobe, Hanna Astrup Larsen, Medill McCormick, Knute Nelson, Theodore Roosevelt, Elihu Root, and William Howard Taft.

Primary election reform, patriotism of the Scandinavian press and church, the wheat farmer during World War I, Non-Partisan League, and women's suffrage are some of the topics discussed in articles, press releases, and letters.

262. GRIMSTVEDT, ABRAHAM. CORRESPONDENCE, 1850–1875. Typescript, 57 pages. P 113.
"Nybygger-breve fra Amerika " (33 letters) were collected and intended for publication by Abraham Grimstvedt, Nissedal, Telemark, Norway. Written in Dane County, Wisconsin; Fillmore County, Minnesota; and Decorah and Lake Mills, Iowa, by Grimstvedt's three sisters and their husbands, the letters give a favorable picture of life in America. Health, farming, school, church and transportation are the topics most often discussed. The letters were never published.

263. GRIMSTVEDT, OLE (d. 1902). REMINISCENCES, 1895. Typescript, 57 pages. P 114.
An earthy and realistic account of a western Dane County, Wisconsin, farmer regarding his hospital life during the Civil War.

264. GRINDELAND, INGEBRIGHT HALSTENSEN. PAPERS, 1824-1931. 5 items. P 111.

Certificates and letters of a Norwegian-born Winneshiek County, Iowa, pioneer.

265. GRØNVOLD, J. CHRISTIAN. (1833–1896). REPORT, 1878. 1 item. P 851.

Newspaper clipping from *Norden* (March 13, 1878): "Virkningen av indvandringen paa de indvandrede nordmænd, af Dr. Chr. Grønvold," a translation of a part of his report in the Minnesota State Board of Health, 6th *Annual Report* (1878). The title of the original is "Effects of Immigration on the Immigrated Norwegians."

Dr. Grønvold, a physician in the Holden community of Goodhue County, was born at Fron, Gudbrandsdal, Norway. He emigrated to the United States in 1865.

266. GRONDAHL, JENS K. (1869–1941). CLIPPINGS, 1914–1924. 8 items. P 115.

Biography and poems by a Norwegian-born editor, state legislator, and poet, Red Wing, Minnesota.

267. GRONDAHL, LARS O. (b. 1880). PAPERS, 1911–1964. 9 items. P 116.

Articles, citations, and autobiography (30 typescript pages) of a Minnesota-born physicist, teacher, research consultant, inventor, and author.

268. GULBRANDSEN, PEER (b. 1907). PAPERS, 1969–1976. 2 items. P 876.

Copy of a clipping from *Østlendingen* (November 9, 1969), about Peer Gulbrandsen, a Norwegian-born artist in the Chicago area. Also a record of an interview with him conducted by Rolf Erickson in 1976.

269. GULBRANDSON, MATHIAS (b. 1858). POEMS. 1 volume, 36 pages, 1875. P 416.

A transcript collection of 22 poems by a pioneer of Manchester, Minnesota.

270. GULLIXSON, ANDRES. PAPERS, 1896–1920. 6 items. P 782.

Letters written to Andres Gullixson while he was a student at Luther College, Decorah, Iowa, and after he was established as a physician at Albert Lea, Minnesota.

271. GUNDERSEN, OSCAR (1861–1941). PAPERS, 1934–1939. 1 box. P 650.

Manuscripts and typescripts of 39 poems in Norwegian; two collections of short stories, "Fra Gutteaarene" and "Brevities," a dramatic sketch, "Alcestis;" and two stories with religious themes, "Expiation" and "Vigilius, Leaves from the Journal of a Roman," a notebook, and three diaries.

Gundersen, a Chicago accountant, wrote two books entitled *Stem-*

ningsbilleder (1891), a collection of poems, and *Ralph Waldo Emerson, En Fremstilling* (1910).

272. GUNDERSON, CARL M. RINGEN. GENEALOGY, 1969. 6 volumes. P 728.
"Norwegian Ancestors of General George Washington," "Famous Americans of Norwegian Descent," "Leif Erikson's Genealogy," "Biography and Ancestry of Andrew Furuseth," and "John Anon 'Snowshoe' Thompson."

273. GUNDERSON, SEVERIN (1854–1947). PAPERS, 1887–1919. 5 items. P 117.
Correspondence and a statement regarding the doctrine of predestination by a Norwegian-born Lutheran clergyman, Mount Horeb, Wisconsin.

274. GUNNULDSON, OLE (1842–1919). GUNNULSON, PEDER G. (1874–1946). PAPERS, 1870's–1933. 21 items and 4 volumes. P 666.
Correspondence, diaries, creamery reports, tobacco pool reports, tax receipts, and assessor's statements (1891) for Town of Christiana, Dane County, Wisconsin. The correspondence deals with farm interests in Yellow Medicine County, Minnesota, and Arvada, Wyoming, and also with the construction of First East Koshkonong Lutheran Church of which Ole Gunnuldson was architect and builder.

275. HAAEIM, SJUR JØRGENSEN. ARTICLE, Christiania, 1842. Typescript, 12 pages. P 118.
A manuscript entitled "Oplysninger om forholdene i Nordamerika især forsaavidt de derhen udvandrede Norskesskjæbne angaar," by a disillusioned Norwegian pathfinder who admonished his countrymen not to emigrate to America. Translated and edited by Gunnar J. Malmin, it was published in *Studies and Records*, 3 (1928).

276. HAAVIK, OLAI (OLAF) LUDVIG (b. 1885). LETTERS, 1962. 2 items. P 852.
Copies of letters between a Norwegian-born Lutheran clergyman and a former parishioner, Jennie Hartmann, containing reminiscences of the Ballard Lutheran Church in Seattle, Washington, and biographical information about Haavik.

277. HAGEN, ANDERS O. (1826–1902). PAPERS, 1859–1878. 12 items. P 119.
Correspondence, autobiography, and a credit record from Klæbo seminarium of a Norwegian-born Lutheran clergyman of St. James and Windom, Minnesota. The letters, written by Michael Borge, W. J. L. Frich, U. V. Koren, B. J. Muus, H. A. Preus, and P. A. Rasmussen relate to Hagen's pastoral call to America, his ministry at St. James, and his call to Windom.

278. HAGEN, O. J. (b. 1872). PAPERS, ca. 1932–1939. 3 items. P 120.

A biographical sketch of, and two articles by a Moorhead, Minnesota, physician.

279. HAGEN, PETRA (1876–1959). DIARY, 1896. 1 volume. P 121.

A diary of a St. Olaf College student containing comments about election of 1896, Foundation Day observance, Alpha Beta Chi programs, dormitory life, college discipline, faculty, students, and courses.

280. HAGEN, SIVERT N. (1872–1966). PAPERS, 1896–1966. 155 items. P 122.

Articles, clippings, and correspondence of a Minnesota-born Luther College graduate and professor of English at Franklin and Marshall College, Lancaster, Pennsylvania.

281. HAGEN, SVEND GULLIKSEN. (b. 1821). PAPERS, 1827–1965. 5 items. P 123.

Vaccination certificate, emigration contract, and correspondence concerning same.

282. HALLING, PER. LETTER, 1908. 1 item. P 124.

Letter by an Ashland, Wisconsin, resident to Norway, containing references to cultural life and national politics.

283. HALVEG, PER. LETTERS, 1909–1913. 2 items. P 125.

Letters written at Ashland, Wisconsin, by Halveg, the secretary of Sæter Lodge, Sons of Norway, discussing politics and cultural interests.

284. HALVERSON, MORRIS. MEMOIRS, n.d. Typescript, 32 pages. P 858.

"Our Norwegian Ancestors of 1868," an account based on the experiences of emigrants from Solør who left Christiania (April 4, 1868) and arrived in Quebec 13 weeks later. Centers around the families of Amund Amundson, Ole Halverson, and Gunder Gunderson, whose journey continued by box car to La Crosse, Wisconsin, and on to areas near Blair, Wisconsin. Their life in the pioneer communities is described up to 1878.

285. HALVORSON, KNUT (1847–1939). PAPERS, 1872–1878, 1955–1960. 3 items. P 126.

Remnants of a diary kept by Knut Halvorson (Knud Halvorsen Brekke), Portage County, Wisconsin, portraying pioneer life in central Wisconsin. Accompanying the diary is a letter by Hannah Halvorson Teslow and a translation of the diary by Malcolm Rosholt, Rosholt, Wisconsin.

286. HAMARS BUDSTIKKE. ARTICLE, 1866. 1 item. P 435.

Copy of an article entitled "Til en smule oplysning for Amerika farere," a signed complaint against American emigration companies in their treatment of Norwegian passengers on board ship.

287. *HAMAR STIFTSTIDENDE*. ARTICLES, 1867. 2 items. P 435.
Copies of notices of arrival in America and of appreciation to shipping lines for safe passage signed by passengers.

288. HAMRAN, HANS. PAPERS, 1933–1963. 22 items and 1 volume. P 127.
A logbook of a Norwegian sailor who together with his brother Harald crossed the Atlantic in 1933 in a 25-foot boat in four months and then continued by water from New York to the Chicago World's Fair (A Century of Progress). Filed with the logbook are letters and pictures. The boat is at the Norwegian-American Museum, Decorah, Iowa.

289. HAMRE, HENRY B. (1856–1933). RECORDS, 1912–1930. 7 volumes. P 684.
Account books and undated prescription books of a Northfield, Minnesota, pharmacist.

290. HAMRE, JAMES S. ARTICLES, 1971–1974. 6 items. P 805.
Articles by a teacher of religion and philosophy at Waldorf College, Forest City, Iowa.

291. HANDE, HALLVARD H. (1846–1887). FOLKLORE, 1871. 1 volume. Typescript, 67 pages. P 128.
Translation of *Segner fraa Bygdom*, by a Norwegian-born Lutheran clergyman and editor, consisting of some forty legends from Valdres, Norway. The translation was done in the 1950's by Hande's granddaughter, M. E. Midelfort, Eau Claire, Wisconsin.
Hande was the editor of *Norden*, Chicago (1874–1882 and 1884–1887), and the author of a play, *Ei Hugvending* (A Change of Heart), based on Valdres superstition and tradition.

292. HANSEN, ANNE M. AND H. J. LETTER, 1853. 1 item. P 435.
Copy of a letter to a relative commending American wages, climate, crops, machinery and tools, food, and work opportunities. Written from Janesville, Rock County, Wisconsin.

293. HANSEN, CARL GUSTAV OTTO (1871–1960). PAPERS, 1862–1958. 17 boxes. P 543.
Correspondence, articles, lectures, reports, clippings, and diaries of a Norwegian-born Minneapolis journalist, musician, lecturer, and author.
Hansen immigrated in 1881. He was a member of the editorial staff of *Minneapolis Tidende* (1897–1935) and the chief editor (1923–1935), contributor to *Skandinaven* (1935–1937), educational director of Sons of Norway (1937–1954). He was director of the Norwegian Glee Club (1912–1945), president of the Norwegian-Danish Press Association, and a founder of Det Norske Selskap and the NAHA. He was a music

critic, book reviewer, biographer of Norwegian Americans, and wrote *My Minneapolis* (1956).

The papers deal with the activities of Norwegian-American singing societies in Minneapolis and other cities, the tribulations of translators, the cultural creativity of Norwegian Americans, the study of Norwegian in the Minneapolis public schools and at St. Olaf College, biographies of Norwegian Americans, and other related subjects.

"Sagas of Today" (a *Minneapolis Journal* column) and "For 50 aar siden," "Det Norske Amerika gjennem Hundred Aar," and "Glimt fra Livet i det Norske Amerika" (*Minneapolis Tidende* columns) are among the clippings.

The collection contains correspondence from significant authors, journalists and scholars of the day. For a list of correspondents, see description catalogue in NAHA Archives.

294. HANSEN, CONRAD J. REMINISCENCES. Typescript, 4 pages. P 944.
"Choosing a Life-Work," an account of how the author became interested in the YMCA, an organization he served from 1919 to 1949.

295. HANSEN, G. ARMAUER (1841–1912). REMINISCENCES, 1910. 1 item. P 806.
Excerpt from the published memoirs of a Norwegian physician who discovered the leprosy baccillus. The excerpt deals with Dr. Hansen's journey in 1887 to St. Paul to work with Dr. Edvard Bøckmann and with his travels in the Middle West.

296. HANSEN, JEAN SKOGERBOE. DISSERTATION, 1972. Typescript, 95 pages. P 910.
"History of the John Anderson Publishing Company of Chicago, Illinois." MA degree, Graduate Library School, University of Chicago.

297. HANSEN, LARS. CORRESPONDENCE, 1876–1924. 6 items. P 129.
Letters from Lars Hansen and nephews, Christiania, Norway, to his brother in Chicago.

298. HANSEN, LESTER W. (1886–1977). AUTOBIOGRAPHY, 1968. Typescript, 475 pages. P 706.
Autobiography of a teacher and railway postal clerk in Hendricks, Owatonna, St. Paul, Minnesota, and Huron, South Dakota. Discusses farm and school life in Minnesota, Civil War experiences of his father, World War I and II, investments in farm and city property, travels, and retirement to St. Petersburg, Florida. Included is a 17-page manuscript, "The Viking Race," by Hansen. He is the author of the *Anderson-Krogh Genealogy*, 1956.

299. HANSEN, PEDER J. (1851–1933). PAPERS, 8 items. P 130.
Papers of a Norwegian-born carpenter and merchant of Sharon, North Dakota, consisting of several poems and his autobiography in which he tells of early houses, land problems, carpentry, and the founding of congregations. Edited by Vigleik E. Boe, 1933.

300. HANSON FAMILY. CORRESPONDENCE, 1891–1896. 11 items. P 131.

Letters written from Norway and from Vienna, South Dakota, by members of the family to relatives.

301. HANSON, ADOLPH M. (1888–1959). PAPERS, 1919–1942. 2 boxes. P 544.

Papers of a Faribault, Minnesota, physician: poems, correspondence, and articles dealing largely with his invention of, and the patent on extract of parathyroid gland, the royalties from which he donated to the Smithsonian Institute.

Hanson was the son of Martin G. Hanson and grandson of Østen Hanson, past presidents of the Hauge Synod. Hanson was a major in the Sanitary Commission during World War I.

302. HANSON, GUSTAV S. RECORDS, 1889, 1891, 1897, 1906. 4 items. P 132.

A Sunday school class attendance record by Gustav S. Hanson, a Norwegian-born pharmacist in Canton, South Dakota.

303. HANSON, HARRY BURTON (1884–1963). PAPERS, 1976. 6 items. P 877.

Genealogical information, a photograph, and clippings describing the work of a Norwegian American who was the chief engineer for the Ford Motor Company and the designer of the Willow Run bomber plant near Detroit, Michigan.

304. HANSON, MARTIN GUSTAV (1859–1915). PAPERS, 1880–1915. 36 items. P 133.

Papers of a Lutheran clergyman: correspondence, reports, letters of call, ordination papers, and the first diploma issued by Red Wing Seminary Department of Theology. The correspondence deals with such topics as Red Wing Seminary and the union movement among Norwegian Lutheran synods. Hanson was president of Red Wing Seminary and also of the Hauge Synod.

305. HANSON, PEDER H. LETTER, 1879. 1 item. P 134.

Letter written by Hanson at New Richmond, Wisconsin, about jobs.

306. HANSON, RASMUS (ca. 1843–1916). CLIPPING, 1864–1900. P 135.

Article from *Bergens Tidende* (October 1, 1960) containing a news story about a collection of America letters and excerpts from several letters by Hanson, a Decorah, Iowa, farmer. There are references to the Civil War, American marriage laws, school, farming, and church.

307. HANSON, RICHARD D. (b. 1934). DISSERTATION, 1970. Typescript, 311 pages. P 607.

"An Analysis of Selected Choral Works of F. Melius Christiansen," degree of Doctor of Education in Music Education, University of Illinois.

308. HARKEY, S. W. (1811–1889). REMINISCENCES, 1888. Typescript, 33 pages. P 556.

"Lutheranism in the West" by a professor of theology at Illinois State University, Springfield, and president of the General Synod, dealing with the separation of Scandinavian Lutherans from the Synod of Northern Illinois. Introduction by Fritiof Ander.

309. HARMONY, MINNESOTA. LOCAL HISTORY, 1928–1946. 4 items. P 136.

Histories of a small community with a predominantly Norwegian population. "Some Early History of This Vicinity" (*Harmony News*, December 6 and 13, 1928) by L. O. Larson, local farmer, contains detailed data concerning persons, farming operations, and social life. "Memories of Early Years of Harmony," by Anna Aaberg Jacobson, deals more exclusively with the village itself as to streets, buildings, persons, and episodes.

310. HARSTAD, BJUG (1848–1933). PAPERS, 1898–1899. 1 volume, typescript, 70 pages. P 668.

Letters and articles written by Harstad, Lutheran clergyman, to the *Pacific Herald*, a Norwegian newspaper in Parkland, Washington, of which he was editor for several years. These letters concern his trip from Tacoma, Washington, to the Yukon during the gold rush period. Harstad gives detailed reports of the route of travel and of the problems and hardships of the expedition, the purpose of which was to secure mining property for the benefit of Pacific Lutheran College, Parkland, of which he was founder and president. Two hand-drawn maps of the routes accompany the papers. Compiled and translated by Oliver Harstad.

311. HARTMANN, HAGBART AMANDUS (1849–1925). LETTER, 1886. Pamphlet, 14 pages. P 556.

Published letter addressed to Pastor T. A. Torgerson, Lake Mills, Iowa, secretary of the Iowa District of the Norwegian Synod, regarding conflicts in church doctrine.

312. HARTMANN, JENNIE B. PAPERS, 1976. 8 items. P 945.

Letters and clippings concerning the Norwegian community in the Northwest and an article, "At the Infirmary" (typescript, 3 pages), by Mrs. Hartmann.

313. HASLER, ALICE. ARTICLE, 1961. 1 item. Typescript, 4 pages. P 137.

A historical sketch of pioneer events in Scandinavia, Waupaca County, Wisconsin.

314. HASTVEDT, KNUDT OLSON. REMINISCENCES, n.d. Typescript, 13 pages. P 138.

"Erindringer om det første norske utvandringsselskabs reise til Texas og fra de første 6 aar af nybyggerlivet der," an account of Hastvedt's trip to Texas in 1846, of Johan Reinert Reiersen's expedition in 1843–1844, and of early frontier life there. Typed from the original manuscript, in the Texas State Historical Association, Austin. It was published in *Studies and Records*, 12 (1941), translated and edited by Clarence A. Clausen.

315. HATGREN, THORA. LETTER, 1874. 1 item. P 139.

Letter from a Hoboken, New Jersey, resident, lamenting her emigration to America and describing conditions as to health, prices, and unemployment.

316. HAUGAN, HERMANA RYE. PAPERS. 3 boxes. P 908.

Papers of a Chicago woman active in the Norwegian organizations in Chicago, a leader in relief work for Norway during and after World War II, and secretary of the Chicago Working Center for Norway (1944–1945).

The collection includes papers of her husband, Reidar Rye Haugan (1893–1972), who came to the United States from Norway around 1920. After working for newspapers in North Dakota, he joined the editorial staff of *Skandinaven* (Chicago). When *Skandinaven* suspended publication in 1941, Haugan, together with John Lindrup, established the Chicago newspaper *Viking*.

317. HAUGAN, TORGEIR HALVORSON (1864–1915). PAPERS. 15 volumes. P 796.

Sermons, sermon outlines and notes, biographical and genealogical materials of a Lutheran clergyman, born in Brunkeberg, Norway. He emigrated to Wisconsin in 1883, taught at Homme Orphan Home and Bethany Indian Mission, and later served a number of congregations in Wisconsin and Minnesota.

318. HAUGE, ANDR. LETTER, 1872. 1 item. P 435.

Copy of letter published September 25 and October 2 in *Addressebladet*. Writing from Leland, Illinois, Hauge deals with farm operations, religious freedom, leisure activities, and homesickness of Norwegian immigrants.

319. HAUGEN, EINAR (b. 1906). PAPERS, 1925–1962. 81 items. P 545.

Correspondence, clippings, and articles (typescript and print) of an author, scholar and former professor of Scandinavian languages, Universities of Wisconsin and Harvard. The collection includes O. E. Rølvaag letters to Haugen.

320. HAUGEN, JOHN E. (1871–1943). CORRESPONDENCE, 1910–1929. 13 items. P 140.

Correspondence and assorted papers of a pharmacist and administrator of the St. Paul Luther Hospital.

321. HAUGEN, KRISTINE (MRS. JOHN) (1878–1965). PAPERS, 1918–1958. 93 items. P 546.
Scrapbooks of clippings from the Norwegian-American press on a variety of subjects, including NAHA, and letters from Ole E. Rølvaag. Mrs. Haugen was correspondent for the Norwegian-American press and was editor of Oppdalslaget yearbook from 1928 to 1935.

322. HAUGEN, MONS. LETTERS, 1871–1874. 2 items. P 142.
Letters by a Goodhue County, Minnesota, farmer to his fiancé regarding her ticket to America and to his parents about farm produce and prices.

323. HAUGEN, NILS P. (1849–1931). PAPERS, 1851–1888. 3 items. P 143.
A letter to a constituent and a speech on tariff by a Norwegian-born Wisconsin attorney and statesman. Haugen was the second Norwegian American in the U.S. Congress.

324. HAUGE'S SYNOD HOME MISSION. CASH BOOK, 1907–1913. 1 volume. P 556.
Record of cash given by congregations and individuals to home missions.

325. HAUGLAND, A. OSCAR. MUSIC, n.d. 2 items. P 558.
Ole E. Rølvaag's poem, "Vaarvise," set to music by professor of music at Northern Illinois University, DeKalb, and a recording tape of same.

326. HAVDAL, OLAF. CLIPPINGS, 1975. P 834.
"Utvandringen fra Orkdal," a series of newspaper articles (copies) published in Sør-Trøndelag, Orkanger, Norway, 1975.

327. HEDEMARK-LIBAK FAMILY. LETTERS, 1880–1913. 77 items. P 852.
Copies and translations of letters from members of the Hedemark and Libak families. Letters from Ole and Otto Hedemark were written to their parents in Norway. The brothers made it possible for their parents and their sister Johanne Hedemark to emigrate. Johanne's letters are addressed to her sister Helene and her husband Hans Libak. Early letters are from Cannon Falls and St. Paul, Minnesota; later letters are from Ransom County, and Lisbon, North Dakota. The translations are by Mrs. John M. Johnson, a daughter of the Libaks.

328. HEG, HANS C. (1829–1863). PAPERS, 1861–1963. 40 items. P 144.
A typescript copy of a letter by Heg; a letter by Olaf I. Rove to Waldemar Ager, quoting August Reymert concerning Heg's contribu-

tion to the Civil War effort; a speech by Julius E. Olson; clippings concerning the Heg monument in Madison, Wisconsin; and genealogies. *The Civil War Letters of Colonel Hans Christian Heg* was published by the NAHA in 1936.

329. HEGLAND HARNESS COMPANY. CATALOGUE, 1928. 1 item. P 146.
Catalogue of a wholesale manufacturer and jobber in Minneapolis, James Hegland, proprietor.

330. HEGLAND, MARTIN (1880–1967). PAPERS, 1902–1968. 3 boxes and 1 scrapbook. P 692.
Papers of a clergyman, author, professor, and director of WCAL, St. Olaf College radio station: articles, correspondence, clippings, pamphlets, photograph albums, and sermons.

331. HEIMARK, J. J. PAPERS, 1869–1965. 3 boxes, including 13 volumes. P 681.
Papers of a Fairmont, Minnesota, physician: correspondence; retail business statements; county and school district orders and receipts; Yellow Medicine County school district treasurer's reports; account books of the Moe grocery store, St. Paul; a translation of B. Aslakson, "Ti maaneders fangenskab i Andersonville;" a family history; and a letter written at Mission, Illinois, in 1869 by Helvik Janson Aske to John Danielson.

332. HEKTOEN, LUDVIG (1863–1951). PAPERS, 1904–1940. 122 items. P 148.
Correspondence, biographies, articles, and pictures of a Chicago physician, pathologist, professor, author, and editor.

Hektoen was professor of pathology at Rush Medical College; first chairman of the Department of Pathology at the University of Chicago (1901–1932); director of the John McCormick Institute for Infectious Diseases; chairman of the Medical Sciences of the National Research Council; executive director of the National Advisory Cancer Council; editor of *Journal of Infectional Diseases* and of *Archives of Pathology*; and author of books and articles.

The papers also include "Optegnelsen angaaende den første bebyggelse af norske paa Coon Prairie og omegn" by P. P. Hektoen, and biographies of Norwegian-American physicians and surgeons.

333. HELJESØN, OLE. PAPERS, 1729–1934. 3 items. P 145.
A Norwegian warranty deed transferring church land to Ole Heljesøn, together with a copy of same and a clipping of an article in *Minneapolis Tidende* by H. Chr. Hjortaas explaining the document.

334. HELLESTAD, OSCAR (b. 1881). PAPERS, 1842–1963. 5 items. P 149.
Emigration papers of a Lutheran clergyman and missionary.

335. HEM, HALVOR O. (1863–1952). ARTICLES, 1938–1945. 2 items. P 150.
Articles concerning a Norwegian-born engineer and inventor. Hem was chief consultant engineer for the Toledo Scale Company.

336. HENDERSON, A. M. (1869–1953). PAPERS, 1937–1952. 26 items. P 151.
Correspondence, memoirs, clippings, and historical sketches of an Iowa farmer, postmaster, and banker.

337. HENDERSON (LØNE), KNUD (1835–1930). NOTES, n.d. 89 items. P 152.
Manuscript material for a book of poems, *Digte om hjemlige tanker* (1928), by a Norwegian-born musician in Chicago and Cambridge, Wisconsin. Includes a short biography.

338. HENDRICKSEN, MARIE ASBJØRNSEN (1875–1959). PAPERS, 1939–1976. 7 items. P 878.
Clippings and letters concerning the needlework artistry of a Norwegian-born housewife who emigrated in 1906 and who lived in Superior, Wisconsin.

339. HENDRICKSON, HERMAN OSKAR (1881–1974). BIOGRAPHIES. 2 volumes. Typescript, 61 and 31 pages. P 769.
Two biographical sketches by a Norwegian-born Lutheran pastor: "Anders Emil Fridricksen (1810–1882); the First Norwegian Lutheran Pastor in Portland, Oregon, 1871–1882," and "Gunder Herlofsen; an Early Norwegian Settler in Kansas."

340. HENDRICKSON, ROY F. (b. 1903). PAPERS, 1943–1946. 8 items. P 153.
Articles and news items regarding an Iowa-born editor, correspondent, author, member of U.S. Department of Agriculture, and his address (1946) at St. Olaf College.

341. HERTSGAARD, OSCAR I. (1883–1979). PAPERS, 1952–1955. 4 items. P 154.
A biographical sketch of Hertsgaard and material on Hallinglag and NAHA.

342. HETLE, ERIK (1873–1962). ARTICLES, n.d. 2 items. P 155.
Articles of a Norwegian-born professor of physics, St. Olaf College: "At snakke norsk paa engelsk" and "Norskdommen og skolerne."

343. HIGHLAND, IRVING H. PAPERS, 1960–1970. 55 items. P 915.
Correspondence and other papers relating chiefly to the Society for the Preservation of Norwegian Culture. The Society, of which Highland was president, was organized to endow a chair in Norwegian studies at the University of Chicago.

344. HILDETEIGEN, NILS GULBRANDSON. GENEALOGY, 1904. 1 item.
P 860.
Copy of *Slægtbog og stamtavler over Slettemoenætten* (191 pages).
Among the Norwegian Americans included in the genealogy are Aagot
Raaen, Gro Svendsen and Ole Nilson.

345. HILL, MABEL PETERSON. ARTICLE, n.d. Typescript, 3 pages.
P 156.
An article concerning Methodist missionaries in Utah.

346. HILLEBOE, GERTRUDE M. (1888–1976). PAPERS, 1820–1968. 13
boxes. P 693.
Correspondence, clippings, articles, brochures, bulletins, school
notebooks, pamphlets, photographs, poems, programs, records, reports,
speeches, and scrapbooks of the dean of women, St. Olaf College
(1915–1958). The material deals with counselling, campus life, student
housing, recruitment, funds solicitation, World War I and World War II
programs at St. Olaf College, and national women's organizations.
Also in the collection are the records of the Roche a Cree Lutheran
Church, Arkdale, Wisconsin; papers of Sjur H. Hilleboe; and correspondence with E. T. Ytterboe family.

347. HILLEBOE, HANS SJURSON (1858–1948). PAPERS, 1875–1944. 2
boxes. P 688.
Articles, catalogues, certificates, correspondence, photographs,
scrapbooks and temperance literature of a Wisconsin-born educator.
Hilleboe was principal of Willmar Seminary, superintendent of Benson, Minnesota public schools, principal of the preparatory department
at Luther College, and professor of education at Augustana College,
Sioux Falls.

348. HILLESLAND, ANTON. PAPERS, 1923. 1 item and 1 volume.
P 158.
Notes (typescript, 7 pages) from interviews held with Swen N. Hes-
kin (1854–1924), a Norwegian-born farmer and lay preacher in the
Goose River settlement in North Dakota, regarding early pioneers and
the Hudson's Bay Company. "The Norwegian Lutheran Church in the
Red River Valley" (1923) is a Master of Arts thesis, University of North
Dakota (typescript, 152 pages).

349. HILTON FAMILY. LETTERS, 1847–1908. 62 items. P 788.
Copies of letters from members of the Hilton family who emigrated to
the United States to relatives at Ullensaker, Norway. The letters are
chiefly from Christopher Jacobson, who emigrated in 1854, to his
brother Hans Jacobson Hilton, and from Hans's son Jacob, who came in
1874 and after a few years settled in Socorro, New Mexico. There are
also some letters from Jacob's brothers Oluf and Christopher from New
Mexico. There are references to August Hilton, the father of Conrad

Hilton. The letters were obtained through Norsk Historisk Kjeldeskrift Institutt, Oslo.

350. HJELLUM, JOHN (b. 1880). ARTICLES, 1927–ca. 1929. 121 items. P 159.
Typescripts of articles, edited by Hjellum, chief of the mailing department of *Skandinaven*, which ran as a serial in that newspaper under the title, "Hvem er hvem blandt norsk-amerikanerne."

351. HJORTAAS, HANS CHRISTIAN GREY (1883–1961). PAPERS, 1933. 3 items. P 160.
Letters and clipping regarding Norsk Slektshistorisk Forening, a Norwegian genealogical association. Hjortaas of the *Minneapolis Tidende* editorial staff was a student of genealogy.

352. HØVERSTAD, HELGE (1870–1945). PAPERS, 1863–1947. 7 boxes. P 547.
Correspondence, articles, lectures, clippings, programs, reports, poems, and biographical sketches of a Norwegian-born Lutheran clergyman.
The correspondence deals with personal problems of friends; church missions in China, Madagascar, and Africa; church politics; relation of church and state; the use of the Norwegian language during World War I; hypnotism and spiritualism; problems as a land owner; and with the Valdres Samband of which he was a founder. Correspondents include Dr. L. W. Boe, Dr. O. M. Norlie, Dr. Einar Haugen, Kristine Haugen, Missionary Harold Martinson, Gov. W. L. Harding (Iowa), and John O. Quale, and members of the Høverstad family both in Norway and in America. There are some copies of letters by Høverstad. The newspaper clippings concern Høverstad's activities, his poems, lectures, and articles.

353. HØVERSTAD, TORGER A. (1868–1943). PAPERS, 1875–1933. 2 items. P 161.
A biography of Mrs. Knute B. Norswing (typescript, 3 pages) and a program for Constitution Day (1933). Høverstad was superintendent of agricultural stations in Minnesota.

354. HØVERSTAD, TORSTEIN. VANG, VALDRES, NORWAY. PAPERS, 1940–1950. 31 items. P 162.
Formal greeting letters from several governmental and private organizations in Norway to the Fellesraad (Common Council) for the *bygdelag* in America on the fiftieth anniversary of the Valdres Samband, together with articles written by Høverstad regarding Johan Falkberget.

355. HOGSTEL, MILDRED. PAPERS, 1976. 2 items. P 827.
"An American at Home in Norway" (typescript, 11 pages), an account of a journey made by a Texan to the homes of her ancestors in Southern Norway. A genealogical compilation (1975) for the families of

Johan and Anna Bronstad and of Berger and Anna Rogstad (typescript, 14 pages).

356. HOIDALE, EINAR (1870–1952). PAPERS, 1930–1934. 7 items. P 163.
Articles and speeches by a Norwegian-born editor, attorney, and congressman from Dawson and Minneapolis, including two speeches made during his campaign for United States Senate on the Democratic ticket, and a biography by Martha Ostenso.

357. HOIE, CLAUS (b. 1911). PAPERS, 1976. 4 items. P 879.
A biographical sketch of Hoie, and photographs and descriptions of paintings made by a Norwegian-born artist who emigrated to the United States in 1924. Hoie served in the 99th Infantry of the United States Army in World War II, a battalion composed of Norwegian nationals and U.S. citizens of Norwegian background. Hoie's work has been shown in different museums in the United States. There is a permanent collection at the Brooklyn Museum.

358. HOLBERG, RUTH LANGLAND (b. 1889). PAPERS, 1975. 3 items. P 946.
Biographical notes with transcription, and a manuscript, "Musings" (typescript, 29 pages). The notes include a bibliography of the 40 children's books written by Mrs. Holberg.

359. HOLAND, HJALMAR RUED (1872–1963). PAPERS, 1908–1963. 54 items. P 164.
Articles, clippings, and pamphlets of a Norwegian-born historian and fruit farmer at Ephraim, Wisconsin. The articles and pamphlets deal with local Door County history, Indians, Robert La Salle, Newport Tower, and the Kensington Rune Stone. The clippings from *Skandinaven* contain three incomplete series of articles: "Billeder fra nybyggerlivet," "Vor nybyggersaga," and "Fra de gamle dage."

360. HOLDEN, GOODHUE COUNTY, MINNESOTA. LOCAL HISTORY, 1876. 1 item, typescript, 5 pages. P 762.
A brief history of Holden Township read at a centennial celebration (July 4, 1876).

361. HOLLAND, BJØRN (1841–1930). PAPERS, 1899–1933. 45 items. P 165.
Clippings, correspondence, and articles of a politician, farmer, merchant and teacher in Iowa County, Wisconsin. The papers concern family, politics, and Norwegian heritage.

362. HOLMES CITY LÆSEFORENING. RECORDS, 1877–1905. 1 volume. P 695.
Constitution and financial records of a reading society at Holmes City, Minnesota, the purpose of which was to establish a library which would promote Christian and civic enlightenment.

363. HOLSETH, MIKEL C. (1845–1926). PAPERS, 1864–1925. 19 items. P 167.
Papers of a Norwegian-born Lutheran clergyman: correspondence, notebooks, and a manuscript of his translation of *Evangelisk Troesgrund* from German to Norwegian.

364. HOLSTAD, SIGURD HENRY (1871–1954). LETTERS, 1941, 1 volume. P 839.
Letters of tribute addressed to Holstad on his retirement as Executive Secretary of the Lutheran Welfare Society, bound into "A Book of Personal Messages to Mr. S. H. Holstad, December 5, 1941." Holstad, a Norwegian-born businessman in Minneapolis, was active in church, community and Norwegian-American affairs.

365. HOLTER, AKSEL H. (1873–1950). ARTICLE, 1925. Typescript, 7 pages. P 168.
"The Influence of Norway in Promoting Skiing" by a Norwegian-born merchant (Ashland, Wisconsin), and an organizer and officer of the National Ski Association of America.

366. HOLTER, SERAF B. FAMILY HISTORY, 1970. 8 pages. P 807.
Treats the emigration of Seraf Holter's grandparents, Christoffer Olson Holter (1827–1866) and Anna Holter (1827–1922), from Nannestad, Norway, in 1862, and their first years in America. They came on *Nordlyset* to Quebec, and went on to Koshkonong, Wisconsin; later to Fillmore County, Minnesota, and finally to Kandiyohi County, Minnesota.

367. HOMME HOMES. PAPERS, 1885–1957. 35 items, including 27 volumes. P 645.
Almanacs entitled *Waisenhus Kalender*, published by Even Johnson Homme, founder of several benevolent institutions in Wittenberg, Wisconsin, containing information on these homes and rosters of Norwegian Lutheran clergymen.

368. HORNTVEDT, LUDWIG (1868–1946). LETTERS, 1888. 2 items. P 169.
Translated copy of letters received by a Kalispell, Montana, farmer from his parents at his departure to America.

369. HOUGEN, JOHN OLAI JENSEN (1857–1927). CORRESPONDENCE, 1884–1900. 15 items. P 170.
Letters written by Lutheran clergymen to Hougen about church affairs, including doctrinal differences. Hougan was a Lutheran clergyman and a contributor to newspapers and journals.

370. HOUGSTAD, HANS CHR. (1834–1915). PAPERS, 1861–1932. 35 items. P 171.
Emigration papers, financial records, diaries, and correspondence of a Norwegian-born farmer who emigrated in 1869.

371. HOUGSTAD, MARTHA HOVE (1867–1945). REMINISCENCES, 1940. 1 item, 73 pages. P 172.
"A Pioneer Family," written primarily for the author's family, relating incidents from the author's life as a daughter of a Worth County, Iowa, farmer; as a college student; and as a teacher of piano and organ in Northwood and Decorah, Iowa, and in Minneapolis.

372. HOUKOM, ANDERS (1861–1938). REPORTS, 1908–1916. 5 items. P 556.
Annual reports of a Norwegian-born Lutheran clergyman to the Augustana congregation at Halstad, Minnesota, concerning ministerial activities.

373. HOUKOM, NELLIE S. JOHNSON (MRS. A.). LOCAL HISTORY, 1948. 53 pages. P 173.
A collection of sketches of pioneer farm life in Muskego and Trempealeau Valley, Wisconsin, dealing with health, travel, Yankee neighbors, and church activity. Mention is made of Marcus Thrane, P. A. Rasmussen, J. B. Frich, and Gjermund Hoyme.

374. HOUKOM, OLAF S. (1850–1920). LETTERS, 1870–1883. 1 volume, typescript, 36 pages. P 174.
Copied letters by Houkom to members of his family in Norway, describing his journey to Coon Prairie, Wisconsin, and discussing his experiences and church relationships at Highland Prairie, Minnesota; Sparta and La Crosse, Wisconsin; and Augsburg Seminary, Minneapolis.

375. HOUKOM, SVENNUNG OLSEN. CORRESPONDENCE, 1856–1891. 9 items. Typescript, 11 pages. P 175.
Letters by relatives and friends in the United States to Houkom and others, written from Coon Prairie and Taylor, Wisconsin; Hampton, Iowa; and Stevens County and Winona, Minnesota. The writers describe their farm buildings and produce; quote prices of crops, livestock, and land; and encourage migration to America. Transcribed by John A. Houkom.

376. HOVDEN, GEORGE JOHNSON (d. 1905). CIVIL WAR DIARY, 1863–1865. 1 volume, typescript, 63 pages. P 853.
The Civil War diary of a Norwegian-born member of the 15th Wisconsin Regiment. Hovden enlisted September 28, 1861, became a Sergeant and later a Second Lieutenant. After the war he married Ragne Snersrud and lived on a farm near Ridgeway, Iowa. The diary was translated by Norma Johnson Jordahl and edited by O. M. Hovde (1971). The original diary is in the Luther College Library at Decorah, Iowa.

377. HOVLAND, PEDER (1831–1912). PAPERS, 1904–1947. 4 items. P 176.

Pamphlets and photographs regarding the life and family of a Norwegian-born cobbler of La Fayette County, Wisconsin.

378. HOYEM, NELL M. DISSERTATION, 1970. Microfilm, 1 reel. P 731.
"John Dahle, Life and Work." Ph.D., Mankato State College, Minnesota.

379. HOYME, GJERMUND (1847–1902). PAPERS, 1888–1902. 14 items and 2 volumes. P 419.
Papers of a Norwegian-born Lutheran clergyman: a memorial article by John O. Hougen; Hoyme's President's Report to the Conference of the Norwegian-Danish Evangelical Lutheran Church in America in 1888; clippings regarding his death; and notebooks. Hoyme was president of the Conference (1886–1890) and of the United Lutheran Church (1890–1902).

380. HUMBOLDT COLLEGE. PAPERS, 1896–ca. 1925. 8 items. P 495.
Brochures and catalogues of a private secondary school with emphasis on business education, founded in 1895 by Jens P. Peterson at Humboldt, Iowa, and moved to Minneapolis in 1914.

381. HUMPHREY, HUBERT H. (1911–1978). PAPERS, 1949–1956. 59 items. P 178.
News letters, news releases, and speeches by a mayor of Minneapolis, a United States Senator from Minnesota, and Vice-President of the United States. His mother was born in Norway.

382. HUSEBY, OLAF (b. 1856). BIOGRAPHY, 1936. 1 item, 2 pages. P 179.
A sketch by Olav Myre about a Norwegian-born liberal book publisher and author from Detroit, Michigan, dealing largely with his career in Norway before emigrating in 1903.

383. HUSET, ASLAUG AAKER (MRS. HALVOR) (1828–1901). PAPERS, 1857–1882. 7 items. P 180.
Deeds, college report cards, and a letter to Mrs. Huset from her brother, Lars Aaker, Alexandria, Minnesota, in which he reports the arrival of Torjus Schibstad, the grandfather of Henrik Shipstead.

384. HUSTVEDT, HALVOR B. (1852–1932). ARTICLES, 1923–1926. 8 items. P 181.
Clippings of articles by a Lutheran clergyman, educator and editor, about life in the Koshkonong (Wisconsin) area: roads, trips to Milwaukee, farm machinery, mills, crops, schools, women's work, wild life, orchards, church, language, politics, relations with the Yankees, Civil War, J. C. Dundas, and about pioneer life in southeastern South Dakota. Also "Missouri flommen i 1881" (typescript, 10 pages).

385.   HUTCHINSON THEOLOGICAL SEMINARY. PAPERS, 1920–1927. 9
    items. P 496.
Catalogues and student journals of a Danish-Norwegian Adventist
institution established in Hutchinson, Minnesota, in 1910.

386.   HVAMSTAD, PER. PAPERS, 1964–1965. 4 items. P 440.
An article about the *Kubberulle* by Hvamstad; a letter from Volin,
South Dakota; and a biography of Ivar Saugen, Lutheran clergyman in
British Columbia.

387.   HYDLE, ODMUND. NOVEL. 1 item, typescript, 166 pages. P 412.
"Bjorn in the New World," an unpublished immigrant story, by a
former teacher, banker, and insurance broker who emigrated in 1906.

388.   HYTTA, CHRISTIAN LEVORSEN. LETTER, 1863. 1 item. P 182.
Letter from a Thunbord, Norway, resident concerning weather,
health, farming, and an inquiry about the Civil War.

389.   IBSEN, JOHAN A. LETTER, 1850. 2 items. P 821.
Typescript copy (9 pages) of a letter from the brother of Henrik Ibsen
to his father, dated May 28, at Milwaukee, Wisconsin. He describes
conditions in Wisconsin, discusses his work as a clerk in a store, wages,
expenses, outlook for farmers, Indians, and the great interest in the gold
rush to California. It is believed that Johan died while crossing the desert
on his way to find gold in California. A translation by Theodore Jorgenson is included.

390.   IBSEN, NIKOLAI (1834–1888). CLIPPINGS. 2 items. P 822.
A clipping from the Estherville, Iowa, *Daily News* concerning the
grave of Henrik Ibsen's brother Nikolai at Estherville. Nikolai Ibsen
came to the United States and settled near Estherville where he owned
40 acres of land. The second item contains some statements made by
Charleton Laird, quoting from sources who had information about
Nikolai Ibsen.

391.   IDUN EDDA FORENINGEN. RECORDS, 1922–1958. 49 items and 1
    volume. P 669.
Records of the Norwegian society at St. Olaf College: minutes, programs, membership lists, and communications.

392.   ILLINOIS, BENEVOLENT SOCIETIES. PAPERS, 1893–1942. 10
    items. P 638.
Constitutions, programs, and reports of several institutions in Illinois.

393.   ILLINOIS STATE UNIVERSITY. PAPERS, 1859, 1920. 4 items.
    P 497.
Reports and a catalogue of a Lutheran academy, college and seminary established at Springfield, Illinois, in 1852.

IN MEMORIAM. See Special Collections, No. 944.

394. INDEPENDENT REALTY COMPANY. PAPERS, 1922–1934. 192 items. P 184.

Papers of a Northfield, Minnesota, firm whose members were George O. Berg, P. O. Holland, Ole E. Rølvaag, Paul G. Schmidt, and J. Jørgen Thompson. The correspondence and reports deal largely with land investments in Northfield and in North Dakota.

395. IOWA BENEVOLENT SOCIETIES. PAMPHLETS, 1914–1924. 2 items. P 639.

Constitution and history.

396. IVERSON, O. B. (1845–1940). ARTICLES, 1920. 7 items. Typescript, 59 pages. P 185.

Transcripts of articles written by a Norwegian-born surveyor, immigration commissioner, and legislator of Stanwood, Washington, which were published in the *Stanwood News*, concerning his work as immigration commissioner, his first trip from South Dakota to Washington to explore the land, and about logging camps, surveying, vegetation, soil, Indians, and settlers.

397. JACOBSEN, NIELS AND WILSON, SJUR D. LETTER, 1864. 1 item. P 435.

Copy of a letter printed in *Aftenbladet*, December 2, by members of Company D of the Sixth Iowa Cavalry Regiment. The letter, written at Fort Rice, Dakota Territory, describes the two-month march against the Indians from Fort Sully to Fort Rice. Jacobsen was a Civil War veteran and later lived at Hills, Minnesota.

398. JACOBSON, ABRAHAM (1836–1910). PAPERS, 1862–1964. 64 items and 4 volumes. P 671.

Articles, correspondence, pictures, and scrapbooks of a Norwegian-born clergyman and farmer. The scrapbooks contain clippings taken largely from *Decorah-Posten*: obituaries, biographical sketches of Dakota pioneers, and items concerning Norwegian pioneer associations, Lutheran church conventions, Det norske selskap, Norsk-danske presseforening i Amerika, and Jacobson's contacts with Abraham Lincoln, *Decorah Posten*, and *Nordlyset*. There are items about Rasmus B. Anderson, L. W. Boe, Gjermund Hoyme, U. V. Koren, Bernt J. Muus, Knute Nelson, Oley Nelson, Halle Steensland, Peer Strømme, Hans G. Stub, and Oscar M. Torrison.

The articles consist of biographies of Winneshiek County, Iowa, pioneers: Jacob Aga, Ole Andreas Anderson, Gunder H. Blegeberg, Ove Christian Johnson Hallan, Thor Halvorson, Tollev Halvorson, Johan Hegg, Christopher T. Hoyme, Andrew O. Lommen, Ole T. Lommen, Lars Iverson Melaas, and Knudt Thompson. The correspondence and other articles concern Jacobson's mission to the Gaspé settlement in the 1860's. Jacobson was the first Lutheran clergyman to preach in Dakota Territory and the first Norwegian in the Decorah area.

399.   JACOBSON, CLARA (1864–1949). PAPERS, 1943. 2 items. P 672.
Manuscript of reminiscences (189 pages) of childhood days spent in the Perry parsonage, western Dane County, Wisconsin. Written in informal style, "Childhood Memories" gives a detailed account of church, school, books, music, dress, entertainment, trips, playmates, guests, and farm employees. Special mention is made of Olaus Jensen Breda, Ole Bull, Aanund B. Dahle, John N. Fjeld, Gulbrand Jensvold, Monona Academy, and the devastating tornado of 1878. Also includes a scrapbook of clippings from *Decorah-Posten* and *Reform*.

400.   JAEGER, LUTH (1851–1925). PAPERS, 1878–1887. 8 items, including 1 volume. P 186.
Papers of a Norwegian-born editor and realtor: correspondence and a scrapbook dealing with such subjects as the cultural life among Norwegian Americans, Norwegian-American press, Bjørnson in America, Scandinavian professorship at the University of Minnesota, Kristofer Janson, and Knute Nelson.
Jaeger was editor of *Budstikken* (1877–1885) and of *The North* (1889–1894), the first English newspaper for Scandinavian Americans.

401.   JANSON, KRISTOFER (1841–1918). PAPERS, 1879–1964. 38 items. P 206.
Papers of a Norwegian author and Unitarian clergyman: clippings, correspondence, and pamphlets. Janson lived in Minneapolis (1881–1893), organized several congregations, including those in Minneapolis and Hanska, and wrote several novels about his Minneapolis countrymen.

402.   JEFFERSON PRAIRIE AND WIOTA (WISCONSIN) AND LONG PRAIRIE AND ROCK RUN (ILLINOIS) PARISHES. MINISTERIAL RECORD BOOK, 1844–1855. 1 volume. P 556.
The membership, baptism, confirmation, communion, marriage, and burial records of Lutheran congregations; the parish reports of J. W. C. Dietrichson, Claus L. Clausen, and Gustav F. Dietrichson; and letters of call to Gustav F. Dietrichson, Gunnulf J. Omland, and Claus F. Magelssen.

403.   JENSEN, BIRGITH (b. 1891). PAPERS, 1976. 58 items. P 880.
Clippings, souvenirs and pictures concerning a Chicago woman and her activities in Norwegian organizations in that city.

404.   JENSEN, CARL C. A. (b. 1878). ARTICLES, 1927. 15 items. Typescript, 142 pages. P 537.
Articles by a Lutheran clergyman concerning Lutheranism in Cerro Gordo County, Iowa, and histories of congregations, hospitals and men's societies.

405.   JENSEN, HANNA BUGGE (MRS. NILS E.) (ca. 1841–1921). PAPERS, 1856–1909. 3 items. P 187.

Papers of a Norwegian-born Lutheran minister's wife at Highland Prairie, Minnesota: reminiscences, the congregation's formal request to the Norwegian Synod for a pastor and her husband's first sermon in the parish. The reminiscences include a description of the journey to America, the parsonage, living conditions, and parish activities.

406. JENSEN, MAGNY LANDSTAD. CLIPPINGS, 1963–1977. P 916.

Copies of clippings about a Norwegian-born poet who came to the United States in 1926, living first in New Jersey and later in California. She has written for newspapers and periodicals and has published *Girdle Stones* (1975), *Wilding Ballads* (1976), and *No Love is Lost* (1977). Some of the poems are based on Norwegian themes. She is a great-granddaughter of the Norwegian poet and hymnwriter M. B. Landstad.

407. JENSENIUS, BERTRAM (1898–1976). PAPERS, 1932–1975. 23 boxes. P 920.

Papers of a Norwegian-American journalist and author, born in Madagascar of Norwegian missionary parents. When he was nine or ten years old he journeyed alone to a home for missionary children in Stavanger, Norway. He was educated in Norway, then lived in France for three years, after which he participated in a race across the Atlantic in 1922, which brought him to the United States. He settled finally in Chicago where he engaged in various occupations. In 1958 he took over the Norwegian weekly newspaper *Viking* and renamed it *Vinland*. He and his wife (Ingrid Hermanson) also ran the Vinland Travel Bureau. He was involved in the many Norwegian clubs and activities in Chicago. A writer of articles, short stories, essays, and plays, he published four books: *Deilig er Jorden* (1948), *Calling on Eternity* (1956), *Misjonærens sønn* (1972), *Misjonærbarna på Korsteig* (1973).

The papers include a broad correspondence, articles, manuscripts, reviews, clippings, and information about the Norwegian-American community in Chicago.

408. JEWELL LUTHERAN COLLEGE. PAPERS, 1897–1935. 2 boxes. P 651.

Account books, catalogues, journals, programs, and reports of a secondary institution founded in 1893 at Jewell, Iowa.

409. JOERGENSON, GUSTAV B. (b. 1883). PAPERS, 1937–1955. 79 items. P 188.

Photographs, programs and articles on the history of Stanwood, Washington, and surrounding area, and early migrations into the Northwest.

Joergenson was a farmer and a son of the pioneer Lutheran clergyman, Christian Joergenson, who left the ministry in 1893 to become a farmer and a leader in the local cooperative movement.

410. JOHANNESEN (STØLSVIG), JOHS. (JOHNSON, J. J.) (1826–1902). PAPERS, 1846–1899, 1917. 133 items. P 189.

Papers of a Norwegian-born Lutheran clergyman and farmer in Winnishiek County, Iowa: correspondence (including a Civil War letter dated November 24, 1864), legal documents, articles, pamphlets, notes and sermons, and an article.

The letters deal largely with theological disputes during the 1860s and 70s and offer comments on Carthage College and Hartwick Seminary. Some of the correspondents are Rasmus B. Anderson, Ole Andrewson, O. J. Hatlestad, Rasmus O. Hill, Jacob Jacobson, and Osmund Sheldahl. The pamphlets are *The Mission of the General Synod* by Simeon W. Harkey (1859) and *Historiske Meddelelser om Den norske Augustana Synode* (1887) by O. J. Hatlestad. A manuscript (139 pages) by Johannesen's daughter, Mrs. Amelia Bakken, entitled "From Bygone Days, History and Reminiscences from Washington Prairie, Springfield Township, Winneshiek County, Iowa," contains names of early settlers, sketches of families, story of the founding of the Norwegian Methodist Congregation and anecdotes relative to the Civil War, country schools, and community life.

411. JOHN ANDERSON PUBLISHING COMPANY. PAPERS, 1854–1955. 34 items. P 193.
Correspondence, anniversary programs, certificates, clippings, pictures, and pamphlets of a Chicago publishing house founded in 1866 by John Anderson (1836–1910). Among the items are the first issue of *Skandinaven* after the Chicago fire in 1871, biographical sketches, letters concerning politics, photographs of the company, "The Story of *Skandinaven*, 1866–1916." Knute Nelson and Victor Lawson were correspondents.

412. JOHNSEN, OLE. LETTER, 1854. 1 item. P 435.
Copy of a letter published in *Arbeider-foreningernesblad*, quoting commodity prices and wages for construction workers, shipbuilders, and fishermen, and encouraging emigration.

413. JOHNSØN, PETER (b. ca. 1786). ARTICLE, 1846. 1 item. P 435.
Copy of an article "Reiseberetning" as it appeared in *Stavanger Amtstidende og Addresseavis* and *Morgenbladet*. Johnsøn, who wrote the article after his return to Norway, was opposed to emigration.

414. JOHNSON, ALFRED B. LETTER, 1881. 1 item. P 190.
Letter by M. H. Messer, Onarga, Illinois, to Johnson regarding the Beaver Creek settlement in Iroquois County, Illinois. Johnson, an early settler in Chicago, was a lumber dealer and during the 1860s a member of the city board of supervisors.

415. JOHNSON (AASEN), ANDREW (1828–1915). PAPERS, 1847–1909. 291 items. P 194.
Mainly correspondence of a Norwegian-born farmer in Wiota, La Fayette County, Wisconsin. The letters, written by relatives and friends from California, Iowa, Nevada, Illinois, Minnesota, South Dakota, and

Wisconsin, present a picture of the migration movement in its various aspects both in country and town. There are letters by a student at Mount Horeb Academy (1895–1896).

416. JOHNSON, CLYDE. ARTICLE, 1973. 1 item. P 808.

An issue of *Inland* containing an article, "Saturday Night on the St. Mary's," the story of a Great Lakes oreboat, captained by Clyde Johnson.

417. JOHNSON, EMIL (1858–1935). PAPERS, 1859–1931. 13 items, including 1 volume. P 191.

Papers of an Erskine, Minnesota, farmer: personal documents, church records, and local histories.

418. JOHNSON, ERIK KRISTIAN (1863–1923). DOCTRINE, 1895. Pamphlet, 16 pages. P 556.

En kort udredning offers an explanation of doctrines in the Hauge's Synod. Johnson was a professor at Luther Theological Seminary, St. Paul.

419. JOHNSON, JOHN ANDERS (1832–1901). PAPERS, 1854–1966. 20 boxes. P 691.

Papers of a Norwegian-born industrialist, inventor, and philanthropist, Madison, Wisconsin: articles, clippings, contracts, correspondence, indentures, patents, pamphlets, receipts, records, reports, scrapbooks, and statements.

Johnson immigrated in 1844 to Walworth County, Wisconsin; moved to Dane County in 1852; to Madison in 1861. He was founder and president of Fuller & Johnson Manufacturing Company, of Gisholt Machine Company, and of Hekla Fire Insurance Company. In 1896, he was elected president of the National Association of Implement and Vehicle Manufacturers.

Johnson was a founder of *Amerika* (1873), a Chicago newspaper. He wrote frequently for newspapers on political, economic, and social topics such as tariff, free silver, temperance, slavery, and education. Besides several pamphlets, his publications include *Det skandinaviske regiments historie* (1869) and *Fingerpeg for farmere og andre* (1888).

Johnson was a member of the Wisconsin legislature in 1857 and 1873–74 and county clerk (1861–69). His philanthropies included the University of Wisconsin, St. Olaf College, and the Gisholt Home for the Aged. The NAHA published *John A. Johnson* by Agnes M. Larson in 1969.

420. JOHNSON, LAURA EDSETH (MRS. SEVERIN) (1876–1962). REMINISCENCES, 1953. 1 item, 4 pages. P 740.

Recollections of a housewife who spent her childhood at Halstad, Minnesota.

421. JOHNSON (KAASA), NELSON (1818–1884). PAPERS, 1900–1962. 9 items. P 192.

Correspondence and articles of a Norwegian-born farmer and Methodist clergyman. The papers include a family history and information on pioneer agriculture and church.

Johnson settled in Winneshiek County, Iowa, in 1850, and for one year was the minister in Cambridge, Wisconsin, in the Willerup Methodist Church, reputed to be the first Norwegian Methodist church.

422. JOHNSON, OLE S. (1843–1935). PAPERS, 1889–1935. 16 items, including 6 volumes. P 548.

Papers of a Norwegian-born farmer and author of Spring Grove, Minnesota: letters and clippings, 4 scrapbooks, and 2 volumes of biographical notes dealing with such subjects as socialism and prohibition. Johnson was the author of three books: *Socialismen* (1906), *Nybyggerhistorie fra Spring Grove og omegn Minnesota* (1920), and *Udvandringshistorie fra Ringerikesbygderne* (1925).

423. JOHNSON, SIMON (1874–1970). PAPERS, 1914–1958. 3 boxes. P 549.

Short stories, novels, and poems in print and in typescript by a Norwegian-born novelist, short story writer, poet, and editor.

Johnson, called "The Poet of the Prairie," has written *Et geni* (1907), *Lonea* (1909), *I et nyt rike* (1914), *Fire fortællinger* (1917), *Fallitten paa Braastad* (1922), and *Frihetens hjem* (1925). He was editor of the Grand Forks *Normanden*, and co-editor of *Decorah-Posten*. "An Immigrant Boy on the Frontier" by Johnson, translated by Nora Solum, appeared in *Studies and Records*, 23 (1967).

424. JOHNSON, THORVALD. REMINISCENCES, n.d. Typescript, 2 pages. P 947.

A brief account by a native of Kongsberg, Norway, who emigrated to America in 1870 and settled in Shawano County, Wisconsin.

425. JOHNSRUD, KNUD (1832–1905). PAPERS, 1855–1871. 8 items. P 196.

Biographical material concerning a Norwegian-born church school teacher at Manitowoc, Wisconsin.

426. JOHNSRUD, ROSANNA GUTTERUD. DRAMA, 1974. Typescript, 25 pages. P 948.

Three-act play, *"Restaurasjonen," the Norwegian Mayflower*, written for the Norwegian-American Sesquicentennial celebration, 1975, at Grand Forks, North Dakota.

427. JONS BJARNASONAR SKOLI (JON BJARNASON ACADEMY). PAPERS, 1913–1933. 6 items. P 499.

Brochures and year books of an institution in Winnipeg, Manitoba, established in 1913 by the Icelandic Lutheran Synod of America and named for its founder.

428. JORDAN, PHILIP D. BIBLIOGRAPHIES, 1961. 2 items. P 707.

Bibliographies of Mt. Pleasant, Iowa, and of Edward Bonney and *The Banditti of the Prairies*. The second item pertains to the Mormons at Nauvoo, Illinois, in the 1840's.

429. JORGENSON, THEODORE (1894–1971). PAPERS. 43 boxes and 7 volumes. P 716.

Correspondence, articles, clippings, diaries, family history, handbooks, lectures, lecture notes, minute book, notebooks, pamphlets, poems, reports, scrapbooks, speeches, and translations of a Norwegian-born professor of Norwegian at St. Olaf College.

Jorgenson immigrated in 1911; was a member of St. Olaf College faculty (1925–1966); author of *History of Norwegian Literature, Norway's Relation to Scandinavian Unionism, Ole Edvart Rølvaag: A Biography* (with Nora O. Solum), *Henrik Ibsen: A Study in Art and Personality, Norwegian-English School Dictionary*. He was the Democratic Farmer-Labor nominee for U.S. Senate, Minnesota, in 1946.

430. JOSEPHSEN, EINAR (b. 1885). PAPERS, 1907–1962. 136 items, including 5 scrapbooks. P 682.

Papers of a Norwegian-born journalist and publicity director: correspondence, articles, and scrapbooks dealing with a variety of subjects such as war, politics, religion, immigration, and Norwegian-American literature. Among his correspondents are Fred Bierman, H. Sundby-Hanson, Sverre Mortensen, and Felix B. Wold. There are World War I letters and letters by Theodore C. Blegen, Knut Gjerset, Birger Osland, Kristian Prestgard, and O. E. Rølvaag.

Josephsen was on the *Skandinaven* staff, circulation manager of *Decorah-Posten*, in the book department of Augsburg Publishing House, publicity manager and later public relations manager of the New York Central Railroad Company, and public relations director of City National Bank, Chicago.

431. KAASA, HARRIS E. PAPERS. Typescript, 54 pages. P 780.

"The Teacher," a translation of Arne Garborg's *Læraren* by Harris Kaasa, a professor of religion at Luther College, Decorah, Iowa.

432. KENSINGTON RUNE STONE. PAPERS, 1911–1955. 37 items and 1 volume. P 198.

Correspondence, articles, and clippings concerning history of, and discussions on the authenticity of the stone.

433. KIÆR, A. N. EMIGRATION, 1864. 6 items. P 435.

Copies of a series of articles entitled "Den norske udvandring til Amerika" that appeared in *Aftenbladet*. Based on reliable sources, the articles contain an analysis of emigration from Norway as to population, districts, ports of exit and entry, ocean travel, illness and deaths, sex, age, economic and social status, geographic location, wealth, causes, and its results in Norway.

434. KILDAHL, JOHN NATHAN (1857–1920). PAPERS, 1882–1913.
402 items. P 205.

Articles, reports, speeches, sermons, and letters of a Norwegian-born Lutheran clergyman, college president, theologian, and author. The letters to his son J. L. Kildahl, offer counsel on pastoral problems and discuss family affairs. Kildahl was the second president of St. Olaf College (1899–1914).

435. KINDEM, ANNA SEKSE (1896–1976). PAPERS, 1938–1968. 124 items. P 713.

Clippings of letters and articles by Mrs. Kindem as well as a few articles by other authors which appeared mostly in the Norwegian newspapers: *Hardanger, Telemark Tidend*, and *Odda Kyrkjeblad*. Written from Northfield, Minnesota, the letters include topics such as prices, employment, politics, crops, Fourth of July, 1939 visit of Norwegian royalty, World War II, memories from Norway, St. Olaf College, Norwegian-American festivities, travel in the United States and Norway. Mrs. Kindem immigrated in 1923.

436. KITTELSBY, AGNES M. (1880–1925). PAPERS, 1894–ca. 1940. 2 boxes. P 550.

Correspondence, scrapbook, and biographical notes of an Iowa-born teacher. Miss Kittelsby taught at St. Ansgar Seminary, Waldorf College, Augustana College, St. Olaf College, and Unity School, Honan, China. Much of the material deals with life at the schools she served.

437. KJØRSTAD-REVLING FAMILY. PAPERS, 1931–1970. 50 items. P 781.

Correspondence, articles, and pictures concerning the Kjørstad-Revling family in America and Norway, compiled chiefly by Asbjørn Hagen, Oslo, and Esther Kjørstad, Evanston, Illinois.

One of the topics discussed is the *blod bryllup* (a bloody wedding) 1823, the subject of Welhaven's poem "Aasgardsreien." See Kjørstad Family History, No. 202.

438. KLAVENESS, EIVIND (1870–1952). PAPERS, 1890–1948. 5 boxes. P 551.

A scrapbook, 10 volumes of correspondence (2408 letters), 9 notebooks, and 43 pamphlets and addresses of a Norwegian-born physician, writer, and lecturer.

Klaveness, who practiced in Brookings and Sioux Falls, South Dakota, and in Minneapolis and St. Paul, Minnesota, held many offices, including president of Vestfoldlag, of Minnesota Leif Eriksen Monument Association, and of Scandinavian Republican State League of South Dakota, and medical director of Sons of Norway and of Surety Fund Life Company. He was founder of Klaveness Corporation (investment bankers representing Klaveness Bank in Oslo); a radio and after dinner speaker; a frequent writer for newspapers and journals on medical and political subjects; and author of two books, *The Enchanted Islands* (1939) and *Norske læger i Amerika 1840–1942* (1943). His correspondence with Richard Olsen Richards of the Richards Trust Company of Huron, South Dakota (3 volumes), reflects the story of that State's politics during the first three decades of the 20th century. For names of correspondents, see description catalogue in NAHA archives.

439. KNUDSON, KNUD (1810–1889). PAPERS, 1839–1944. 4 items. P 199.

Papers of a Norwegian-born blacksmith, farmer, and prospector: a printed diary of Knudson's trip from Drammen to Detroit, and a typescript translation (17 pages) by C. O. Solberg. Included are two letters by Solberg concerning Knudson and his emigrant party.

440. KNUTSEN, ALFRED (1888–1954). PAPERS, 1935–1938. 50 items and 2 volumes. P 424.

Correspondence and 2 scrapbooks of a collector and researcher among Norwegians in America. Knutsen returned to Norway in 1912. The scrapbooks contain a newspaper serial, "Haringer i Amerika gjennom 100 år" (1937–1938), which gives a detailed account of Norwegian Americans from Hardanger.

Knutsen collected thousands of clippings, conducted an extensive correspondence, and interviewed emigrants home on visits. He gave his scrapbook library to the University of Oslo.

441. KNUTSON, HAROLD (1886–1953). ARTICLES, 1945–1946. 33 items. P 200.

Releases entitled "Observations from Washington" by a Norwegian-born, Wadena, Minnesota, Republican Congressman.

Knutson was a member of the House of Representatives (1917–1949), was House whip (1919–1925), and for a time was chairman of the House Ways and Means Committee. Earlier he was editor of the *Wadena Pioneer-Journal*.

442. KNUTZEN, JOHAN FRIDERICH. DOCUMENT, 1760. 1 item. P 201.

Paper issued by King Friderich V, granting citizenship in Mandal to Knutzen of Christiansand.

443. KOFFSTAD, NIELS C. AND SKRABELSRUD, JOHANNES CHR. LETTER, 1853. 1 item. P 435.

Copy of a letter from Illinois, published in *Arbeider-foreningers blad*, which details writers' modes of travel from Quebec to Chicago and lauds the good living and ample work opportunities. There is a reference to the Ole Bull colony.

444. KOMPAS, JUNE (b. 1920). PAPERS, 1976. 54 items. P 881.

Biographical information about a Norwegian-American woman who grew up in the home of her immigrant grandparents, Peter and Martha Petersen, at Manistee, Michigan.

445. KOREN, ULRIK V. (1826–1910). PAPERS, 1888–1927. 9 items. P 203.
Lectures and sermons on doctrine by a Norwegian-born Lutheran clergyman at Decorah, Iowa.

446. KREFTING, LAURITS W. PAPERS. 3 items. P 835.
Bulletins of a research biologist of the United States Fish and Wildlife Service, St. Paul, Minnesota. Included are two Technical Bulletins in the Forestry Series of the Agricultural Experiment Station, University of Minnesota.

447. KROGNESS, SAMSON MADSEN (1830–1894). PAPERS, 1853–1894. 3 boxes. P 794.
Correspondence (4 volumes of copybooks), 3 volumes of ministerial records, a scrapbook, a diary, notes, and manuscripts of a Lutheran clergyman, born and educated in Norway, who emigrated to the United States in 1866. He was Secretary of the Norwegian Augustana Synod (1870–1874 and 1876–1882), member of its Board of Education (1869–1870, 1880–1884) and of the Israel Mission Central Committee (1884–1892). He founded and edited *Almueskoletidende* (1861–1866). He was an able writer and translator, and at various times served as editor of *Missionsvennen, Budbæreren, Den Norske Lutheraner, Ebenezer*, and *Luthersk Kirketidende*. He also edited reports and yearbooks for the church. His 8000 volume library and his manuscript dealing with the history of the Norwegian Lutheran church in the United States were destroyed by fire in 1879.

448. KVAMME, VERA JOYCE FOX. GENEALOGY. 11 volumes. P 764.
Ancestral forefathers of Vera Joyce Kvamme (Mrs. J. P.) compiled by Carl M. R. Gunderson.

449. LA CROSSE LUTHERAN HOSPITAL. REPORTS, 1905–1923. 3 items. P 621.
Annual reports of a hospital founded in 1899 in La Crosse, Wisconsin, by a corporation, some of whose members were affiliated with the Norwegian Synod.

450. LANDSVERK, OLE G. PAPERS, 1953–1969. 23 items. P 724.
Papers of the owner of Landsverk Electrometer Company, Glendale, California: clippings, correspondence and articles regarding the Kensington stone. Alf Monge and Landsverk are the authors of *Norse Medieval Cryptography in Runic Carvings* (1967), and other related works.

451. LANGELAND, KNUD (1813–1888). PAPERS, 1869–1888. 26 items. P 204.
Articles, correspondence, and legal papers, of a Norwegian-born journalist and author, containing Langeland's views on political issues of the day, his attack on the Norwegian Synod, and his defense of the

common school. The legal papers concern the ownership and financial policies of *Skandinaven* of which he was first editor (1866). Langeland is the author of *Nordmændene i Amerika* (1888).

452. LANGLAND, HAROLD S. (b. 1898). BIOGRAPHY, 1968. Pamphlet, 34 pages. P 195.
A biography of Samuel S. Langland (1855–1928), Norwegian-born Seattle attorney.

453. LANGLAND, JOSEPH (b. 1917). PAPERS, 1963–1964. 4 items. P 207.
A biography and critique of a second-generation Norwegian-American poet and professor of English at the University of Massachusetts. Langland spent his early life in northeastern Iowa and has authored two volumes of poems, *The Green Town* (1956) and *The Wheel of Summer* (1963).

454. LANGUM, HENRY (b. 1882). ARTICLES, n.d. 2 items. Typescript, 5 pages. P 208.
"Thoughts about Life" and "When Old Age Comes" by a Lutheran clergyman and high school teacher.

455. LARSEN, ERLING (1909–1976). ARTICLES, 1955–1956. 10 items. P 209.
Articles appearing in *Sparks*, official publication of Minnesota State Automobile Association, by a professor of English at Carleton College. The articles deal largely with Minnesota, its lakes, rivers, birds, history, mines, Indians, and museums.

456. LARSEN, GUNHILD ANDRINE JACOBSDATTER (MRS. TOBIAS) (1835–1934). REMINISCENCES, 1923, 1925. Typescript, 5 pages. P 210.
Recollections of a Norwegian-born Lutheran minister's wife: her passage across the Atlantic, life in Muskego in the 1840's and 1850's and her wedding (November 3, 1856). There are comments on *Nordlyset*, the presidential election of 1856, Søren Bache, Claus L. Clausen, J. W. C. Dietrichson, Elling Eilesen, Even Heg, John J. Landsverk, and H. A. Stub.

457. LARSEN, GUSTAV A. (1859–1934). CORRESPONDENCE, 1881–1931. 5 items. P 211.
Letters of call to a Lutheran clergyman and related correspondence.

458. LARSEN, KAREN (1879–1961). PAPERS, 1881–1961. 54 items. P 602.
Diplomas and decorations presented to Laur. Larsen, Hanna Astrup Larsen, and Karen Larsen; clippings, pamphlets, and photographs, including an album.

459. LARSEN, MAGNUS (b. 1870). LETTERS, 1887–1899. 21 items. Typescript, 34 pages. P 212.

Copies of letters by a Norwegian-born draftsman and designer who rose from coal shoveler to designer for Tiffany. Larsen is critical of the inequalities in American society and gives detailed accounts of unpleasant experiences in metropolitan New York.

460. LARSON, AGNES M. (1892–1967). CORRESPONDENCE, 1952–1961. 18 items. P 213.

Letters to Larson, professor of history at St. Olaf College, from former students in the armed services.

461. LARSON, C. W. (b. 1881). ADDRESS, 1927. Typescript, 14 pages. P 214.

Manuscript of an address delivered by the Iowa-born chief of the Bureau of Dairy Industry of the United States Department of Agriculture before the American Institute of Cooperation in Chicago, dealing with cost and improvements in methods of milk production, and the role of the cooperative.

462. LARSON, CHRISTIAN (1840–1919). BIOGRAPHY, 1917. Manuscript, 23 pages. P 215.

Autobiography of a Norwegian-born Iowa farmer and father of Laurence M. Larson, professor of history at the University of Illinois.

463. LARSON, CLIFFORD. BIOGRAPHY, n.d. Typescript, 6 pages. P 216.

A biography of Peder Borderud (1818–1890), the author's grandfather, who settled with his family at Kindred, North Dakota, in 1871. Topics treated are the trek from St. Ansgar, Iowa, to the Red River Valley, purchase of land, beginnings of the new settlement and its institutions, and relations with the Indians.

464. LARSON, EVER. PAPERS, 1824–1889. 22 items. P 217.

Correspondence and personal papers of an Ashippan, Wisconsin, resident, including those of Ole Tollefson, Racine, Wisconsin.

465. LARSON, LAURIS (1862–1935). PAPERS, 1885–1951. 1 item and 13 volumes. P 218.

Daily weather records at Perley, Minnesota, and a biography of Larson.

466. LARSON, LEWIS A. (1850–1909). PAPERS, 1864–1965. 11 items. P 219.

Papers of a Norwegian-born Methodist clergyman: correspondence; Civil War letters by his father, a Goodhue County, Minnesota, farmer; diaries (1882, 1886); clippings; and a biography by Lester W. Hansen.

467. LAWRENCE, CARL G. (b. 1871). PAPERS, ca. 1969. 8 items. P 699.

Papers concern the dedication of Carl G. Lawrence Library, Southern State College, South Dakota. Lawrence was a South Dakota educator.

468. LEE, JOHANNES J. SR. (1839–1926). POEMS, n.d. 10 items. P 222.
Poems in manuscript by a Norwegian-born farmer, surveyor, poet, and artist at Lake Park, Minnesota.

469. LEE, LARS. LETTER, 1863. 1 item. P 435.
Copy of a letter by the postmaster at South Bend, Minnesota, giving an account of an Indian outbreak in the Norwegian settlement at the South Branch of Watonwan River and including names of those killed and injured.

470. LEE, LUDVIG HALVORSEN. LETTERS, 1928. 4 items. P 223.
Letters to Karl Holm, Brooklyn, New York, by a prisoner at Sing Sing as he awaits execution.

471. LEE, NELS A. (1841–1916). PAPERS, 1862–1898, 1930. 4 items. P 220.
Papers of a Norwegian-born farmer in Dane County, Wisconsin: three letters, one of which is a Civil War letter by Berge O. Lee, Deerfield, and a clipping relative to the history of the Gilderhus family.

472. LEE, OLAV (1859–1943). PAPERS, 1880–1938. 139 items. P 221.
Papers of a Norwegian-born professor, clergyman, and author who taught languages and religion at St. Olaf College (1894–1934): articles and translations of songs, biographies of F. Melius Christiansen and B. J. Muus, and a historical sketch of St. Olaf College. "Grandpa Lee" by Ingmar A. Lee, Jr. is included.

473. LEIF ERIKSON MEMORIAL VIKING COMPLEX. PROPOSAL, 1963. Typescript, 16 pages. P 817.
Copy of a plan to create a monument to Leif Erikson: "A Proposal to the Norwegian People and Their Fellow Citizens of Chicago" by Arnold A. Tweten & Associates, Public Relations.

474. LELAND, RAGNVALD (1865–1936). SCRAPBOOKS, 1898–1929. 3 volumes. P 652.
Clippings largely from the Norwegian-American press regarding such subjects as Det Norske Selskab, New Norse, medicine, Skandinavisk-Amerikansk Lægeforening, and Norwegian literature.

475. LENKER, JOHN NICHOLAS (1858–1929). PAPERS, 1911–1929. 11 items. P 224.
Correspondence, sermons, articles, and two scrapbooks of a Lutheran clergyman. The clippings in the scrapbooks deal with the study of Scandinavian languages in the public schools.

476.   LIBERG, O. P. LETTER, 1863. 1 item. P 435.

Copy of a letter reprinted in *Morgenbladet* from *Emigranten* dealing with the Indian attack on the Norwegians at Watonwan River, Minnesota.

477.   LIEBERG, P. O. (1859–1943). PAPERS, 1871–1943. 6 items. P 226.

Correspondence and biography of a Pasadena, California, merchant. Lieberg's parents were members of Ole Bull's colony in Pennsylvania.

LEIF ERIKSON. See No. 190.

478.   LINDBERG, DUANE R. PAPERS. 2 items. Typescript, 87 and 13 pages. P 751.

"American Saloon and American School" (1970), a study of the attitudes of the Norwegian Lutheran clergy toward American environment, their role in ethnic cultural maintenance and influence on institutional structure of Upper Plains society, and "Perceived Ethnicity among Lutheran Pastors and Parishes in North Dakota."

479.   LINDELIE, ANDREAS H. (1866–1943). REMINISCENCES, 1935–1936. 29 items. P 227.

Reprints of a series of articles, which appeared in *Decorah-Posten*, entitled "Nogle erindringer og betragtninger," by a Norwegian-American editor of *Normanden* (Grand Forks), plantation owner in Cuba and Honduras, and proprietor of a travel bureau in Florida. Topics discussed include politics and temperance and such personages as Knute Arnegaard, Alexander Bull, Hans A. Foss, M. Falk Gjertsen, Kristofer Janson, Simon Johnson, Knute Nelson and Peer Strømme.

480.   LIPSCHUTZ, WENDY. STUDENT PAPER, 1976. 1 item. P 883.

"Norwegian Americans in La Salle County, Illinois, 1825–1926," a 43-page paper prepared at Northwestern University, Evanston, Illinois. The author reports some general information, but primarily records her interviews with five residents of La Salle County, two of whom were descendants of the Sloopers.

481.   LISBON GENERAL STORE, LISBON, ILLINOIS. ACCOUNT BOOKS, 1854–1882. 2 volumes. P 685.

Business records of a general retail mercantile store, including prices of produce and items of merchandise. Records for the period after 1856 are incomplete.

482.   LISBON SEMINARY (EIELSEN SEMINARY). PAPERS, ca. 1920. 2 items. P 500.

Historical sketch and a report of an institution at Lisbon, Illinois, that operated for one year (1855–1856).

483.   LJONE, ODDMUND. RADIO SCRIPTS. 22 volumes, typescript. P 790.

Scripts for three series of programs given over Norwegian broadcast-ing under the cover title *Nybyggerne* (Pioneers). The first two series involve seven episodes, the third has eight. Each episode approximates 30 pages.

484. LOE, HANS NILSEN (1840–1875). PAPERS. 6 items. P 747.
Diary and account books of a wagon-maker who came to America in 1862.

485. LØVENSKJOLD, ADAM. REPORT, 1847. I item. P 435.
Copy of an excerpt from the report by the Norwegian-Swedish consul in New York to his government on the Norwegian settlements in the West (October 15), and published in *Morgenbladet* (November 22). The report contains data on housing, water supply, forests, soil, health, wages, prices, taxes, crops, farm stock, wild life, American freedom, church situation, especially in Luther Valley and Koshkonong, Wiscon-sin, and number of families in each settlement.

486. LOKKE, CARL L. (1897–1960). PAPERS, 1861–1965. 8 boxes. P 554.
Articles, clippings, correspondence, diaries, maps, notes, and photo-graphs collected by an archivist, author, and educator. The material concerns the Lars Gunderson family, and the career of the Monitor Gold Mining and Trading Company of Alaska. The Papers formed much of the basis for *Klondike Saga* by Lokke, published posthumously by The NAHA in 1965.

487. LOKKEN, OLE J. (1882–1962). SCRAPBOOK, 1948–1953. P 228.
A collection of pictures and descriptions of churches in Trøndelag, Norway.

488. LOSS, HENRIK V. ZERNIKOW (1861–1938). PAPERS, 1906–1911. 5 items. P 229.
Papers of a Norwegian-born, Philadelphia consulting engineer and inventor of hydraulic machines, including an all-steel wheel to be used on railway cars.

489. LUNDY, GABRIEL (b. 1886). BIOGRAPHY, 1963–1968. 2 items. P 230.
Two typescript biographical sketches (6 and 8 pages) of a professor of agricultural economics at South Dakota State College, Brookings.

490. LUTHER ACADEMY. PAPERS, 1888–1926. 12 items. P 501.
Catalogues and reports of an institution founded at Albert Lea, Min-nesota, in 1888.

491. LUTHER COLLEGE. PAPERS, 1872–1965. 7 boxes. P 555.
Bulletins, catalogues, reports, clippings, programs, brochures and directories of a Decorah, Iowa, men's college, founded in 1861 and made co-educational in 1936.

492. LUTHER HOSPITAL AND TRAINING SCHOOL. PAPERS, 1916–1925. 6 items. P 622.
Correspondence, history, and reports concerning an institution in Eau Claire, Wisconsin, founded in 1908.

493. LUTHER INN. PAPERS, 1915–1918. 63 items. P 632.
Correspondence and reports regarding a Lutheran home for girls in Mason City, Iowa, founded about 1914.

494. LUTHERAN BIBLE INSTITUTE. CATALOGUE, 1927. 1 item. P 502.
Catalogue of a school founded in 1919 in St. Paul and later moved to Minneapolis.

495. LUTHERAN BIBLE SCHOOL. PAPERS, 1912–1938. 18 items. P 503.
Catalogues and reports of a Bible school founded by the church of the Lutheran Brethren in 1903, located in Wahpeton and Grand Forks, North Dakota, each in turn, and then moved to Fergus Falls, Minnesota, in 1935.

496. LUTHERAN BROTHERHOOD INSURANCE COMPANY. CORRESPONDENCE, 1936. 88 items. P 556.
Correspondence between C. O. Teisberg, Assistant Superintendent of Agents, and men's clubs within congregations regarding membership in the insurance company.

497. LUTHERAN CHURCH. PAPERS, 1881–1946. 4 boxes. P 556.
Articles, clippings, correspondence, records, scrapbooks, and reports regarding the Lutheran church among Norwegian Americans, dealing with bilingualism, doctrine, education, history, and with controversial figures like Bjørnstjerne Bjørnson, Hjalmar H. Boyesen, Bernt J. Muus, and Kristofer Janson. Among the correspondents are Rasmus B. Anderson, Ole A. Buslett, Johannes B. Frick, Severin Gunderson, Ole Juul, Ole L. Kirkeberg, Amund Mikkalsen, Hans G. Stub, and Martin Ulvestad.

498. LUTHERAN CHURCH IN AMERICA. ARTICLES, 1851–1859. 2 items. P 435.
Copies of articles published in *Christiania-posten* (April 25, 1851, and February 10, 1859) containing a general review of the Lutheran Church meeting at Luther Valley, Wisconsin (January 5, 1851), constitution of the newly-organized synod, resolutions regarding baptism, confirmation, and conversion; analysis of the Lutheran church in America as to national background and synodical affiliations; and detailed data regarding Norwegian ministers and their parishes.

499. LUTHERAN DEACONESS HOME AND HOSPITAL, CHICAGO. PAPERS, 1896–1962. 1 box. P 618.
Correspondence, constitution, history, journals, legal documents, and reports of a Chicago institution opened in 1897.

500. LUTHERAN DEACONESS HOME AND HOSPITAL, MINNEAPOLIS. PAPERS, 1889–1939. 1 box. P 619.

Correspondence, catalogues, histories, and reports of a Minneapolis institution founded in 1888 under the leadership of Sister Elizabeth Fedde of Brooklyn, New York.

501. LUTHERAN HISTORICAL CONFERENCE. NEWSLETTER, 1966– 1973. 8 items. P 786.

An incomplete file of the newsletter (typescript) distributed by the Lutheran Historical Conference, organized in 1962 at Chicago, Illinois, to provide cooperation among persons concerned with the research, documentation and preservation of resources relevant to Lutheranism in America.

502. LUTHERAN LADIES' SEMINARY. PAPERS, 1898–1920. 34 items. P 504.

Catalogues, journals, pictures, and reports of a Red Wing, Minnesota, school (1894–1920).

503. LUTHERAN MISSIONARY TRAINING SCHOOL. PAPERS, 1913– 1922. 4 items. P 507.

Catalogues and reports of a school founded in 1919 in Minneapolis to train mission and parish workers.

504. LUTHERAN NORMAL SCHOOL. PAPERS, 1914–1928. 11 items and 8 volumes. P 508.

Catalogues, journals, correspondence, historical sketch, and reports of a teacher training institution founded in 1892 at Madison, Minnesota.

505. LUTHERAN NORMAL SCHOOL. PAPERS, 1899–1931. 2 boxes. P 505.

Brochures, correspondence, reports, and student publications of an institution founded in Sioux Falls, South Dakota, in 1889.

506. LUTHERAN PUBLISHING HOUSE. PAPERS, 1908–1915. 55 items. P 231.

Minutes of the board of publication, financial reports, and correspondence of the Norwegian Synod's publishing house in Decorah, Iowa, with a branch office in Minneapolis.

507. LUTHERAN THEOLOGICAL SEMINARIES. PAPERS, 1899–1947. 2 boxes. P 506.

Articles, catalogues, correspondence, history, and records of several Lutheran theological seminaries founded by Norwegian Americans.

508. LYSENG, ENGEBRET AND HOLDAHL, ELLING OLSEN. PAPERS, 1704–1968. 14 items. P 539.

Documents pertaining to E. Lyseng estate and Elling Olsen Holdal estate, and a Lyseng family chart.

509. McMahon, Ruth Lima. Papers, 1886–1976. 1 box. P 844.
Correspondence, articles, clippings and accounts concerning the settlement of Griggs County, Dakota Territory (1881) and pioneer life there. Letters written by Mrs. McMahon's parents, Ole Lima (1860–1931) and his wife Martha (1868–1900), make up the bulk of the collection. Translations of most of the letters and accounts are by Mrs. McMahon.

510. Madagascar Missions. Scrapbook, 1897–1912. 1 volume. P 793.
Newspaper clippings of letters from missionaries, hymns, and reports regarding the missions in Madagascar. Some of the clippings are from papers published in Norway. For names of writers, see description catalogue in NAHA Archives.

511. Madland, Øistein (b. 1917). Biography, 1976. 1 item. P 861.
Information about a Norwegian seaman who came to the United States in 1959. The account deals with his experiences in the Norwegian underground and service with the British in World War II.

512. Madson, Hans. Papers, 1847–1931. 29 items. P 234.
Emigration papers, tax receipts, and certificate of naturalization of a Norwegian-born farmer of Manitowoc County, Wisconsin.

513. Magelssen, Thora (d. 1968). Scrapbook, 1923–1932. 1 volume. P 710.
Compiled by a Rushford, Minnesota, teacher and homemaker, containing letters by Knut Gjerset, Kristian Prestgard, and O. E. Rølvaag. The clippings pertain to them and to Adolph Gunderson, Ragnvald Nestos, Henrik Shipstead, Ola M. Levang, and the Magelssens.

514. Magnus, M. H. Clipping, 1908. 1 item. P 696.
An article from *Ørdbladet* (August 8) by Colonel Magnus concerning the limitation of emigration from Norway to America.

515. Malmin, Gunnar J. (b. 1903). Papers, 1925. 20 items. P 235.
Letters, clippings and articles by a professor of music at Pacific Lutheran University, Parkland, Washington. "Source Material Relating to the Emigration of 1825" was published in *The American Scandinavian Review*, 13 (June, 1925). "The Society of Friends in Norway and Their Relations to the Early Norwegian Emigration to America," "Norwegian Music in America," and "Norwegian Archives" are unpublished manuscripts. Clippings from *Decorah-Posten*, "Norsk Landnam i U.S.," were written by Malmin.

516. Mandt, Torgeir (Tarjei) G. (1845–1902). Papers, 1870's–1965. 8 items. P 686.
A poster and clippings of Norwegian-born industrialist and inventor concerning his Wagon Works started in 1865.

517. MARKERS MENIGHETS SØNDAGSSKOLE, FARIBAULT, MIN-
NESOTA. RECORDS, 1901–1902, 1910–1912. 1 volume. P 428.
Attendance records of teachers and pupils of the Sunday school of
Markers congregation, together with reports of receipts and disburse-
ments.

518. MARTIN LUTHER CHILDREN'S HOME. PAPERS. 3 items. P 633.
Constitution and brochure of a Stoughton, Wisconsin, institution
founded in 1889.

519. MAURITZSEN, JOHANNES. POEMS, 1839–1841. 1 volume. P 425.
Poems copied by Mauritzsen.

520. MEHUS, MIKKEL. LETTER, 1883. 1 item. P 236.
Letter written at Newburgh, North Dakota, dealing largely with the
drinking problem among Norwegian settlers.

521. MEHUS, O. MYKING. PAPERS. 11 items. P 917.
Copies of articles by and about an educator, administrator, public
servant, and leader in Norwegian-American organizations.

522. MELAND, RASMUS J. (1869–1961). PAPERS, 1896–1957. 2
boxes. P 557.
Correspondence, clippings, articles, reports and notes of a Lutheran
clergyman. Much of the material concerns the activities of Nordfjordlag
and related cultural enterprises, for example, early attempts to found a
Norwegian-American archives. Included is a collection of anecdotes
submitted to Meland by clergymen for *Pioner presters saga*, a publication never realized. Among these anecdotes are reminiscences (typescript, 7 pages) by Mary Nelsen Wee (Mrs. M. O.) under the title
"Church Union."
Meland was author of *John J. Maland and Marie Brekke Genealogy*
(1959), co-author of *Norske settlementer og menigheter i Sherbourne,
Benton og Mille Lacs Counties, Minnesota* (1903), and editor of several
Nordfjordlag annuals.

523. MELLBY, OLE A. (1843–1917). PAPERS, 1872–1944. 6 items.
P 237.
Papers of a Norwegian-born Lutheran clergyman: correspondence,
receipts, and a biography of Mrs. Mellby by C. A. Mellby, a son; letters
are by H. A. Preus, U. V. Koren, T. Bjørn, and Mrs. C. A. Mellby.

524. MELLEM, GULDBRAND (1849–1922). BIOGRAPHY, 1923. 3
items. P 238.
Clippings and a translation (typescript, 25 pages) of an article that
appeared in *Decorah-Posten*, January 2, 1923, concerning a
Norwegian-born farmer in Worth County, Iowa. The sketch touches on
subjects such as chinch bugs, logging in Missouri, slavery, caravan to
Iowa from Rock Prairie, Wisconsin, Indian visits, purchase and sale of
land, public service, and the slavery question in the church.

Part of Mellem's land became the site for Northwood. For a time he was considered the largest landowner in Iowa. The translation was done by Mrs. Brede Wamstad, a granddaughter.

525. MEN'S FELLOWSHIP CLUB OF CARPIO. MINUTES, 1924–1925. 1 volume. P 741.
Constitution and minutes of a men's club connected with St. John's Congregation, Carpio, North Dakota.

526. MICKELSEN, MICHAEL (1863–1949). PAPERS, 1891–1947. 195 items. P 239.
Correspondence, articles, and clippings of a Norwegian-born Lutheran clergyman. The clippings treat subjects such as temperance, language problems, and the Norwegian Memorial Church. Many of the letters are from charity institutions, including Homme Home for the Aged, Wittenberg, Wisconsin, and Ebenezer, a Home for the Aged, Minneapolis.

527. MIDELFORT, CHRISTIAN FREDRIK. PAPERS. 1 volume. Typescript, 302 pages. P 770.
"Non-Migration and Migration in Twenty-five Hundred Families" by a physician at the Gundersen Clinic, La Crosse, Wisconsin. A statement in the preface reads: "One of the purposes of this study . . . is to throw light on the non-migratory families, their physical and mental illnesses." The study is based on clinical histories of patients seen by the writer over a twenty-year period (1950–1970). The patients come from Minnesota, Iowa and Wisconsin. Dr. Midelfort is the author of *The Family in Psychotherapy*, New York, 1957.

528. MIDTLIEN, JOHN N. (1877–1966). PAPERS, 1911–1952. 112 items. P 244.
Correspondence of a Norwegian-born Lutheran clergyman and "A Christmas at the Old Parsonage in Coon Valley" (typescript, 5 pages) by Midtlien and translated from the Norwegian by L. A. Mathre in 1965. A large number of the letters are from Martin Norgaard, a mathematics teacher. The remaining letters concern his duties as a parish minister.

529. *MIDWESTERN OBSERVER*. NEWSPAPER, 1934. 3 items. P 802.
Issues nos. 1, 3, and 4 of a monthly published and edited by Trondby Fenstad (Chicago), a second generation Norwegian. Only four or five issues were published. Claimed to be a journal of liberal opinion.

530. MIKKELSEN, NILS. LETTER, 1866. 1 item. P 435.
Copy of a letter printed in *Hamars Budstikke*. An appeal for settlers, this letter written at Holmes City by the first Norwegian in Douglas County, Minnesota, describes the topography, vegetation, and wild life and gives the names of the Norwegians already in the county.

531. MINNEAPOLIS KREDS NORSK-LUTHERSKE LÆRERFORENING. RECORDS, 1893–1900. I volume. P 429.
The constitution and minutes of the Minneapolis Norwegian Lutheran Teachers' Association.

532. MINNEHAHA ACADEMY. CATALOGUE, 1924. I volume. P 509.
Catalogue of a Minneapolis school founded in 1913 by Northwestern Young People's Covenant (Swedish).

533. MINNESOTA BENEVOLENT SOCIETIES. PAPERS, 1902–1955. 37 items. P 640.
Brochures, constitutions, and reports.

534. MINNESOTA COLLEGE. PAPERS, 1915–1926. 25 items. P 510.
Catalogues, student publications, and programs of a Lutheran secondary institution founded in 1904 in Minneapolis by the Minnesota Conference of the Augustana Synod.

535. MINNESOTA, FILLMORE COUNTY. TAX RECEIPTS, 1861–1877. 18 items. P 240.
Tax levies on land ranging from 80 to 320 acres.

536. MINNESOTA, GOODHUE COUNTY. PAPERS, 1901–1943. 9 items. P 241.
Clippings and church programs regarding Goodhue County pioneer history.

537. MINNESOTA NORMAL AND BUSINESS COLLEGE. REPORT, n.d. I item. P 511.
Report about a school in Minneapolis (1898–1900) operated by Martin L. Tuve and Gabriel Loftfjeld.

538. MINNESOTA SCHOOL AND BUSINESS COLLEGE. POEM, 1896. I item. P 512.
Poem about the school by a student.

539. MJØSENLAGET. PAPERS, 1916–1938. 17 items and 7 volumes. P 720.
Records, reports, yearbooks, and clippings.

540. MOE, ANDREW B. BIOGRAPHY, n.d. Typescript, 5 pages. P 242.
By a Norwegian-born pioneer concerning his father, Iver B. Moe, founder of Poulsbo, Washington, and its first postmaster. Deals also with the trip across the mountains from Miles City, Montana, to Seattle, and with logging in Washington.

541. MOHN, FREDRIK VOSS (1856–1942). PAPERS, 1838–1938. 83 items. P 245.
Articles, correspondence, clippings, and legal papers of a Norwegian-born physician of Los Angeles, dealing with cultural and

medical subjects. Mohn was professor at California Ecletic Medical College; wrote *Før doktoren kommer* (ca. 1890); and was interested in socialized medicine.

Correspondents include Elisabeth Koren, Christian Michelsen (Oslo), O. S. Sneve, Gabriel Tischendorf (Bergen), and Johs. B. Wist.

542. Mohn, Thorbjørn N. (1844–1899). Papers, 1884–1919. 3 boxes, including 9 volumes. P 715.

Letters, clippings, and brochures of a Norwegian-born educator and clergyman. Mohn emigrated in 1852 and was president of St. Olaf College (1874–1899).

The letters by Mohn (ca. 3000 in 8 letter books) deal with matters relative to St. Olaf College and to the Lutheran church: conduct, housing, and recruitment of students; employment of teachers; student and teacher recommendations; appeals for funds; establishment of a seminary at St. Olaf; anti-Missourian and union movements in the church; and status of St. Olaf in relation to the church. For names of correspondents, see description catalogue in NAHA Archives.

543. Molee, Elias (1845–1928). Papers, 1911–1928. 15 items. P 243.

Clippings, pamphlets, and articles of a Muskego-born language reformer, farmer, teacher, and writer. The articles (manuscript and typescript) deal with language reform and the author's career, including childhood days in Muskego.

544. Monona Academy. Reports, ca. 1920. 2 items. P 513.

Reports regarding a Lutheran co-educational institution (1876–1881) in Madison, Wisconsin.

545. Monson, Clara (Mrs. Martin O.) (b. 1888). Papers, 1871–1964. 43 items. P 247.

Correspondence, family histories, and memoirs of a La Fayette County, Wisconsin, housewife. The letters, written from the Wiota and Luther Valley settlements, deal with farming, housing, dress, epidemics, school, church and social activities in pioneer days. The histories are of the Synstelien, Tollefsrude, and Brenum families. The memoirs (typescript, 21 pages) were written primarily for her family.

546. Mordt, Anders L. Papers. 13 items and 1 volume. P 824.

Copies of papers relating to the history of Anders L. Mordt Land Co., Guymon, Oklahoma. Mordt, a promoter of Oslo, a Norwegian settlement in Hansford County, Texas, in the early 1900's, advertised extensively in the Norwegian-American newspapers, urging settlers to buy land from him. He hoped to build a city which would compare with the Norwegian capital. The city was never built, but the area was populated by Norwegian farmers who came from the Mid-west. They organized the Oslo Lutheran Church at Gruver, Texas. A history of this congregation is included.

547. *MORGENBLADET*. EMIGRATION, 1849–1866. 14 items. P 435.
Copies of articles dealing with causes and effects of emigration, emigration agents, cholera, social position of Norwegian Americans, Know-Nothingism, Americanization, and interviews with passengers.

548. MORGENSTIERNE, WILHELM T. M. (1887–1963). PAPERS, 1940–1952. 40 items. P 667.
Articles, biography, reports, and speeches by Norway's New York Consul General, envoy extraordinary, and ambassador to the United States, 1929–1962.

549. MORMONS, SCANDINAVIAN. PAPERS, 1950–1958. 9 items. P 248.
Pamphlets, articles, and 1850–1860 census records concerning Scandinavian Mormons. One pamphlet (1950) contains articles and the program held in Salt Lake City commemorating the centennial of the introduction of Mormonism into the Scandinavian countries. Included are articles by William Mulder.

550. MOTZFELDT, LUDWIG (1847–1928). CLIPPINGS, 1908–1934. 3 items. P 249.
Clippings providing information about Motzfeldt who emigrated to Chicago about 1872, established a trading post in Forest County, Wisconsin, and married a Chippewa Indian girl. Included is a 3-page biographical statement on Ketil Johnsen Melstad Motzfeldt.

551. MOUNT HOREB ACADEMY. REPORT, ca. 1920. 1 item. P 514.
Roster of teachers at a Lutheran institution in Mount Horeb, Wisconsin (1893–1898). See also the Andrew Johnson (Aasen) Papers and the Christian Thompson scrapbook, Nos. 415 and 859.

552. MURI, CHRISTIAN J. (1871–1943). BIOGRAPHY, ca. 1939. Typescript, 3 pages. P 250.
An autobiographical sketch of a Montana rancher.

MUSIC. See Special Collections, No. 945.

553. MUUS, BERNT JULIUS (1832–1900). PAPERS, 1771–1946. 3 boxes. P 559.
Articles, clippings, correspondence, lectures, sermons, and notes of a Norwegian-born clergyman and the founder of St. Olaf College.

554. MYRVIK, OLE A. (1871–1952). HISTORY, 1933, 1949. 1 volume, 23 pages. P 251.
Family and church histories prepared by Myrvik, a farmer, born in North Dakota of Norwegian parents. The family history gives an account of the journey from Montreal to Minnesota, and includes comments on travel by covered wagon, land sharks, snowstorms, diseases, schools, and prices of commodities and crops. The history of St. Stephen Lutheran Church, Milton, North Dakota, includes the names of

the founders and pastors and the history of the auxiliary societies. Both accounts are written in Norwegian.

555. NÅLSUND, BERNHARD. FAMILY HISTORY, 1975. 1 item. Typescript, 32 pages. P 828.
"Butli, gården og slekten" by Bernhard and Jon Ivar Nålsund, Trondheim, 1974.

556. NAESETH, GERHARD B. (b. 1913). PAPERS, 1844–1845; 1962. 5 items and 2 reels of microfilm. P 413.
Two reels of microfilm of passenger lists of vessels arriving at New York, June 19–August 31, 1844, and June 2–July 15, 1845, together with a typewritten transcript of the Norwegian portions of these films compiled by Naeseth. The roster (over 1000 names) includes names of ships, dates of sailings, and ages and occupations of immigrants. Reprints from *Norsk Slektshistorisk Tidsskrift*, "Nordmenn i De Forenede Stater," and from *The Norseman*, "In Search of the Past," a description of Vesterheim Genealogical Center.

557. NAESS, ANDERS PEDERSEN. POEM. 1 volume, 52 pages. P 763.
Manuscript (1750?), bound in pigskin, containing six poems (hymns) under the title "Den første sang."

558. NANSEN, FRIDTJOF (1861–1930). PAPERS, 1918–1961. 26 items. P 253.
Articles, clippings, and pamphlets concerning a Norwegian Arctic explorer, scientist, humanitarian and diplomat, dealing largely with Nansen's lecture in Chicago in 1929 and the Nansen centennial in 1961. An article by Nansen, entitled "Amerikansk idealisme," is included.

559. NAPOLEONIC WARS. CORRESPONDENCE, 1807. 2 items. P 254.
Letters written to families at home in Norway by men in military service at Christiansand during the Napoleonic wars.

560. NATIONAL SKI ASSOCIATION OF AMERICA. PAPERS, 1911–1942. 125 items. P 673.
Minutes, reports, membership lists, bulletins, and histories of an association, organized in 1904.

561. NELSEN, FRANK C. DISSERTATION, 1968. 1 volume, 270 pages. P 725.
"The American School Controversy among the Norwegian-Americans, 1845–1881." Ph.D., Michigan State University.

562. NELSON, CARL (1873–1932). PAPERS, 1926–1978. 13 items. P 949.
Memoirs, poems, humerous squibs and biographical data of a talented Norwegian-American editor and poet, who lived at Cando, North Dakota. Includes a biography (8 pages), a tribute by Knut Wefald (5 pages), memoirs (33 pages), and poems (56 pages) by Nelson (all in

typescript), and a compilation of his "Ole Axhandle" articles (12 pages).

563. NELSON, FRANK G. PAPERS, 1976–1977. 3 items. P 909.
Manuscripts and copies of articles by a professor at the University of Hawaii, Hilo, Hawaii: "Following the Pathfinder, a Norwegian Account of Western Missouri in 1848," a translation of an America letter from Peder Nielsen Kalvehaven, with introduction by Frank Nelson, and "A Danish Account of Missouri in 1839."

564. NELSON, JACOB A. (1886–1958). PAPERS, 1933–1939. 5 items. P 255.
"John Hanson and the National Domain" (typescript, 22 pages) by an Iowa attorney, and brochures announcing the publication of Nelson's book, *John Hanson and the Inseparable Union* (1939). John Hanson was "President of the United States in Congress Assembled" (1781–1782).

565. NELSON, KNUTE (1842–1923). PAPERS, 1860–1966. 40 items. P 257.
Papers concerning a Norwegian-born attorney and statesman: clippings, correspondence, genealogy, and speeches. Nelson was a member of the Wisconsin and Minnesota legislatures, governor of, and United States senator from Minnesota.

566. NELSON, OLEY (1844–1938). PAPERS, 1893–1943, n.d. 20 items. P 258.
Papers of a Civil War veteran: pamphlets, speeches, sketches of Nelson's life, and GAR mementoes. Included is a pamphlet entitled *The Controversy As to the Responsibility of the Augsburg Board of Trustees to the United Norwegian Lutheran Church of America from 1890 to 1893* by Oley Nelson and Ole O. Onstad.
Nelson, a Slater, Iowa, farmer, merchant, and legislator, was Commander-in-Chief of the GAR in 1935.

567. NELSONE, NELSON (1800–1886). LETTER, 1848. 1 item. P 259.
Letter written in English by Nelsone (most often known as Nelson Nelson Hersdal) of Norway, La Salle County, Illinois, to Joseph Mann, Orleans County, New York, describing his farming operations and Mormon and Jansonist activities in the community. Nelsone was a Slooper.

568. NERHEIM, SIVERT (b. 1898). PAPERS, n.d. 6 items. P 732.
Genealogical material and two typescript articles, "The Farm at Nerheim at Ølen, Sunnhordaland" (25 pages), and "My First Journey to America" (2 pages).

569. NESSEIM (NESHEIM), LARS NIELSSEN (1792-ca. 1885). PAPERS, 1838–1961. 28 items and 7 volumes. P 560.

Two volumes of immigrant letters written during the 1840's to friends and relatives in Voss, Norway, copied by Nesseim, a resident of Voss. The correspondence, scrapbooks (clippings) and pamphlets concern these letters.

Among the letters are some by Elling Eielsen, one by Sjur Jorgensen Haaheim in defense of Bishop Jacob Neumann's opposition to Norwegian emigration, and one from John Haldorsen Kvilekval, Knute Nelson's uncle.

For data on Lars Nielssen Nesseim, see K. A. Rene, *Historie om Udvandringen fra Voss og Vossingerne i Amerika* (1930).

570. NEUTSON, KNUTE (1851–1949). PAPERS, 1941–1947. 3 items. P 260.

Papers of a Norwegian-born insurance man and chief promoter of the Minnesota Credit Union Law of 1925: a biography, his story of the Jesse James raid in Northfield, and a review of his book *Memoirs of a Pioneer* (1938).

571. NEW EFFINGTON, SOUTH DAKOTA. LOCAL HISTORY, 1963. 1 volume, 160 pages. P 927.

A commemorative booklet noting the fiftieth anniversaries of the communities of New Effington, Claire City, and Hammer. Norwegian immigrants were among the early settlers in the area. The volume includes a number of biographies and photographs.

572. NEW YORK BENEVOLENT SOCIETIES. PAPERS, 1924–1949. 7 items. P 641.

Histories and reports of four institutions.

573. NIELSEN, HAGBARTH (1867–1947). PAPERS, 1899–1952. 20 items. P 261.

Reminiscences from mining days in Alaska and the Yukon (1899–1902), and several poems by a Norwegian-born miner and dairyman. Nielsen emigrated in 1893 and lived in California.

574. NILSEN, OLA (1834–1912). LETTERS, 1866–1880. 2 items. P 884.

Letters from Ola Nilsen to his father, Nils Knudsen Gudmundsrud, Aal, Hallingdal, Norway. Translated into the English and compiled into booklet form (typescript, 67 pages) by Theressa Lundby, a granddaughter. A short biography (typescript, 4 pages) is included. Nilsen emigrated in 1866.

575. NILSEN, OLE M. (1844–1933). PAPERS. 7 items and 1 volume. P 676.

Scrapbook, poems, speeches, and correspondence of a Lutheran clergyman.

576. NISSEDAHLE. PAPERS, 1928–1961. 9 items. P 262.
Material regarding a Norwegian folk museum at Mount Horeb, Wisconsin, established by Isak Dahle, Chicago.

577. NJAA, SVEN HANSON (b. 1870). BIOGRAPHY, 1964. 13 pages. P 950.
Article, "Fra Jaeren til praeriens misjonsmark," published in *Jul i Rogaland* (1964). Njaa emigrated from Rogaland in 1892. Treats chiefly his early experiences and his stay in Canada, after which he served a Northwood, North Dakota, parish for fifty years.

578. NORA LODGE NO. 1. RECORDS, 1860–1965. 3 boxes and 2 volumes. P 653.
Records and pamphlets of a Norwegian cultural and benefit society in Chicago. Norwegian Society Nora was organized July 18, 1860; renamed Nora Lodge No. 1, Knights of the White Cross in 1863; and merged with the Sons of Norway in 1938.

579. NORBECK, PETER (1870–1936). PAPERS, 1910–1936. 9 items. P 263.
Speeches by a United States senator from South Dakota on agriculture, immigration, and Iceland's parliament millenial.

580. NORDIC ARTS, NORTHFIELD, MINNESOTA. PAPERS, 1936–1970. 8 items. P 843.
Minutes, clippings, histories, sewing and cooking guides of two women's organizations. The second club, organized in 1939, was dissolved in 1950.

581. *NORDISK TIDENDE.* LOCAL HISTORY, 1924–1941. 20 items. P 283.
Pamphlets published by *Nordisk Tidende*, including a history of Norwegians in Boston and detailed facts about Brooklyn Norwegians as to homes, shops, income, clubs, churches, building trades, newspapers, background, and savings.

582. *NORDLYSET* AND *MAANEDSTIDENDE*, RACINE COUNTY, WISCONSIN. RECORDS. 1 volume. P 432.
Subscription list of *Nordlyset* (1847–1849) and *Maanedstidende* (ca. 1851) organized according to states, counties, and post offices; *Maanedstidende* treasury reports; and a short essay on the *Skandinaviske presseforening*. Filed with the volume are short essays, presumably by L. H. Langland.

583. NORDRAAK, RIKARD (1842–1866). PAPERS, 1934–1935. 5 items. P 266.
Papers concerning the composer of the music for Norway's national anthem by the Norwegian journalist, Alf Dus, consisting of correspondence and the manuscript (21 pages) of his musical radio drama entitled "Rikard Nordraak."

584.   NORGE SKI CLUB, CHICAGO (1905). PAPERS. 11 items. P 928.
Letters, clippings and a fiftieth anniversary program of a Chicago ski club.

585.   NORLIE, OLAF MORGAN (1876–1962). PAPERS, 1848–1958. 7 boxes. P 561.
Articles, bibliographies, clippings, correspondence, essays, notes, programs, reports, scrapbooks, statistics, and verse of an author, editor, educator, and clergyman.
The collection includes annotated bibliographies on Elling Eielsen and the Beaver Creek, Illinois, settlement; biographical sketches of prominent Norwegian-Americans; essays on the lodge; statistics and data on Bible translations, church schools, and immigration; typescript of the report to the Norwegian government by Consul General Adam Løvenskjold after his visit to America in 1848; and an essay on the similarities between the Norwegian and Indian languages.

586.   NORMAN, AMANDUS (1866–1931). SERMON, 1895. 1 item. P 809.
"Hva er tro?" a sermon preached at the Nazareth Church, Minneapolis. Norman was influenced by Kristofer Janson and succeeded him at Nazareth Church. He later served the Unitarian congregation at Hanska, Minnesota.

587.   THE NORSE-AMERICAN CENTENNIAL. PAPERS, 1923–1929. 7 boxes and 2 volumes. P 562.
Correspondence, minutes, financial records, reports, programs, clippings, pictures, pamphlets, and scrapbooks of an association incorporated in 1925 in St. Paul, Minnesota, to supervise the observance of the arrival of the first group of Norwegian immigrants in America. The collection describes in detail the management of the celebration and gives data on observances in Chicago, Canada, Boston, and Brooklyn. Letters and essays reveal the loyalty of Norwegian-Americans to their cultural heritage and the rivalry among area groups of Norwegians in America. The celebration was initiated by the *bygdelags*.
The chief officials were Gisle Bothne, S. H. Holstad, J. A. Holvik, Elisa P. Farseth, and Mrs. Wm. O. Storlie. Correspondents include Juul Dieserud, Knut Gjerset, Hanna Astrup Larsen, and O. M. Norlie. The centennial received nationwide press coverage.

588.   NORSE AMERICAN CENTENNIAL DAUGHTERS OF ST. PAUL. PAPERS, 1922–1946. 342 items and 1 volume. P 275.
Articles, brochures, clippings, correspondence, and reports of a Norwegian-American society organized in 1925 following the Norse American centennial celebration in Minneapolis that year. It has supported the Minnesota Leif Erikson Monument Association, entertained visiting royalty from Norway and promoted library, music, museum, and welfare projects.

589. NORSK-DANSKE PRESSEFORENING I AMERIKA. PAPERS, 1895–1938. 1 box. P 563.

Minutes, reports, correspondence, and clippings of the Norwegian-Danish Press Association of America organized in 1895. The collection deals with such subjects as immigration, influence of the press on the preservation of the Norwegian heritage and Americanization of immigrants, history of the Association, and annual meetings. The name of the society was changed to the Norwegian and Danish Press Association in 1938.

590. NORSK EVANGEL. LUTHERSKE MENIGHEDER I RICE COUNTY, MINNESOTA. MINISTERIAL BOOK, 1869–1911. 1 volume. P 556.

Incomplete ministerial records of membership, communicants, confirmations, marriages, baptisms, and burials.

591. NORSK LÆSE-OG SAMTALEFORENING, SILVANA, WASHINGTON. RECORDS, 1884–1895. 2 volumes. P 433.

Minutes of a society organized to provide for its members a library and an opportunity to discuss current topics, such as women's suffrage, temperance, taxes, presidential elections, fire insurance, the new literature, farming vs. logging, and causes of economic depressions. A copy of the constitution, lists of members, library records, and financial accounts are also included.

592. DET NORSK LUTHERSKE LANDSFORBUNDET. PAPERS, 1928–1936. 4 items. P 267.

Report of the Lutheran Landsforbundets annual meeting in the Luther Valley, Wisconsin, church (June, 1936) and clippings and program.

593. DEN NORSKE DRAMATISKE FORENING I CHICAGO. RECORDS, 1868–1871. 1 volume. P 674.

Minutes, financial reports, by-laws, and programs of the society's dramatic productions.

594. DET NORSKE SELSKAP I AMERIKA (1903–1976). PAPERS, 1903–1976. 4 boxes and 1 volume. P 564.

Correspondence, reports, and records of a Norwegian society organized January 28, 1903, for the preservation and the promotion of Norwegian culture in America. Treats subjects such as the Sigvald Quale declamatory contests, folk festivals, Norwegian literature, memorial monuments, and Norwegian-American history.

The society published a journal, *Kvartalskrift* (1905–1922), edited by Waldemar Ager. The society was merged with the Norwegian-American Historical Association in 1976. In 1977 the Association published *Cultural Pluralism versus Assimilation*, edited by Odd S. Lovoll, a volume of essays translated from *Kvartalskrift*.

595. DET NORSKE SKYTTERLAG. PAPERS, 1900. 13 items. P 265.

Papers of a Chicago Norwegian-American sharpshooters society.

596. DEN NORSKE SYGEFORENING "NORDLYSET" AV CHICAGO. PAPERS, 1893–1944. 3 boxes. P 654.
Constitution, reports, and record books of a Chicago social and sick benefit society.

597. NORSTOG, JON (1877–1942). PAPERS, 1903–1941. 38 items. P 268.
Five issues of *Dølen*, a journal of poetry written and published by a Norwegian-born author and farmer at Watford City, North Dakota, and clippings concerning him.

598. NORTH DAKOTA BENEVOLENT SOCIETIES. PAPERS, 1912–1951. 126 items. P 642.
Brochures, journals, and reports.

599. NORTH DAKOTA, CASS COUNTY, SCHOOL DISTRICT NO. 45. TEACHER'S REGISTER, 1885–1892. 1 volume. P 687.
Records of pupil attendance, the course of study, textbooks, property, and visitors.

600. NORTH DAKOTA HOSPITALS. PAPERS, 1902–1925. 10 items. P 623.
Northwood Deaconess Hospital catalogue, Rugby Hospital history, and Grand Forks Deaconess Hospital constitution.

601. NORTH DAKOTA, WATFORD CITY. LOCAL HISTORY, 1964. 1 volume. P 718.
Watford City, North Dakota compiled by the Golden Jubilee Book Committee on the fiftieth anniversary of the community's founding. Profusely illustrated, the volume consists of historical sketches of clubs and institutions, and of family histories.

602. NORTHWESTERN COLLEGE. JOURNAL, 1920. 1 item. P 516.
Official organ of a secondary school, Fergus Falls, Minnesota, operated by Swedish Lutherans in the Northwest.

603. NORTHWESTERN COLLEGE. REPORTS, 1922. 2 items. P 517.
Reports of a Lutheran secondary institution at Velva, North Dakota (1910–1912).

604. NORWAY, ROYAL FAMILY. PAPERS, 1929–1958. 3 boxes. P 566.
Articles, brochures, correspondence, pictures, and programs dealing largely with royal visits to the United States in 1939 and 1968.

605. NORWAY IN WORLD WAR II. PAPERS, 1940–1948. 3 boxes. P 565.
Papers concerning Norway and World War II consisting of brochures, clippings, correspondence, manuscripts, pamphlets, and pictures.

606. NORWEGIAN ALMANACS, 1858–1910. 6 items. P 269.
Almanacs published by Hostetter, Pittsburgh; Dr. D. Jayne, Philadelphia; and *Norsk Folke Calender*, Madison, Wisconsin.

607. NORWEGIAN-AMERICAN CHAMBER OF COMMERCE (1915). PAPERS. 7 items. P 862.
Assorted papers of a corporation, organized in New York City chiefly for the purpose of promoting business interests between Norway and the United States.

608. NORWEGIAN AMERICA LINE. ESSAYS, 1937–1964. 1 box. P 567.
Essays by St. Olaf College students receiving awards from the Norwegian America Line in their annual essay contests.

609. NORWEGIAN-AMERICAN HISTORICAL ASSOCIATION (1925). PAPERS, 1925–1970. 67 boxes. P 1000, P 1001, P 1002.
Financial, secretarial and publication records of an association organized in 1925 to maintain archives and to publish books relating to Norwegian migration to America.
Consists of minutes; annual reports; correspondence, statements on editorial and financial policies, on purpose and service of the organization; manuscripts; publication bids and contracts; book reviews of NAHA publications; catalogues; pamphlets and brochures. Use of the papers pertaining to publication requires the permission of the NAHA editor.

610. NORWEGIAN-AMERICAN HOSPITAL. PAPERS, 1894–1939. 8 items. P 624.
Brochures, constitution, yearbook, and history of a Chicago hospital founded in 1891.

611. NORWEGIAN-AMERICAN MUSEUM, DECORAH, IOWA. PAPERS. 2 boxes. P 726.
Clippings, articles, newsletters, circulars, directories, reports, and correspondence.

612. NORWEGIAN-AMERICAN WOMEN'S CLUB OF DETROIT. PAPERS, 1940–1941, 1950. 178 items. P 286.
Correspondence, records, and clippings of a society organized to raise relief funds for Norway.

613. NORWEGIAN AMERICANS IN POLITICS. PAPERS, 1890–1965. 40 items. P 271.
Brochures, clippings, and speeches concerning such subjects as anarchism, immigration, Leif Erikson Day, and the Bennett law.

614. NORWEGIAN CLUBS. PAPERS, 1869–1966. 66 items. P 280.
Brochures and programs of varied Norwegian-American organizations in the United States.

615. NORWEGIAN CLUBS, CHICAGO. PAPERS, 1921–1978. 1 box. P 278.
Papers of a variety of Chicago organizations: art, athletic, dance, social, student, and theater.

616. NORWEGIAN-DANISH METHODIST EPISCOPAL CONFERENCE. PAPERS, 1870–1958. 7 items. P 272.
A report of the women's foreign mission society, and articles on the history of the Methodist church among Norwegian Americans.

617. NORWEGIAN-DANISH THEOLOGICAL SEMINARY. CATALOGUE, 1925. 1 volume. P 518.
Catalogue of an institution founded in 1875 in Evanston, Illinois, by the Norwegian-Danish Educational Society of the Methodist Episcopal Church.

618. *NORWEGIAN EMIGRANT SONGS AND BALLADS* (1936). NOTES, 1836–1936.
Manuscripts and notes used by Theodore C. Blegen, Martin B. Ruud and Gunnar J. Malmin in their preparation of *Norwegian Emigrant Songs and Ballads*.

619. NORWEGIAN HOSPITAL SOCIETY, ST. PAUL HOSPITAL. PAPERS, 1914–1928. 15 items. P 625.
Brochures and reports of an institution in St. Paul, Minnesota, founded in 1901.

620. NORWEGIAN IMMIGRATION. STUDENT PAPERS, 1926–1929. 31 items, 31 folders. P 287.
General statements, genealogies, family histories, and histories of pioneer settlements by students studying under O. E. Rølvaag.

621. NORWEGIAN LANGUAGE. ARTICLES. 6 items. P 273.
Assorted commentaries.

622. NORWEGIAN LITERARY SOCIETY OF CHICAGO, INC. (DET LIT-TERÆRE SAMFUND). PAPERS, 1925–1975. 4 boxes. P 279.
Papers of a literary society (also known as Delisa): programs; clippings; secretarial, financial and library records; manuscript volumes which were the genesis of the yearbook *Forum* (1925–1926) and the literary journal *Norden* (1928–1933) published by the society; as well as copies of *Forum* and some scattered issues of *Norden*.

623. NORWEGIAN LITERARY SOCIETY OF MINNEAPOLIS. MINUTES, 1929–1951. 1 volume. P 434.
Secretary's record of a society organized in 1929 to promote Norwegian-American literature.

624. NORWEGIAN LUTHERAN BETHESDA HOME. PAPERS, 1916–1949. 28 items. P 634.

Brochures and reports of a Chicago institution for the aged founded in 1907.

625. NORWEGIAN LUTHERAN CHILDREN'S HOME SOCIETY. PAPERS, 1900–1943. 32 items. P 635.
Constitution, history, journals, and reports of a Chicago institution founded in 1896.

626. NORWEGIAN LUTHERAN CHURCH OF AMERICA, SOUTHERN MINNESOTA DISTRICT. MINUTES, 1917–1934. 1 volume. P 556.
Minutes of the home mission committee and related committees.

627. NORWEGIAN LUTHERAN DEACONESSES' HOME AND HOSPITAL, BROOKLYN. PAPERS, 1895–1960. 114 items and 39 volumes. P 617.
Brochures, catalogues, histories, and reports of an institution in Brooklyn, New York. The hospital, started in 1883 under the leadership of Sister Elizabeth Fedde, merged with the Lutheran Hospital of Manhattan in 1956 and became known as Lutheran Medical Center.

628. NORWEGIAN LUTHERAN TEACHERS ASSOCIATION OF AMERICA. PAPERS, 1917–1931. 12 items and 1 volume. P 556.
Correspondence and minutes of a society organized to promote parochial schools.

629. NORWEGIAN MUTUAL INSURANCE COMPANY, WORTH COUNTY, IOWA. RECORDS, 1881–1890. Microfilm, 1 reel. P 886.
Business records of a mutual insurance company in Worth County, Iowa.

630. NORWEGIAN NATIONAL LEAGUE, CHICAGO. PAPERS, 1899–1961. 21 items. P 277.
Programs and reports of a Norwegian organization founded in Chicago in 1899 to unite Norwegian societies in that region in order to support projects of common concern.

631. NORWEGIAN NATIONAL LEAGUE, MINNEAPOLIS. PAPERS, 1927–1956. 14 items. P 284.
Programs and reports.

632. NORWEGIAN OLD PEOPLE'S HOME SOCIETY OF CHICAGO. PAPERS, 1896–1962. 2 boxes. P 644.
Constitution, journals, and reports of an institution incorporated in 1896.

633. NORWEGIAN PICTURE POST CARDS (ca. 1925). 32 items. P 274.
Cards showing interior views and costumes at the time the first Norwegians settled in the United States.

634. NORWEGIAN SINGING SOCIETIES. PAPERS, 1890–1952. 3 boxes. P 570.

Pamphlets, song books, brochures, and concert programs of Norwegian singing societies throughout the country.

635. NORWEGIAN STUDENTS' AMERICA CHORUS, 1925. 14 items. P 833.
Correspondence, records, clippings and other information concerning the visit to Minneapolis of a choral group from Norway.

636. NORWEGIANS IN THE UNITED STATES. SCRAPBOOKS, 1923–1926. 4 volumes. P 697.
Scrapbooks of clippings of articles by W. Ager, R. B. Anderson, G. M. Bruce, L. M. Gimmestad, H. R. Holand, C. G. O. Hansen, Haldor Hanson, S. B. Hustvedt, Torstein Jahr, Gunnar Malmin, O. E. Rølvaag, J. C. Roseland. Subjects include Leif Erikson, Kensington stone, Norwegians in Canada, Norwegian Moravians in Pennsylvania, Civil War, Norwegian-American press, Quakers in Iowa, and the Sloopers. Biographies of Knud Henderson, Nils Otto Tank, J. C. Dundas, Nils P. Haugen. Histories of several congregations: LaSalle County, Illinois; Big Canoe, Iowa; Koshkonong and York, Wisconsin; Norway Lake, Minnesota.

637. NYGAARD, KAARE K. PAPERS, ca. 1969. 4 items. P 733.
Biographical information on a Norwegian-born surgeon and sculptor.

638. OAK GROVE SEMINARY. PAPERS, 1908–1941. 10 items and 30 volumes. P 519.
Correspondence, catalogues, and reports of a Lutheran secondary school established in Fargo, North Dakota, in 1906.

639. ODIN LYCEUM BUREAU, INC. PAPERS, 1917. 5 items. P 294.
Papers of Norwegian-American chautauqua and lyceum, Minneapolis. Gisle Bothne, Nicolay Grevstad, Jacob A. O. Preus, and Theodor S. Reimestad were among the promoters and lecturers.

640. ODLAND, GUNDER THEODOR (1856–1935). DIARY, 1882–1914. 1 volume. P 791.
Diary of an emigrant from Stavanger beginning April 15, 1882, the day he left Norway for America. The diary presents a complete record of his early experiences with data on weather, expenses, letters, church attendance, visits, friends, and his work. He provides an account of earnings and expenditures at the close of each year.
Odland returned to Norway in 1888, married Olena Haaland, and they returned to his homestead (160 acres) in Sargent County, North Dakota. The Odlands moved to Eagle Bend, Minnesota, in 1892. The diary reveals a progressive entry of English expressions mixed with the Norwegian, indicative of the gradual Americanization process.

641. ODLAND, LISA. POEMS, n.d. 1 volume, typescript, 158 pages. P 417.
Collection of poems entitled "The Mystic Star."

642. ODLAND, THOMAS (b. 1875). PAPERS, 1894, 1908. 5 items. P 895.
Emigration documents of an emigrant from Tysvær, Norway.

643. ØIHAUGEN, OLE T. LETTER, 1866. 1 item. P 435.
Copy of a letter signed by Øihaugen and others, published in *Addressebladet*. The authors complain about treatment and conditions on ship passage to America.

644. ØSTERUD, OLE OLSON (1820–1909). PAPERS, 1833–1909. 1 box. P 689.
Correspondence, diaries, legal papers, and pamphlets of a Norwegian-born artisan and farmer of Ostrander, Minnesota, who emigrated in 1854. The correspondence (1854–1894) consists of letters from Norway, a Civil War letter, and letters from New Ulm, St. Peter, Spring Valley, Walnut Grove, Preston, Hurdal, Red Wing, Minnesota; Coon Prairie, Sparta, Muskego, Wisconsin; and Revillo, Dakota Territory, and contains references to prices, house construction, crops, railroad building, disease, school teaching, migration, activities on the Mississippi River, and Wisconsin pineries.

645. ØSTREM, OLE O. (1835–1910). REMINISCENCES, 1858. Typescript, 10 pages. P 289.
Typewritten copy of an article based on a diary recounting the experiences of a sea voyage in 1857. Østrem was a Lutheran clergyman.

646. OFTEDAHL, MARIA (MRS. EINAR L.) (1861–1948). REMINISCENCES, 1930. 5 items. P 290.
Articles and clippings of a Cottonwood, Minnesota, housewife dealing with childhood memories, the "snow winter" of 1880–1881 in Lyon County, and local church history.

647. OFTELIE, TORKEL (1856–ca. 1943). PAPERS, 1904–1957. 44 items. P 291.
Articles, poems, letters, and clippings of a Norwegian-born writer and editor of *Telesoga*. The articles and poems contain biographical sketches of immigrants from Telemark, Norway, and accounts about Indians. "Rispur og Sogur" is a collection of folk stories. A letter from Peder Ydstie, Minnesota poet, discusses the family life of Kristofer Janson.
Oftelie was also editor of *Ugeblad* and of *Rodhuggeren*, both in Fergus Falls, Minnesota. Halvdan Koht called Oftelie the best saga writer among Norwegian Americans.

648. OHME, THOR (b. 1891). AUTOBIOGRAPHY, 1975. Typescript, 68 pages. P 863.
"From the Cradle to the Grave, a Few Notes from Traveling Through Life " by Thor Ohme, born in Oma, Hardanger, Norway, emigrated in 1909. The account covers travels, work, attendance at Augsburg Col-

lege (1911–1912); service as an airplane mechanic in World War I; employment by the Minneapolis Post Office (1921–1956); and activity in Norwegian-American affairs.

649. OIEN, JOHN G. CLIPPINGS, 1881–1953. 10 items and 7 volumes. P 411.
Clippings and articles, collected by a Chicago attorney, relating to Norwegian American topics.

650. OLESEN, JOHN Y. HISTORY, 1952. Booklet, 47 pages. P 864.
"History of Norway and the Norsemen " published by Mr. Olesen, a civil engineer.

651. OLESON, SOREN (d. 1898). LOCAL HISTORY, 1898. 1 item. P 295.
A historical sketch of early Norwegian settlers in Marshall County, Iowa, including Oleson, by C. R. West.

652. OLSEN, EMILY VEBLEN (ca. 1865–1953). PAPERS, 1885–1941. 1 box. P 571.
Papers of the wife of a Lutheran clergyman and sister of Thorstein and Andrew A. Veblen: a history of St. Ansgar congregation; sermon by her father-in-law, Johan Olsen; a tribute to Claus L. Clausen by her husband, Sigurd Olsen; a letter by Ole Nilsen; memoirs and biographies of her husband and her father-in-law by Mrs. Olsen; and an album of photographs.

653. OLSEN, JOHN W. (b. 1864). AUTOBIOGRAPHY. Typescript, 34 pages, n.d. P 609.
The story of a Danish-born state superintendent of schools in Minnesota, dean of the Agricultural College (Minnesota), and lecturer.

654. OLSEN, M. M. FAMILY HISTORY, 1936? 39 pages. P 929.
Copy of a pamphlet, *Minder og erfaringer*, published in Copenhagen, dealing with a Norwegian immigrant family in Wisconsin, who brought up one son to become a physician in a Seventh-day Adventist health care institution and four to become Seventh-day Adventist ministers.

655. OLSEN, MICHAEL L. (b. 1944). STUDENT PAPER, 1966. 1 item. Typescript, 70 pages. P 296.
"Scandinavian Immigrant Farmer Participation in Agrarian Unrest in Western Minnesota," a paper fulfilling requirements for graduation with distinction in the field of history, St. Olaf College.

656. OLSEN, NIELS H. F. (1890–1962). PAPERS, 1859–1959. 1 box. P 572.
Albums, clippings, genealogies, letters, and legal papers of a Norwegian-born engineer, Dearborn, Michigan.

657.   OLSEN, NILS A. (1886–1940). CATALOG, 1971. P 814.
Catalog of Nils A. Olsen Papers, prepared by James T. Steensvaag, Iowa State University Library. Nils Olsen was connected with the Bureau of Agricultural Economics, U.S. Department of Agriculture (1925–1935).

658.   OLSEN, OLAF (b. 1871). PAPERS, 1841–1961. 11 boxes and 2 volumes. P 573.
Correspondence, articles, reports, drawings, diaries, log-books, notebooks, clippings, and pamphlets of a Norwegian-born machinist and engineer.
The correspondence deals with such topics as problems in engineering, sea disasters, strikes and labor problems, drought, farm crops, recreation, and religion. In a letter dated September 29, 1890, Olsen describes his journey from Oslo to Laredo via ship and rail. Most of the letters by Olsen are to his wife. The articles include biographies of members of Olsen's family and also treat Yukon gold rush experiences. One diary concerns his immigration journey to America.
Olsen was a shop machinist in Laredo (Texas), Wilmington (Delaware), and Philadelphia; a machinist on English ships and in the American Revenue Cutter Services; and after 1900 an engineer with coastal trade steamship lines. He was a member of the Socialist Party.

659.   OLSON, ELEANORA (1870–1946). MONOLOGUE. 1 item. Typescript, 3 pages. P 297.
A dialect monologue entitled "Sogne-Kjerring" by a Chicago and Minneapolis reader (declaimer) and singer.

660.   OLSON, FLOYD B. (1891–1936). CLIPPINGS, 1932–1935. 9 items. P 298.
Information regarding the political career of Olson.

661.   OLSON, GILBERT (b. 1841). REMINISCENCES, 1932. 1 item, 12 pages.
Recollections of a Norwegian-born pioneer at Sawyer, Wisconsin, dealing with his life in Norway before emigration and with such topics as church, roads, and Lake Michigan traffic.

662.   OLSON (LANGRUD), HANS (1820–1896). DIARY, 1870. 2 items. P 300.
An account of the journey Olson took in 1870 from Dodgeville, Wisconsin, to Coal Creek, Kansas. Towns on the route of travel and the supply of grass and water for his cattle are the chief topics. A typewritten translation is included (8 pages).

663.   OLSON, JACOB (1854–1937). PAPERS, 1933–1935. 8 items. P 301.
Papers of a Norwegian-born farmer in Bosque County, Texas: articles, pictures, a letter, and a poem by Franklin Petersen. The articles by

Olson give information on Texas pioneers: names, dates of arrival, house construction, farm operations, Cleng Peerson, and the Civil War. Other articles concern Gustaf W. Belfrage, Swedish entomologist of Bosque County.

664. OLSON, JULIUS E. (1858–1944). PAPERS, 1902–1930. 27 items. P 302.

Clippings and pamphlets that contain speeches made by Olson at Norwegian-American festivals, and also an Olson family history. Olson was professor of Scandinavian languages at the University of Wisconsin (1884–1935).

665. OLSON, LUDWIG EDWARD (b. 1916). BIOGRAPHY. 2 volumes, typescript. P 783.

Two biographical sketches: "Grandpa Made Knives" (21 pages) concerns Knut Langedal Olson (1845–1933). Rolf H. Erickson is a co-author. "Grandpa Went to War" (26 pages), an account of Samuel C. Onson (1840–1903) who served in the 21st Wisconsin Infantry.

666. OLSON, PAUL A. (1873–1954). PAPERS, 1931–1952. 1 item and 3 volumes. P 414.

Papers of the editor and publisher of *The Story City Herald*, Story City, Iowa. A biography (typescript, 5 pages) and three booklets on local history.

667. ONSAGER, LARS (b. 1913). CLIPPING. 1 item. P 896.

"Yale's First Faculty Nobelist," an article about a Norwegian-born professor of theoretical chemistry at Yale University who received the Nobel Prize in Chemistry in 1968. Onsager came to the U.S. in 1928.

668. ONSTAD, ANDREW. PAPERS, 1801–1929. 20 items. P 292.

Legal papers and correspondence regarding family affairs of a Norwegian-born grocer of Green Bay, Wisconsin.

669. ORE, ØYSTEIN (1899–1968). ARTICLES, 1956, n.d. 3 items. P 293.

Manuscript material of "Norwegian Emigrants with University Training 1830–1880" published in *Studies and Records*, 19 (1956). Also commentary on the play, *Broder Ebben i fødelandet eller amerikareisen* (1839) (typescript, 12 pages). A copy of the play is included. Ore, born and educated in Norway, was professor of mathematics at Yale University.

670. OSLAND, BIRGER (1870–1963). PAPERS, 1887–1955. 24 boxes. P 574.

Correspondence, clippings, reports, and manuscripts of a Norwegian-born Chicago investment banker, philanthropist, and author. He was an official in various enterprises of Charles H. Wacker (1893–1911); founder and president of Birger Osland and Company, investment bankers (1911–1940); general Western manager of the Norwegian America Steamship Line (1911–1923) and for many years a member of its board of representatives; secretary-treasurer of Lake Otis Groves, Inc.; director of Scandinavian Trust Company of New York until its merger with New York Trust Company; and vice president of Chicago Security Dealers Association.

From 1917 to 1919 Osland was an attaché with rank of major in the Military Intelligence Division of the U.S. Army, stationed in Christiania, and also a member of the U.S. Food Administration, Copenhagen. He was a trustee of the Century of Progress Exposition; member of the Norwegian-American World's Fair Auxiliary Committee; treasurer of the NAHA for 25 years; director and also president of the Norwegian-American Hospital; and national treasurer of Norwegian Relief, Inc., during World War II.

The correspondence, about half of which are letters by Osland, deal with business enterprises, civic interests, philanthropy, and family. Topics discussed include city, state, and federal politics; banking and investments; Osland's work as organizer of American financial participation in the Norwegian America Line in 1911–1912; and the participation of Norway and Norwegian Americans in the Century of Progress Exposition.

Includes material on the various Chicago Norwegian organizations and institutions: Arne Garborg Klub, Den Norske Quartet Klub, Det Norske Nationalforbund, Den Norske Klub, Dovre Klub (politics), Sleipner Athletic Club, Norwegian Fish Club (businessmen's luncheon group), American Norwegian Chamber of Commerce, Norwegian Pioneers Club, Norwegian-American Athletic Association, Norwegian Literary Society, Norwegian People's Academy, Norwegian Players, Norwegian Singers' League, Norske Skiklub, Norwegian-American Hospital, Norwegian Old People's Home, and several non-church-affiliated institutions.

Osland wrote frequently for the press about his civic interests, including articles on Chicago Norwegians. He promoted the compilation of his family genealogy, *Aasland-ætten*, by Ola Aurenes (1947); and he wrote his own biography, *A Long Pull from Stavanger*, published by NAHA in 1945.

671. OUSDAL, ASBJØRN P. (1879–1959). PAPERS, 1935–1951. 34 items and 10 volumes. P 678.

Papers of a Norwegian-born osteopathic physician and surgeon of Santa Barbara, California. The clippings, correspondence, pamphlets, scrapbooks and pictures, including a three-act play, "Vinland Saga" (1937), by Ousdal, deal with the founding of Norroenn Federation of America and its promotion of Leif Erikson Day. They deal also with Ousdal's fossil museum. Ousdal is the author of *Our Revolting Society* (1945).

672.   OUTLOOK COLLEGE. PAPERS, 1917–ca. 1922. 6 items. P 520.
Correspondence, historical sketch, and reports of a Lutheran secondary school founded in 1916 at Outlook, Saskatchewan.

673.   PACIFIC COAST NORWEGIAN SINGERS ASSOCIATION. PAPERS, 1903–1969. 2 boxes. P 727.
Concert programs and related items.

674.   PACIFIC LUTHERAN UNIVERSITY. PAPERS, 1908–1956. 1 box. P 575.
Brochures, bulletins, catalogues, minutes, programs, and history of a Parkland, Washington, school founded in 1894.

PAMPHLETS. See Special Collections, No. 946.

675.   PARK REGION LUTHER COLLEGE. PAPERS, 1914–1928. 17 items and 9 volumes. P 522.
Bulletins, catalogues, student journals, programs, and reports of the Fergus Falls, Minnesota, school founded in 1892.

676.   PASTORAL CONFERENCE, 1884. MINUTES, 1885. 1 volume, 134 pages. P 556.
Protokol over prestekonferencens forhandlinger, a record of a clerical conference in Decorah, Iowa.

677.   PAULSEN, GUNDER (1821–1872). REMINISCENCES, 1872, 1944. 2 items. P 719.
Copy of *Minder fra Tiden omkring Aaret 1830 til 1848* published in 1872, and a typescript translation of same (132 pages). Reminiscences from attorney Paulsen's childhood and youth in Solør, Norway.

678.   PAUST, BENJAMIN A. (b. 1880). PAPERS, 1969. 4 items. P 270.
A letter and three typescript articles: "An Immigrant and His Progeny," "My Summers on the Farm," and "My Four Years at the University of Wisconsin," by a Minneapolis realtor.

679.   PEDERSEN, CARL O. (1887–1972). PAPERS, 1925–1926. 20 items and 1 volume, typescript, 346 pages. P 303.
Clippings and pamphlets of a Norwegian-born Lutheran clergyman, and a manuscript dealing with the observance of the Norse-American Centennial in the United States and Norway.

680.   PEDERSEN, JENS CHRISTIAN (b. ca. 1859). PAPERS, 1865–1900. 3 items. P 304.
Vaccination certificate, a diary of a trip from Christiania to New York, and a poem written on board ship in 1898.

681.   PEDERSON, MAREN POL (MRS. ANDREAS) (1849–1935). BIOGRAPHY, 1956. Typescript, 9 pages. P 305.
Biography of a Norwegian-born boarding house operator and

housewife written by two granddaughters. The story includes life in Norway before emigration, hardships at sea on a trip to Hawaii via Cape Horn, and making a living in Hawaii and California.

682. PEDERSON (SABØ), PAUL (1824–1898). PAPERS, 1852–1891. 5 items. P 306.
A biography, emigration and citizenship papers, and a pastoral letter of call of a resident of Renville County, Minnesota.

683. PEERSON, CLENG (1782–1865). PAPERS, 1806–1964. 69 items and 1 volume. P 308.
Correspondence, legal documents, clippings, pictures, and biography concerning a Norwegian-American pathfinder.
The papers include copies and transcripts of Peerson letters, an emigration paper, and Texas warranty deeds; a biography by Rasmus B. Anderson, an article by Theodore C. Blegen, and pamphlets concerning the Bishop Hill colony.
Peerson, the founder of the first Norwegian settlements in New York, Illinois, Iowa, and Missouri, spent his last years in Texas, and was buried there in Bosque County.

684. PERSON, MRS. NELS U. LETTERS, 1925–1929. 16 items. P 930.
Letters addressed to Mrs. Nels U. Person, Columbus, North Dakota, from relatives in Norway. Many of the letters are undated and fragmentary.

685. PETERSEN, BERTHE C. (1872–1941). PAPERS. 17 items. P 818.
Copies of clippings concerning a Norwegian-born Chicago resident. Mrs. Petersen was active in Norwegian National League, President of the Federation of Norwegian Women's Societies, served on the Norse-American Centennial Committee, and promoted the idea of Leif Erikson Day.

686. PETERSEN, FRANKLIN (1862–1939). PAPERS, 1889–ca. 1939. 5 items and 1 volume. P 772.
Manuscripts of three sea stories (169, 93, and 267 pages) by a Norwegian-born New York City editor, poet, and railroad employee, two of which are known to have been published in 1938 in *Decorah-Posten* and *Skandinaven*, and four poems. Petersen was editor of *Nordisk Tidende* (1907–1911), founder of *Det nye Norge* in 1911, and author of two collections of poems.

687. PETERSON, C. STEWART. SCANDINAVIAN SETTLEMENTS, 1938. Typescript, 6 pages. P 307.
Survey of early Scandinavian settlements in 28 states.

688. PETERSON, HENRY J. (1880–1957). BIOGRAPHY, 1935. 1 item. Typescript, 3 pages. P 310.
A biographical sketch of Aven Nelson (1859–1952), president of the University of Wyoming and professor of Botany at the same institution.

689. PETERSON, SAMUEL P. CLIPPINGS, 1926–1930. 5 items. P 311.
Clippings of articles by a Norwegian-born meteorologist in the United States weather bureau at Wichita, Kansas, recounting his experiences at sea for several years during the 1890's.

690. PETTERSEN, CARL WILHELM (b. ca. 1843). PAPERS, 1866–1886. 17 items. P 312.
Poems (presumably by Pettersen), and correspondence of a Madelia, Minnesota, bricklayer who immigrated in 1867.

691. PETTERSON, SØREN (1833–1917). CHURCH HISTORY, 1915. 1 volume, 46 pages. P 556.
Den gamle grund, a discussion of the approaching merger of the Norwegian Synod, the United Church, and the Hauge Synod of which Petterson was a member.

PHOTOGRAPHS. See Special Collections, No. 947.

692. PHYSICIANS AND SURGEONS. ARTICLES, 1925–1957. 21 items. P 313.
Articles by and about seven Norwegian-Americans in the field of medicine: H. A. Eckers, Gunnar Gundersen, Olaf Jenson Hagen, Carl Alfred Ingerson, Hendrik J. Svien, Orin P. Thorson.

693. PIERSON, HARRIET. LETTERS, May 24, 1846. 2 items. P 314.
Letters written in English from Hartland, Michigan, to Sarah and Nancy Austin, Orleans County, New York, regarding family affairs.

694. PINE LAKE SCANDINAVIAN CONGREGATION. PAPERS, 1841–1963. 36 items. P 315.
Correspondence, clippings, pictures, and records of a Scandinavian congregation near Oconomowoc, Wisconsin, affiliated with the Protestant Episcopal Church. The papers deal with matters relative to building a church, securing a minister, electing officials, and living conditions. Two of the correspondents are John G. Gasmann and Jackson Kemper. John J. Johnson includes reminiscences in his correspondence.

695. PIONEER SOCIAL CLUB OF CHICAGO, 1878. HISTORY, 1966. Booklet, 44 pages. P 866.
History of the club and biographical sketches of its members.

696. PLEASANT VIEW LUTHER COLLEGE. PAPERS, 1905–1942. 30 items and 1 picture album. P 528.
Brochures, catalogues, journals, and pictures of an Ottawa, Illinois, secondary school founded in 1896.

697. POEMS, 1840–1952. 363 items. P 316.
Poems in manuscript and in print by different authors, including S. O. Braaten, John Benson, Borghild Dahl, Lauritz P. Dommersnaes, Bernhard H. J. Habel, Ole E. Hegstad, John Heitman, Palmer J. Hertsgaard,

N. J. Hong, Kristofer Janson, M. R. Odegaard, Didrick J. Orfield, Olav Refsdal, Ditlef G. Ristad, Soren Roinestad, Per Sivle, Carl K. Solberg, Oscar J. Sorlie, Henrik Voldal and Rolf Fjelde.

698. PRESTGARD, KRISTIAN (1866–1946). PAPERS, 1884–1945. 4 boxes. P 577.

Correspondence, manuscripts and scrapbook of a Norwegian-born journalist and author. He was co-editor and editor of *Decorah-Posten* (1897–1946); co-editor and publisher of *Symra* (1905–1914); editor of *Norske Kvad* (1906); translator of *Fra Livet i Vestjylland* by Jakob Jakobsen (1894); author of *Nansenfaerden* (1896); *Skrøneboka* (1911), *En Sommer i Norge* (1928), *Streiftog, Stemninger og Skildringer* and *Fjords and Faces* (1937); and a founder of NAHA and a member of its board of editors (1925–1933).

The letters by Prestgard and those by his correspondents deal largely with such subjects as the language controversy both in Norway and America, the tour of Norway by twelve American newspaper men in 1927, Knut Gjerset's unfinished dictionary of Norwegian-American biography, the writings of Ole E. Rølvaag, Norwegian-American His-torical Association, the merging of *Minneapolis Tidende* and *Decorah-Posten* in 1935, genealogy, immigration history, and gladioli. He gained a reputation as a horticulturist by developing 30 new varieties of gladioli.

The Ola K. Stokkestad letters to Prestgard (1884–1897) are unique in that they treat not the economics of rural areas, but cultural pursuits mainly in the city. The Arne Odd Johnson letters (1934–1938) deal with editorial and publication problems connected with using the Prestgard-Ivar Kleiven correspondence as basic material in a history of the migra-tion of Norwegians to America. The John Heitman letters (1928–1945) are primarily about the problems of translating, editing, and publishing *Fjords and Faces*, the English version of *En Sommer i Norge*.

Among the other correspondents are Rasmus B. Anderson, Henry Armstrong, Mrs. L. M. Boomer, Th. Caspari, Borghild M. Dahl, Juul Dieserud, P. J. Eikeland, Johan Falkberget, Arne Garborg, C. J. Ham-bro, J. C. M. Hanson, Hjalmar R. Holand, Halvdan Koht, Hanna As-trup Larsen, Fritjof Nansen, John Norstog, Julius Olson, Franklin Peter-son, Ragnhild Prestgard, A. N. Rygg, Ludwig Saxe, Th. H. Svanøe, A. A. Veblen, Henry A. Wallace.

699. PREUS, JOHAN CARL K. (b. 1881). CHURCH HISTORY, 1965. Typescript, 45 pages. P 318.

"Transition from Norway's State Church to an American Free-Church" is a study of the early efforts of the Reverend Herman A. Preus and his Spring Prairie, Bonnet Prairie, Norway Grove, and Lodi parish in Dane and Columbia Counties, Wisconsin, to orient themselves to American church life.

700.   PROTOKOL FOR DEN EVANGELISK LUTHERSK PRESTEKONFERENS
       VED STILLEHAVSKYSTEN, 1890–1912. MINUTES. 1 volume.
       P 556.
Records of the Evangelical Lutheran Ministers' Conference on the
Pacific coast.

701.   PSALMODICON CHARTS, n.d. 9 items. P 319.
Manuscripts of musical scores for a Norwegian one-string instrument.

702.   QUAKERS, NORWAY AND AMERICA. PAPERS, 1967–1968. 2 vol-
       umes. P 709.
"Det norske Kvekersamfunns historie" (typescript, 89 pages) by
Anne Emilie Jansen has a chapter about Norwegian Quaker emigration
to America.

703.   QUALE, SIGVALD (1890–1909). CLIPPINGS, 1909, 1924. 2 items.
       P 897.
Clippings concerning a gift to Luther Hospital, Eau Claire, Wisconsin, by Sigvald Quale.

704.   QUALEY, CARLTON C. (b. 1904). PAPERS, 1972. 2 items. P 810.
"Ethnic Studies and Higher Education" (typescript, 8 pages), and *On
Being an Ethnic Historian* (pamphlet, 12 pages) by a scholar in the field
of ethnic studies.

705.   QUAM, NELS (b. 1894). AUTOBIOGRAPHY. 1 item. Typescript, 91
       pages. P 931.
Autobiography of a Norwegian-born retired school superintendent,
and for a time superintendent of Ebenezer Home in Minneapolis
(1946–1962). Includes descriptions of his childhood and youth in Nor-
way, his emigration to the United States in 1913, his school-days at
Jewell Lutheran College and at St. Olaf College, his experiences in both
World Wars and his work in the Iowa schools and at the Ebenezer
Home.

706.   QUAM PRACTICAL BUSINESS COLLEGE. CATALOGUE, ca. 1925. 1
       item. P 521.
Catalogue of a business school founded in 1917 in Minneapolis by
Robert J. Quam.

707.   QUESTAD, CARL (1815–1886). PAPERS, 1830–1957. 213 items.
       P 737.
Correspondence, historical sketches, and legal papers of a
Norwegian-born Texas rancher, who emigrated in 1851.

708.   RAAEN, AAGOT (1878–1957). PAPERS, 1929–1950. 25 items.
       P 320.
Clippings and articles treating local pioneer life in North Dakota of a
public school teacher in North Dakota. Raaen wrote *Grass of the Earth*

(1950), published by NAHA; *Measure of My Days* (1953); and *Hamarsbøn-Raaen Genealogy* (1954).

709. RAMBERG, SEVERT H. (1844–1920). BIOGRAPHY, 1912. Type-script, 29 pages. P 321.

"Biografi av Hans Helliksen Ramberg (1817–1890) og hans familie" is an anecdotal account of the family's migrations from Norway to Wisconsin, Minnesota, Kansas and back to Wisconsin (1855 to 1864).

710. RAMSTAD, ANDERS WILLIAM (b. 1891). PAPERS, 1973. 2 volumes. P 867.

Biographical sketches of the life of a Norwegian-American clergyman and educator who served as a teacher and administrator at Pacific Lutheran College from 1925 until his retirement in 1961. The sketches were written by his wife, Emma Kvindlog Ramstad.

711. RASMUSSEN, GERHARD (1857–1943). PAPERS, 1876–1946. 3 boxes. P 579.

Articles, autograph books, clippings, correspondence, diaries, notebooks, reports, and sermons of a Lutheran clergyman.

Among his papers are materials on Lutheran Deaconess Home and Hospital in Chicago, Augsburg Seminary, St. Olaf College, the use of the English language in the church (1893), Lisbon cultural conditions, the merger movement among Norwegian Lutherans, and sketches of his father's life (P. A. Rasmussen).

Among his correspondents are Nils C. Brun, Markus O. Bøckman, Theodor H. Dahl, Peder Dreyer, Thore Eggen, Peder J. Eikeland, Nils J. Ellestad, Severin Gunderson, Bjørn Holland (his mother's brother), Hans C. Holm, Even J. Homme, Mikel C. Holseth, John N. Kildahl, Laur. Larsen, Gerhard Lenske, Lars Lund, W. A. Passavant, L. H. Schuh, Hans G. Stub, Peder Tangjerd, Martin E. Waldeland, and Carl M. Weswig.

Most of the letters by Rasmussen are to his parents and to Gjermund Hoyme.

712. RASMUSSEN, HENRY E. (b. 1867). PAPERS, 1910–1920. 5 items. P 610.

Letters to Rasmussen regarding the J. J. Hill gift to the St. Olaf College Endowment Fund (1913) and the Peter Norbeck gift to the Augustana College Endowment Fund (1920).

713. RASMUSSEN, MATHILDE (1865–1952). FAMILY HISTORY, 1945. Typescript, 45 pages. P 611.

"A Brief History of the P. A. Rasmussen Family" includes material on their Norwegian background; activities of parishes in Illinois, Wisconsin, Iowa, Minnesota, and Missouri; life in the Lisbon (Illinois) parsonage; synodical affairs; and family anniversaries and memorials.

714. RASMUSSEN, PAUL A. (b. 1895). ADDRESSES, 1936. 2 items.
P 322.
Two WCCO addresses given by the Minnesota state budget commis-
sioner.

715. RASMUSSEN, PETER A. (1829–1898). PAPERS, 1830–1941. 1
box. P 578.
Correspondence, reports, articles, pamphlets, and clippings of a
Norwegian-born Lutheran clergyman, author, and editor.
Rasmussen immigrated in 1850; was a parochial school teacher
(1850–1852); minister, Lisbon, Illinois (1854–1897); president, Eielsen
Seminary, Lisbon (1854–1855); organizer of Lisbon Society for Publication of Textbooks and Devotional Books (1856); editor of *Kirkelig
Tidende* (1856–1861) and of *Opbyggelseblad* (1877–1887); and author
of books and articles treating theological subjects.
Some of the topics discussed are education, foreign and home mis-
sions, theological doctrine, union of synods, lay activity in the church,
recruitment of pastors from Norway, St. Olaf College, Augsburg Semi-
nary, and life in the Lisbon settlement.
Among the correspondents are Ludvig M. Biørn, August Cramer,
Nels J. Ellestad, E. S. Holland (his brother-in-law), Gjermund Hoyme,
Gisle Johnson, John N. Kildahl, J. Landsverk, N. J. Laache, Olaus
Nielsen, and Friedrich A. Schmidt. Many of the letters are by Rasmussen.

716. RAY, OLAF E. (1856–1943). PAPERS, 1898–1944. 2 boxes.
P 580.
Papers of a Norwegian-born attorney and etymologist: correspondence, clippings, journals, pamphlets, and notes for his book *Vore
navne* (1944).
Ray wrote frequently for the local press on civic matters. His chief
interests were the Leif Erickson discovery of America and the etymol-
ogy of Norwegian names. He represented Sons of Norway at the Mille-
nary of the Duchy of Normandy festival in June, 1911.

717. REAR, ESTEN E. BIOGRAPHY, ca. 1922. Manuscript, 8 pages.
P 612.
A sketch of Haldor Ostensen Rye and his family of North Aurdal,
Valdres, Norway, who immigrated to Wisconsin in 1852.

718. RECORD BOOK, 1853–1871. 1 volume, 66 pages. P 323.
An unidentified account of an emigration journey from Norway to
Muskego, Wisconsin, to Stillwater and ending in Brownsville, Minnesota, in 1855. Also contains irregular farm and household accounts
(1853–1871).

719. RED WING SEMINARY. PAPERS, 1887–1933. 12 boxes. P 581.
Correspondence, records, catalogues, photographs, and histories of a

Lutheran Seminary founded in 1879, consisting of an academy and a divinity school. Gradually college courses were added and in 1917 both college and theological departments were merged with St. Olaf College and Luther Theological Seminary respectively.

The correspondence deals with the problems of the post-merger period, recruitment of students, employment and salaries of teachers, and the organization of new departments.

720. REECE, ANDREW A. (1873–1943). PAPERS, n.d. 3 volumes, typescript, 631 pages. P 418.

Unpublished manuscripts of a Norwegian-born Lutheran clergyman: the first, a drama entitled "Pastor Brown," deals with the problem of building a church in a pioneer Minnesota congregation divided into State Church and dissenter groups. The second (unfinished), entitled "A Norseman in the Melting Pot," recounts the experiences of a young Norwegian immigrant in Chicago and the Fox River settlement and his visit to the homeland after nine years in America.

721. REIERSEN HELENA. LETTER, 1860. P 324.

Typescript copy of a letter by Helena Reiersen, Shreveport, Louisiana. It deals with slaves, railroad building, and her husband's business (commission merchant), and refers to the Bache family and to Elise Waerenskjøld.

722. REIERSEN, JOHAN REINERT (1810–1864). PAPERS, 1844–1846. 1 item and 1 volume. P 325.

Papers of the Norwegian-born founder of the Brownsboro, Texas, settlement: a bound volume of twelve issues of *Norge og Amerika* and a copy of an article which appeared in *Morgenbladet* (July 11, 1844). Both items aim to treat conditions among Norwegians in America in such a manner as to arouse people of Norway to free themselves of non-democratic restraints.

723. REIERSON, I. JOHANNES AND OLSON, REIER. BOND, April 27, 1886. P 326.

Document reminiscent of the Norwegian *kaar brev* drawn up in Waupaca County, Wisconsin, stipulating conditions under which the father conveyed his farm to his son.

724. REYMERT, AUGUST (1851–1932). PAPERS, 1832–1927. 6 boxes. P 391.

Correspondence, clippings, articles, reports, and photographs of a Norwegian-born New York attorney.

The correspondence deals largely with family affairs in America, Norway, and Scotland. The letters by James Denoon Reymert, August's uncle, first editor of *Nordlyset* (1847), first Norwegian-American member of a state legislature (Wisconsin), and attorney, deal with opportunities for law practice on the American frontier. Ole Bull was also a correspondent.

Other items include biographical sketches of family members, a family chart, and an article about Hans Balling, the portrait painter. See *Studies and Records*, 12 (1941).

725. RIPPY, NELS ANDERSON. LETTER, 1883. 1 item. P 898.
Letter from Newark concerning the trip back to the United States after a visit in Norway signed by forty travellers from Bergen.

726. RISTAD, DITLEF G. (1863–1938). PAPERS, 1880–1938. 6 boxes. P 582.
Papers of a Norwegian-born poet, educator, lecturer, and Lutheran clergyman: correspondence; manuscripts of articles, lectures, poems, and sermons by Ristad; clippings of articles by and about him and subjects in which he was interested; and records of organizations he supported. The papers are largely from the period 1920 to 1938. Most of the letters by Ristad deal with church activity.

The papers deal with such subjects as church union; Grundtvigianism; church school problems; organization and finances of the church; the Norwegian Museum at Decorah, Iowa; the collecting, research, publication, and financial program of NAHA; Norwegian-American exhibit at the Century of Progress, Chicago; restoration of the Trondheim Cathedral; and the preservation of Norwegian culture in America.

Ristad was a minister at Edgerton and Manitowoc, Wisconsin; president of three church schools; editor of *Wisconsin Tobacco Reporter*; first president of the NAHA; president of Trønderlag; and president of the Eastern District of his church (1936–1937).

Correspondents include J. A. Aasgaard, Waldemar Ager, T. C. Blegen, L. W. Boe, Arne Fjellbu, L. M. Gimmestad, Knut Gjerset, Carl G. O. Hansen, Einar Haugen, Jacob Hodnefield, Hjalmer R. Holand, M. A. Holvik, U. V. Koren, Laur. Larsen, R. Malmin, O. M. Norlie, Jon Norstog, Torkel Oftelie, Julius E. Olson, Birger Osland, E. J. Oyen, Kristian Prestgard, C. K. Preus, Ove J. H. Preus, Carlton C. Qualey, O. E. Rølvaag, A. N. Rygg, Peder Tangjerd, I. B. Torrison, and Johs. B. Wist.

727. RITTER, MATTIE W. PAPERS, 1867–1869. 2 items. P 327.
A diary and a teacher's certificate.

728. ROALQUAM, HALVARD (1845–1926). PAPERS, 1848–1935. 3 boxes. P 583.
Papers of a Norwegian-born clergyman and educator: letters, reports, lectures, diary, account books, an autobiography (typescript, 74 pages), a scrapbook of material dealing with church controversies, addresses given at St. Olaf College Founder's Day (1905, 1906), and letters regarding synodical activities. Most of the letters by Roalquam are to his wife. Roalquam was a teacher at Luther College (1878–1886); principal at Grand Forks College (1891–1893).

729. ROAN, CARL MARTIN (1878–1946). FAMILY NARRATIVE. Typescript, 325 pages. P 773.

"The Immigrant Wagon," by a Minneapolis physician, is chiefly the story of his immigrant parents. Roan's father, Ole Roen Johnson (1825–1903) came from Valdres to Wisconsin in 1852; Roan's mother, Beret Eggen (1832–1907), came from Trondhjem diocese to Wisconsin in 1853. After their marriage they moved to Minnesota.

730. ROCKSTAD, ANDRES (1847–1932). PAPERS, 1817–1931. 6 items and 1 volume. P 342.

Correspondence and biographical notes regarding a Norwegian-born citizen of California.

731. ROE, HERMAN (1886–1961). PAPERS, 1918–1961. 89 items. P 328.

Family history, reports, speeches, correspondence, clippings, articles, and brochures of the editor of the *Northfield* (Minnesota) *News* (1910–1961).

Roe was president of the Minnesota State Fair, member of the board of governors of the Minnesota Agriculture Society, secretary of the Minnesota Editorial Association, and president of the National Editorial Association.

732. RØLVAAG, OLE EDVART (1876–1931). PAPERS, 1899–1956. 49 boxes. P 584.

Correspondence; notebooks; manuscripts of novels, articles, book reviews, lectures and poems; clippings; scrapbooks, essays; and general commentary on Rølvaag as author, educator, and cultural leader.

Correspondence: Rølvaag carried on a voluminous correspondence in both English and Norwegian on subjects such as guidance to students and aspiring writers, assistance to teachers planning courses in Norwegian, the place of Norwegian culture in American life, defense of realism in his novels, the arts of writing and translating, church affairs, immigration history, problems of publication and distribution, state and national politics, and promotion of organizations. His correspondents (approximately 1300) included land prospectors, farmers, students, teachers, editors, artists, historians, theologians, poets, novelists, diplomats, publication houses, and lecture bureaus. A list of Rølvaag's main correspondents is available in the description catalogue in the NAHA archives.

Manuscripts: Complete or fragments of Rølvaag's published works, including manuscripts of translations of Rølvaag novels done by others. Complete or fragments of unpublished manuscripts such as articles, poems, stories, and lectures (public and classroom). The titles of some of these are "Individualiteten," "Kildahl ved St. Olaf," "Hvis det er sandt," "When a Novelist Is in a Hurry," "Our Racial Heritage," "On Writing," "On Books," "Books and Folks," "Thoughts of Thinking People," "Nils og Astri," "Tøis," and "The Romance of a Life." The collection includes manuscripts by other authors forwarded to Rølvaag: "The Peer Strømme I Knew" by Helen Egilsrud; "My Visit to St. Olaf in 1878" by Susie C. Ellsworth; "Pioneer Life in Brown County, Minnesota" by Einar Hoidale; "Rølvaag, nordmann og amerikaner" by Gudrun Hovde Gvåle.

Organizations: Because the preservation of Norwegian culture and its inculcations into American life was Rølvaag's major interest, his papers also relate to the many organizations he supported: Nordlandslag; For Fædrearven; Norsk Luthersk Landungdomsforbund: Det Litterære Samfund; Det Norske Selskap; the Society for the Advancement of Scandinavian Study; and the Norwegian-American Historical Association, which he helped found in 1925, and was its first secretary and archivist.

Scrapbooks (17 volumes) consist mainly of clippings and most of them are classified according to topic: reviews of separate Rølvaag novels, reviews in European papers, articles by Rølvaag, clippings about Rølvaag, memorials and tributes, "Bjarne Blehr and Norwegian-American authors," an extended debate in *Duluth Skandinav*.

733. RØNNING, NILS N. (1870–1962). PAPERS, 1903–1955. 2 boxes. P 585.
Letters, clippings, and notes of a Norwegian-born journalist and author. Includes reviews of Rønning's books, notes on Hans Nielsen Hauge and Elling Eielsen, and historical sketches of Homme Home for Boys, Wittenberg, Wisconsin. The reports and articles include materials on fiddlers, sketches of Torkel Oftelie and Th. N. Mohn, and a statement of the value of bilingualism to the Norwegian American by Anna Thykesen.

Rønning was editor of *Ungdommens Ven, Familiens Magasin, The Friend*, and *Telesoga*.

Correspondents include Richard Beck, Theodore C. Blegen, J. A. Holvik, Hanna Astrup Larsen, K. O. Lundeberg, O. M. Norlie, D. G. Ristad, Mrs. O. E. Rølvaag.

734. ROINESTAD, SOREN C. (b. 1887). LOCAL HISTORY, 1963. Typescript, 83 pages. P 331.
"A Hundred Years with Norwegians in East Bay," by a Norwegian-born San Francisco builder and contractor, treats churches, societies, festivals, programs, leading Norwegian Americans in education, industry, government, and art.

735. ROLLAG, AUSTIN K. (1854–1941). PAPERS, 1933–ca. 1938. 4 items. P 330.
Papers of a Norwegian-born farmer at Garretson, South Dakota, including a letter to H. H. Einung containing family history; a golden anniversary booklet; and two articles, "Da Professor Koren kom til Beaver Creek menighett" (typescript, 3 pages) and "Da Jamesbrødrene drog gjennem Syd Dakota" (typescript, 3 pages).

736. ROLLAG, GRACE (MRS. OLE). (1851–1943). REMINISCENCES, 1929. 12 pages. P 329.

"Erindringer fra gamle dage" recounts pioneer experiences mostly at Beaver Creek, Minnesota, dating from 1873, the year of her marriage.

737. RONNEI BUSINESS COLLEGE. REPORT, n.d. 1 item. P 523.

Report about a school at Devils Lake, North Dakota (1902–1906), operated by Sylvester P. Ronnei.

738. ROOD, PAUL. PAPERS, 1978. 1 item, 15 pages. P 932.

List of source materials available in the State Historical Society at Madison, Wisconsin, which relate to Norwegian Americans.

739. ROREM, EDWARD (1880–1963). BIOGRAPHY, 1974. 1 volume, typescript, 75 pages. P 784.

"The biography of Edward Rorem, Pastor, Educator, Administrator " by his grandson, Paul Edward Rorem. Rorem's work included service as a parish minister, the presidency of Madison Lutheran Normal School (1921–1927) and the superintendency of Sunset Home, Story City, Iowa (1943–1954).

740. ROSDAIL, OVE (1809–1890). LETTERS, 1847–1849. 2 items. P 332.

Two letters to Rosdail, La Salle County, Illinois. One from Lars Ellickson, Company G, 1st Regiment, Illinois Infantry, Santa Fe, New Mexico, concerns the death of Rosdail's brother-in-law. The other from Ole Johnson, Kendall, New York, concerns sale of land.

741. ROSHOLT, MALCOLM (b. 1907). PAPERS, 1963–1968. 9 items. P 443.

A translation of J. W. C. Dietrichson's *Reise blandt de norske emigranter*, a history of St. Michael's Hospital, Stevens Point, Wisconsin, and a serial in *The Iola Herald* (1965–1970) entitled *From the Indian Land*. The latter, based largely on Thor Helgeson's *Fra Indianernes lande* (1915), plat books, and town, school, and church records, relates the history of Norwegian settlements in Waupaca County, Wisconsin. Includes some biographical and genealogical material. Rosholt is a free lance writer from Rosholt, Wisconsin.

742. ROSSING, LARS A. (1845–1913). PAPERS, 1866–1963. 2 boxes and 5 volumes. P 586.

Correspondence, clippings, pamphlets, scrapbooks, and account books of a Norwegian-born merchant at Argyle, Wisconsin, dealing with merchandising, church, local history, and family interests. The L. A. Rossing general merchandise store was founded in 1870.

743. ROSVALD (SOLVESON), HALVOR (1823–1904). PAPERS, 1849–1935. 3 items and 1 volume. P 333.

Papers of a Norwegian-born farmer, Dodge County, Wisconsin: an itinerary and account book, and biographical sketches of Halvor and his brother, Engebret S. Roswell, Whitewater, Wisconsin. The papers contain data on the brothers' California expedition together with Hans C. Heg.

744. ROVE, OLAF I. (1864–1940). PAPERS, 1910–1913. 41 items. P 334.
Correspondence, articles, pictures, and reports of a Norwegian-born Milwaukee attorney containing historical data on Norwegian social, cultural, and philanthropic societies in the United States. Rove was the Norwegian vice consul in Milwaukee from 1906 to 1935, and was a founder of several Norwegian societies.

745. ROWBERG, ANDREW A. (1887–1969). SCRAPBOOKS, 1939–1960. 2 volumes. P 335.
Clippings from *Decorah-Posten*, containing a serial entitled "Norske døbenavne; deres betydning og oprindelse" (1887) by Bernt Støylen, Norway; and clippings regarding Vinland, the Norse discovery of America, and related topics. Rowberg was editor of the *Northfield Independent* for ca. 40 years and the compiler of a biographical file of some 125,000 items which he gave to NAHA. See No. 942.

746. RUDE, OLE. CORRESPONDENCE, 1874, n.d. 13 items. P 336.
Discussion of economic and church conditions.

747. RULLAND, KNUD OSTENSEN (1813–1892). CORRESPONDENCE, 1850–1863. 5 items. P 444.
Civil War and other letters received by Rulland, Coon Prairie, Wisconsin.

748. RUNDAHL (ROUNDAL) KNUTSON (KNUDSEN), OLE (1812–1876). PAPERS, 1847–ca. 1864, n.d. 8 items. P 337.
Emigration papers, correspondence, and biographies of a Norwegian-born Coon Valley, Wisconsin, farmer.

749. RUSTE, ERICK OLSEN (1854–1924). PAPERS. 4 items. P 951.
Biographical sketch of a Norwegian-American clergyman by Sofie Ruste, a poem by E. Ruste, a letter, and a "folk song" by Anton Amundson.

750. RUUD, MARTIN B. (1885–1941). ARTICLE, 1935. 1 item. Typescript, 2 pages. P 338.
"The Second Generation" by a professor of English at the University of Minnesota. Comments on the death of *Minneapolis Tidende* and the need for Norwegian Americans to preserve their cultural heritage.

751. RYGG, ANDREAS N. (1868–1951). PAPERS, 1944. 4 items. P 339.
A scrapbook of clippings from *Nordisk Tidende*, concerning Norwegians in the Boston area; membership lists of two Norwegian societies; a

sea narrative; and an article concerning Karel Hansen Toll, Schnectady, New York. Rygg was a Norwegian-born editor of *Nordisk Tidende*, Brooklyn, New York, and author of *Norwegians in New York* (1941).

752. RYNNING, JENS (1778–1857). ARTICLES, 1839. 2 items. P 340.
A typescript copy (12 pages) of an article by a Norwegian clergyman that was published in *Morgenbladet* (October 10, 1839). It includes the Hans Barlien letter which announced the death of the author's emigrant son, Ole Rynning, and offers criticism of the emigration movement. Includes also a reprint of Jacob S. Worm-Müller's address on Ole Rynning (July 4, 1937).

753. RYNNING, OLE (1809–1838). PAPERS, 1896–1937. 8 items. P 341.
Material concerning a prominent early immigrant: biographies and copies of the Ole Rynning Centenary programs held in 1937 at St. Olaf College and at Snaasa, Norway.

754. SAERVOLD, OLA JOHANN (1867–1937). PAPERS, 1840–1941. 4 boxes and 1 volume. P 587.
Biographical miscellany, correspondence, articles, clippings, and account books of a Norwegian-born, American-educated, Minneapolis resident, world traveler and lecturer, journalist and linguist, farmer and sailor.
Saervold was a sailor on the Great Lakes (1886–1889); a student at Luther College (1889–1895); a correspondent for *Inter-Ocean* (Chicago) (1895–1898); a lecturer and newspaper correspondent who described his travels in Norway (1899–1910); a farmer on the ancestral farm in Strandvik, Midthordland, Norway, which he equipped and operated according to American standards (1910–1918); a traveler and correspondent for *Skandinaven* (1921–1925). He was the author of four books: *Erling* (1898), *Det store stævne i Camrose, Canada* (1926), *Reisebreve*, 3 volumes (1926), and *The Discovery of America* (1931).
His papers contain transcripts of legal documents dealing with the history of Saervold (farm); his Luther College report cards; a recipe book (manuscript) from the Lutheran Ladies' Seminary (Red Wing, Minnesota), domestic science course (1908–1909); and manuscripts entitled "Prestehjemmenes plads i vort folkeliv," "Kirken og det norske sprog i Amerika," and "What is the Matter with Minnesota and Why" (a study of taxation). Correspondents include B. E. Bergeson, L. W. Boe, Juul Dieserud, Einar Hoidale, Peter Norbeck, and Henrik Shipstead.

755. SAGENG, HALVOR O. (1873–1949). BROCHURES, ca. 1910–1912. 2 items. P 343.
Brochures concerning the Sageng combination gasoline thresher, invented by Sageng in 1908.

756. St. Ansgar Seminary. Papers, 1918. 3 items. P 524.
Letter and reports concerning a Lutheran secondary school in St. Ansgar, Iowa (1878–1910).

757. St. Olaf College. Papers, 1874–1966. 22 boxes. P 647.
Brochures, bulletins, clippings, pamphlets, photographs, minutes and record books of an educational institution founded by Norwegian immigrants at Northfield, Minnesota, in 1874. The papers deal mostly with non-curricular activities such as festivals, anniversaries, musical and Norwegian-Americana programs.

758. Sandaker, Arvid. Speech, 1971. Typescript, 8 pages. P 899.
"The America Fever" delivered by a native of Slemmestad, Norway, at the annual convention of Landingslaget, Mayville, North Dakota.

759. Sandbeck, Oscar P. (1890–1976). Papers, 1957–1967. 4 items. P 952.
Pamphlets by a native of Trent, South Dakota, expressing his views about creation and human life. Two letters to Dr. H. M. Blegen give further expression to his ideas.

760. Saugstad, Christian T. (1838–1897). Lecture, 1893. Booklet, 42 pages. P 556.
"Augsburgs historie" given at Bardo Church, Polk County, Minnesota.

761. Saugstad, Jesse E. Biography, ca. 1963. Typescript, 77 pages. P 734.
"A Mountain Is Named " is about the author's great uncle, Christian Saugstad, and his founding of a Norwegian colony in Bella Coola, British Columbia.

762. Scandinavian Lutheran Seamen's Mission. Papers, 1899–1946. 3 boxes. P 656.
Records of services to seamen, of gifts by American contributors to the Mission in San Francisco, and related correspondence.

763. Scandinavian Sisters of America (1921) Newsletter, 1934. 2 items. P 868.
Two monthly letters issued by a lodge with headquarters in Superior, Wisconsin.

764. Scanpresence II Conference, 1977. Papers, 1977. 1 box. P 919.
Papers of an "Action Conference on the Scandinavian Presence in America, Minneapolis, Minnesota, October 6–8, 1977."

765. Schaefer, Frederic (1877–1955). Correspondence, 1928–1940. 6 items. P 344.

Correspondence of a Norwegian-born engineer and inventor, Pittsburgh, Pennsylvania, dealing with Det Norske Selskap.

766. SCHEFSTAD, JERMIA (1871–1912). BIOGRAPHY, 1974. Typescript, 29 pages. P 811.

Biography of a Norwegian-born violinist who emigrated from Norway in 1888; studied at the Leipzig conservatory (1894–1899); returned to live at Grand Forks, North Dakota. He died at age 41. The biography, originally written in the Norwegian language by Sam Fossland, is translated by Gyda Fossland.

767. SCHERN FAMILY. LETTERS, 1886–1937. 12 items. P 900.

Copies of letters written by various members of the family in the United States and in Norway, giving information about family events.

768. SCHEVENIUS, CARL. TRAVEL, 1964. Typescript, 5 pages. 1 item. P 933.

"We Took A Trip," a report of a tour to Europe and Africa by the Reverend Carl Schevenius and his wife. In Norway the couple visited friends and relatives.

769. SCHILLING, W. F. REMINISCENCES, 1935. Booklet, 51 pages. P 446.

Article in pamphlet form entitled "Up and Down Main Street Forty Years Ago" includes reminiscences of a Northfield, Minnesota, farmer, editor, and antique collector.

770. SCHIOTZ, FREDRIK A. (b. 1901). PAPERS, 1925–1954. 3 items. P 345.

A manuscript of Schiotz's book, *Release* (1935); a history of the Lutheran Student Association of America; and a biographical sketch of Schiotz, a former president of the American Lutheran Church.

771. SCHMIDT, FRIEDRICH AUGUST (1837–1928). PAPERS, 1848–1926. 3 boxes. P 588.

Correspondence, clippings, and articles, written in English, German, Latin, and Norwegian, of a German-born Lutheran clergyman, theologian, author, and editor.

Among the subjects discussed are doctrines concerning absolution, assurance, conversion, and election; position and participation of the laity in doctrinal disputes and clerical leadership in such controversies; Augsburg College and St. Olaf College; and the union movement that led to the 1917 merger. There are only two letters by Schmidt.

Among the correspondents are M. O. Bøckman, C. L. Clausen (February 2, 1863), N. J. Ellestad, O. J. Hatlestad, P. P. Iverslie (December 27, 1883), Kristofer Janson (March 31, 1891), J. N. Kildahl, U. V. Koren, Laur. Larsen, A. Mikkelsen, Th. N. Mohn, B. J. Muus, J. A. Ottesen, H. A. Preus, P. A. Rasmussen, Halvard Roalkvam, H. A. Stub.

772. SEBJØRNSEN (OVERDALEN), LARS. LETTER, 1843. 1 item. P 435.
Copy of a letter written to relatives from Koshkonong Prairie, Wisconsin, which gives specific information regarding wages, prices, money economy, topography, religious freedom, weather, health, and reputation of the Norwegians in the area.

773. SEBO, MILDRED M. NARRATIVE, 1954. 3 items. Typescript, 33 pages. P 613.
A history of the Sebu-Myhre family, an account of the family's centennial celebration and of their first Christmas in America, by a La Molle, Minnesota, resident.

774. SEMMINGSEN, INGRID (b. 1910). PAPERS, 1966–1974. 3 items. P 614.
Citation for honorary degree, Dr. of Letters, St. Olaf College (1974), prepared by Kenneth O. Bjork. Review of Gudrun Hovde Gvåle's biography of Rølvaag and "A Shipload of German Emigrants and their Significance for the Norwegian Emigration of 1825." Dr. Semmingsen is professor of American history at the University of Oslo.

775. SERUM, A. O. (1849–1927). PAPERS, 1871–1927. 3 boxes and 1 volume. P 589.
Correspondence, reports, speeches, articles, clippings, and account books of a Norwegian-born farmer at Halstad, Minnesota. The papers include school district reports; articles and letters on early days in the Red River Valley; correspondence with Fuller and Johnson, farm machinery company, Madison, Wisconsin; and personnel at Augsburg and Augustana (Marshall, Wisconsin) seminaries. The clippings include items on synod controversies and letters from World War I servicemen.
Serum held state and church offices, spoke on crop production, suffrage, monopoly, co-operatives, and local history, was the first teacher in his district, the first president of the *Selbulag*, and the author of "Nybyggerliv i Red Riverdalen" in *Selbygbogen*, 2 (1931).

776. SETHER, GULBRAND. CLIPPINGS. 2 items. P 934.
Clippings and a letter concerning a Norwegian-born artist and author who lived and worked in Chicago.

777. SEVAREID, ERIC (b. 1912). ARTICLE, 1956. 1 item. P 348.
Article, appearing in *Collier's* (May 11, 1956), entitled "You Can Go Home Again," recounts his experiences on a visit to his native Velva, North Dakota.

778. SHIPSTEAD, HENRIK (1881–1960). PAPERS, 1931–1946. 47 items. P 349.
Letters, reports, and speeches of a United States senator from Minnesota (1923–1947). His parents were born in Norway.

779. SIEWERS, KARL. CORRESPONDENCE. 1 item. Typescript, 84 pages. P 792.

"Expedition from Christiania," a collection of letters, compiled and translated by Karl Siewers, Chicago. The letters center around Lyder Siewers and his wife Thrine Brandt Siewers. Siewers (1830–1907) taught at Luther College (1863–1877), Decorah, Iowa, and was editor of *Decorah-Posten* from 1877 until his death in 1907. Mrs. Siewers (1844–1909), a talented pianist, died in Norway. The letters reflect an upper class tradition, and reveal the joys, but also the frustrations and financial hardships of frontier life. Some biographical commentaries accompany the letters.

780. SIHLER, ERNEST G. W. (b. 1900). PAPERS, 1968. 3 items. P 698.
A chart of Lutheran synods comprising the American Lutheran Church; translation of abbreviations, words, and phrases found in O. M. Norlie, *Norsk lutherske menigheter i Amerika, 1843–1916*; and a translation key to rubrics in parochial reports of Norwegian Lutheran synods.

781. SILJAN FAMILY. PAPERS, ca. 1936. Typescript, 7 pages. 2 items. P 350.
A biography of O. G. U. Siljan (1870–1936), Lutheran clergyman in Madison, Wisconsin, and a genealogy of the Gullickson (Graue) family, Voss, Norway (1240–1906), of which his wife was a member.

782. SIMLEY, IVER (1869–1937). PAPERS, 1860–1928. 66 items. P 351.
Correspondence of a Norwegian-born merchant, banker, and realtor at Black Earth, Wisconsin. The letters, dealing largely with family and religious matters, were written at Black Earth and Amery, Wisconsin; Decorah, Iowa; and Benson, Minnesota. Congressman Ole J. Kvale was a correspondent. Of interest is an auction bill issued by Simley's father just before his emigration in 1869.

783. SIMONSON, INGEBRET (1843–1931). DIARY, 1870–1874. 1 item. P 753.
Diary kept by Simonson, translated in 1969 by three of his daughters. Covers his last year in Norway, part of the trip to America and the first years at Hanley Falls, Minnesota.

784. SIMUNDSON, SIMUND O. (b. 1870). DIARY, 1908, 1909. 1 volume. P 347.
A Lutheran clergyman's daily account of journeys from Kenyon, Minnesota, to Kalispell, Montana, and from Kenyon to Ashland, Oregon.

785. SINGSTAD, OLE (1882–1969). PAPERS, 1929–1946. 10 items and 2 volumes. P 367.
Reports of a Norwegian-born engineer to New York City Tunnel Authority, and to Washington Toll Bridge Authority, and articles on engineering problems.

786. SJØMANNSHJEMMET EIDSVOLD. ARTICLES, n.d. Typescript, 2
    pages. P 352.
Article regarding erection of a seaman's home at Katnook, Westches-
ter County, New York.

787. SJOLANDER, CARL A. (1851–1934). PAPERS, 1852, 1871. 2
    items. P 353.
A testimonial issued by the parish pastor in 1852 to Sjolander's par-
ents on their departure to America, and the constitution and by-laws of
the Hekla Fire Insurance Company, Madison, Wisconsin, incorporated
March, 1871, possibly the only such society operated by Norwegian-
Americans. Sjolander lived in Onalaska, Wisconsin.

788. SKAALEN SUNSET HOME. NEWSLETTER, 1952. 1 item. P 636.
Information (8 pages) about an institution founded at Stoughton, Wisconsin, in 1899.

789. SKARD, SIGMUND. REPORT, 1944. 1 volume, typescript 96
    pages. P 447.
A report by a Norwegian scholar on the Scandinavian collection in the
Library of Congress.

790. SKARTVEDT, GUDMUND (1852–1915). PAPERS, 1880–1928. 1
    box. P 658.
Account books and legal papers of a Norwegian-born realtor, insurance agent, and farmer at Canton, South Dakota.

791. SKAVLEM, HALVOR L. (1846–1939). FAMILY HISTORY, 1915.
    245 pages. P 829.
Copy of a family history, *The Skavlem and Odegaarden Families*, by
Halvor Skavlem, Janesville, Wisconsin.

792. SKØRDALSVOLD NIGHT SCHOOL. REPORT, n.d. 1 item. P 525.
Report of a school operated in Minneapolis (1902–1914) by Johannes
J. Skørdalsvold.

793. SKOUGAARD, LORENTZ SEVERIN (1837–1885). LETTER, n.d. 1
    item. P 355.
A letter by Kristen Kvamme, Lutheran clergyman at Ossian, Iowa, to
Ole E. Rølvaag, containing a sketch of Skougaard of New York City,
concert soloist, voice teacher, and friend of Alfred Corning Clark, who
published a Skougaard biography in 1885.

794. SLOOPER SOCIETY OF AMERICA. PAPERS, 1840–1961. 1 box.
    P 657.
Articles, correspondence, clippings, pictures, programs, and reports
of a society formed in 1925, whose members are descendants of those
Norwegians who emigrated in 1825 on the sloop *Restaurationen*. Includes a thesis (23 pages) presented at Wagner College, "The Descendants of Lars Larson, 'Slooper', in the New World" (1955), by Dorrit
Weill.

795. SMELAND, ASLAK NELSON. PAPERS, 1855–1867. 3 items. P 356.
Copy of a letter and typescript and translation copies of another, both from Four Mile Prairie, Texas, by a cobbler, describing geography, government, settlements, health, farming, Indians, church, and school. Also a biography of Smeland (typescript, 12 pages) by his great grand-daughter, Mildred Hogstel.

796. SMELAND, H. G. (b. 1872). PAPERS, 1932. Booklet, 39 pages. P 761.
Reconstruction and Readjustment, Stockton, California, deals with reorganization of the U.S. government and calls for social and economic reform. Smeland emigrated in 1892.

797. SØNNELAND, SIDNEY GAYLORD (1891–1978). PAPERS. 14 items. P 752.
Papers of a Norwegian-American physician who practiced in Los Angeles, California, and who established the S. G. Sønneland Foundation at the University of Oslo, Norway, in 1972.

798. SØNNICHSEN, S. ENGELHART (1878–1961). PAPERS, 1899–1945. 1 box. P 659.
Professional documents, pictures, plans, correspondence, and clippings of a Norwegian-born architect.
Sønnichsen, educated in Norway and Germany, emigrated in 1902; was architectural draftsman for various firms; opened his own office in Seattle in 1916; and was designer for engineering and transportation companies during World War II.

799. SØNNICHSEN, YNGVAR (1875–1938). PAPERS, 1896–1937. 73 items and 3 volumes. P 420.
Biography, clippings, correspondence, and pictures dealing with the career of a Norwegian-born artist.
Sønnichsen, educated in Norway, Belgium, and Paris, emigrated in 1904. His most well-known works are his picture panels in New Brunswick (Canada) church windows, portraits of Roald Amundsen and Ole Bull, murals in Seattle's Norway House, and his Alaska Landscapes. He is a brother of architect S. Engelhart Sønnichsen.

800. SØRHUS, H. J. REMINISCENCES, 1865. 1 item, 30 pages. P 901.
Account of an emigrant journey from Stavanger to Winona, Minnesota, via Quebec.

801. *SØRLANDET*. ALBUM. 1 volume. P 815.
Photographs, charts, and commentary concerning the training ship which made an expedition to Chicago in 1933 as a feature of the "Century of Progress" exposition.

802. SØRNES, RASMUS. CLIPPING. 1 item. P 954.
Article from a Norwegian newspaper describing an astronomical

clock, made by Rasmus Sørnes, which was bought by Seth G. Atwood and donated to the city of Rockford, Illinois.

803. SØYLAND, CARL (b. 1894). PAPERS, 1916–1976. 4 boxes and 1 volume. P 845.

Articles, clippings, correspondence, manuscripts, unpublished research notes, lectures, and a scrapbook of a Norwegian-born journalist and author, who came to the United States about 1920 to study music, but who found the life of a "tramp-journalist" more interesting. He travelled all over the world writing for newspapers, sometimes using the pseudonym Viggo Vey. He edited *California Vikingen* (1924–1925) in Los Angeles. In 1926 he began his association with the Brooklyn, New York, newspaper *Nordisk Tidende*, of which he was chief editor (1940–1962). He is the author of two books, both published in Norway: *Langs landeveien* (1929) and *Skrift i sand* (1954).

804. SOLBERG, CARL K. (1872–1954). PAPERS, 1886–1958. 14 boxes. P 590.

Correspondence, articles, poems, pamphlets, diaries and notebooks of a Lutheran clergyman, poet, author, and lecturer. The diaries cover most of the period between 1892 and 1945, including Solberg's student career at St. Olaf College and United Lutheran Church Seminary. Among the articles are such titles: "The Restoration of Israel," "Do We Need a Chair in English Bible in Our Seminary?" "Spiritualism," "Our Greatest Enemy" (temperance), and "A Scene from College Life" (St. Olaf College).

Solberg was parish minister in South Dakota, Chicago, and Minneapolis. Among his books are *A Brief History of the Zion Society for Israel* (1928), *Scriptural Evangelism* (1935), *In Quiet Moments*, and *Sacred Verse* (1940).

805. SOLBERG, ELIZABETH RONNING (b. 1911). AUTOBIOGRAPHY, 1967. 1 volume, 91 pages. P 12.

Covers farm and village life in North Dakota, working career in Evanston, Illinois, and years as an invalid in California.

806. *SOLSTRAALA*. JOURNAL, 1934–1938. 2 volumes. P 890.

Solstraala, a handwritten journal prepared for Bondeungdomslaget in Chicago, edited by Aasmund Rørvik.

807. SOLSTAD, LARS (1866–1932). AUTOGRAPH BOOK, 1886. 1 item. P 157.

Statements and messages to Solstad by classmates at Klæbo Seminary, Norway. Solstad, born at Børsskogning, Trondheim, Norway, was a banker and merchant in Woodville, Wisconsin.

808. SOLUM, CHRIS (1865–1954). PAPERS, 1920–1937. 47 items. P 357.

Correspondence, reports, and clippings of a Norwegian-born shoe manufacturer and merchant of Racine, Wisconsin. The papers deal largely with matters pertaining to the Scandinavian American Fraternity and the Sons of Norway, especially the latter's sponsorship of the Colonel Hans C. Heg monument. Letters include comments on the unemployment situation in Merrill, Wisconsin, during the 1930's. A copy of a letter (July 30, 1862) by Colonel Heg to James Denoon Reymert is also included.

809. SOLUM, GUSTAV (1871–1955). PAPERS, 1952–1953. P 358.
Correspondence of a Seattle resident and one-time president of the Numedal og Kongsberglag, regarding a *bygde* book for Sandsvær, then being prepared in Norway.

The papers include a roster of the names of emigrants to America from Sandsvær and Kongsberg (1866–1925) as they appeared in Kongsberg *Laagendalsposten*. The roster includes addresses, dates of sailings, and occasionally the names of ships.

810. SOLUM, NORA O. (1889–1971). PAPERS, 1904–1969. 3 boxes. P 744.
Correspondence, manuscripts, diaries, and research notes of a professor of English at St. Olaf College (1919–1960), author, and translator. Co-author of *Ole Edvart Rølvaag: A Biography* (1939); translated Rølvaag, *Peter Victorious* (1929), *The Boat of Longing* (1933); and Lise Lindbaek, *Norway's New Saga of the Sea* (1969).

811. SONGE, KJØSTEL TORJESEN. PAPERS, 1852–1853. 2 items. P 359.
A letter written to his brother Elef in Chicago, describing his farm buildings and produce at Wautoma, Wisconsin, in 1853; and a certificate of birth.

812. SONS AND DAUGHTERS OF NORWAY BUILDING ASSOCIATION OF MINNEAPOLIS INC. PAPERS, 1920–1958. 3 boxes. P 721.
Correspondence, minutes, and financial reports of a group composed of several Sons of Norway and Daughters of Norway lodges organized to provide a place for lodge meetings. The Association was dissolved in 1958.

813. SONS OF NORWAY. (1895) PAPERS, 1907–1958. 4 boxes. P 591.
Correspondence, clippings, constitution, reports, and souvenir programs of a Norwegian-American lodge dealing largely with purposes, policies, and the organization of new branch lodges. Several of the pamphlets contain historical sketches.

814. SONSTEBY, JOHN J. (1879–1941). PAPERS, 1871–1937. 73 items. P 360.
Correspondence, copies of official records, military correspondence, city of Chicago official correspondence, minutes of meetings of Chicago Common Council, excerpts from the *Journal of the Illinois Legislature*, and notes from various publications, concerning the Chicago fire (Oc-

tober 8-9, 1871), and the part played by the Norwegian National Guard of Chicago organized September 30, 1870. The papers, which include a list of names of the members, deal largely with the problem of compensation for services rendered during the 13 days following the fire. Sonsteby, chief justice of the Chicago Municipal Court, gathered this material for a projected monograph on the Norwegian Guard.

815. SOUTH DAKOTA HOSPITALS. PAPERS, 1919–1925. 6 items. P 626.
Sioux Falls Lutheran and Watertown Luther hospitals.

816. SPERATI, CARLO A. (1860–1945). BIOGRAPHY, 1970. Typescript, 9 pages. P 771.
Biographical sketch by Barbara L. Bauman. Sperati had a distinguished career as a teacher of music, band director and choral director at Luther College, Decorah, Iowa.

817. SPOKANE COLLEGE. PAPERS, 1906–1929. 76 items and 14 volumes. P 534.
Publications, reports, and a history of a Lutheran school founded in 1905 by Norwegian Americans and merged in 1929 with Pacific Lutheran College, Parkland, Washington.

818. STADE, C. M. NARRATIVES, n.d. Typescript, 289 pages. P 361.
Three unpublished narratives by Stade of Hopkins, Minnesota: "The First Norwegian Stades," "Van Der Ostade," and "In a Highland Valley."

819. STANGELAND, CHARLES E. (1881–1942). ARTICLE, 1910. 1 item. P 197.
"Scandinavian and American Culture," an address before Det Norske Selskab in Washington, D.C. January 26, 1910.
Stangeland was a professor of political economy at the State College in Pullman, Washington, and professor at the University of Berlin.

820. STAVANGER BOARDING SCHOOL. JOURNALS, 1903–1905. 15 items. P 526.
Issues of the *Stavanger Mirror* published by a boarding school near Le Grand, Iowa, founded in 1890 by the Society of Friends.

821. STAVSETH, REIDAR. CLIPPINGS, 1975. 12 items. P 812.
A series, "I Midt-Vesten," which appeared in *Addresseavisen*, Trondheim, Norway, featuring Norwegian Americans and their institutions in the Middle West. Stavseth travelled in this area in 1975.

822. STEEN, ADOLF. BIOGRAPHY, 1951. Typescript, 3 pages. P 362.
"Nils Paul Xavier, 1839–1918, the Kautokeino-Lapp Who Became Minister in Amerika " by Adolph Steen and translated by Magdalene Xavier Visovatti, a granddaughter of Xavier.

823. STEENE, HANS TØNNESEN (b. 1813). TRAVEL, 1854. Typescript, 36 pages. P 363.

A copy of *Beretning om en 3 Aars Reise i Amerika foretagen i Aarene 1849 til 1852 iblandt de norske Emigranter i de Forenede Stater i Nordamerika*, an account of the author's preaching and teaching journey in Illinois and Wisconsin from 1849 to 1852.

824. STEENSLAND, HALLE (1832–1910). PAPERS, 1901–1923. 5 items. P 364.

Biographical sketches and articles entitled "Hard Times and How They May Be Avoided" and "Erindringer" by a Norwegian-born merchant and banker in Madison, Wisconsin.

825. STEENSLAND, OLE (1842–1903). PAPERS, 1900–1963. 8 items. P 365.

Papers of a western Dane county, Wisconsin, farmer; biographical data; an address given at a reunion of the Fifteenth Wisconsin Infantry at Scandia Hall, Chicago (August 29, 1900), in which Steensland recounts his Civil War Experiences including those at Andersonville prison; and a temperance lecture given at Perry, Wisconsin.

826. STEFFERUD, JACOB (1889–1968). PAPERS, 1916–1964. 6 boxes and 3 volumes. P 592.

Articles, brochures, clippings, correspondence, reports, and scrapbooks of a Norwegian-born Minneapolis resident.

Stefferud was chief clerk for the Norwegian America Line in their New York and Minneapolis offices, acting consul for Norway, and commissioner for Nordmanns-Forbundet.

827. STENE, GABRIEL (1856–1945). CLIPPINGS, 1922–1936. 10 items. P 366.

Clippings of articles by a Wisconsin-born farmer at Norway Lake, Minnesota, containing reminiscences from pioneer days.

828. STENGEL, E. LETTER, 1903. Typescript, 5 pages. P 789.

Copies of a letter from E. Stengel to his daughter Martine who emigrated to San Francisco in 1882, to join her husband who had emigrated a year earlier.

829. STENSWICK, OLE. LETTER, 1902. 7 pages. P 955.

Copy of a letter written from Two Harbors, Minnesota, to Sigrid Iverson (a cousin) after he had returned from a visit to his home area in Norway a year earlier.

830. STEPHENS (HUSTVEDT), OLAF B. (1850–1947). PAPERS, 1890–1940. 109 items and 2 volumes. P 677.

Papers and scrapbooks of a farmer, school teacher, and book store proprietor, consisting mostly of reminiscences about pioneer life in eastern Dane County, Wisconsin, southeastern Dakota, and Luther College.

The anecdotes concern neighbors and relatives, wild life, and farm buildings, and machinery. There are references to R. B. Anderson, Kristofer Janson, Laur. Larsen, and Halvor Kostveit (reputed to have killed Joseph Smith).

831. STOLEE, MICHAEL J. (1871–1946). THEOLOGY, n.d. Pamphlet, 16 pages. P 556.
The Danger of Modernism to Our Church written after 1924 by a professor of missions at Luther Theological Seminary, St. Paul, Minnesota.

832. STOLEN, LENA KJELLESVIG (MRS. KNUT) (1869–1937). PAPERS, 1857–ca. 1932. 4 items. P 369.
Emigration papers, a letter, and a genealogy of the Anon Kjellesvig family.

833. STORSETH, JOHN (1863–1946). PAPERS, n.d. 2 boxes. P 593.
Manuscripts of a Norwegian-born farmer, lumberman, and self-taught student of literature and religion: "Old Homes and New" and its Norwegian counterpart *Fra gammel og ny tid i Norge og Amerika*, an autobiography, depicting the problems of the adjustments between the Norwegian and the American cultures; "The Ancients" and "The Mysteries of Space," sketches on science and astrology; "Djaevelskab," a collection of sketches. Excerpts from the autobiography were published in *Studies and Records*, 13 (1943).

834. STORWICK, EVANGELINE. DRAMA, 1975. Typescript, 51 pages. P 935.
"Norwegian Immigrant Drama, The Sloopers " written by Mrs. Storwick and presented in Silvana, Washington (October 25, 1975), as part of the Norwegian-American Sesquicentennial celebration. Includes pictures, programs, and clippings related to the production.

835. STOUGHTON ACADEMY AND BUSINESS INSTITUTE. REPORTS, ca. 1892–1922. 43 items. P 527.
Reports regarding a Lutheran school at Stoughton, Wisconsin (1888–1900).

836. STOYLEN, SIGVALD. PAPERS, 1965. 5 items. P 380.
"Marcus Thrane i Amerika" and "The Kensington Rune Stone" by a Norwegian-born teacher in the Minneapolis schools, and clippings concerning Norwegian-American writers.

837. STRAND, SVEIN (1852–1945). PAPERS, 1910–1921. 4 items. P 370.
Manuscript of a biography of Claus L. Clausen, pioneer minister in the Norwegian Lutheran church, published in *Symra* 9 (1913); two printed articles; and a letter to O. M. Norlie. Strand was a Lutheran clergyman and Clausen's son-in-law.

838.   STRØMME, PEER O. (1856–1921). PAPERS, 1888–1921. 8 items and 1 volume. P 371.
Travel letters, biographies, clippings, and poems of an author, journalist, and lecturer.

839.   STUB, HANS ANDREAS (1822–1907). LETTERS, 1848–1862. 4 items. P 435.
Copy of letter dated August 21, 1848, written to a theological association in Stavanger, dealing with the events and costs of the journey to America in 1848, the Fourth of July celebration in New York City, and the reconciling of differences between parties within the Muskego congregation in the matters of church government and liturgy. The second letter, also to the theological association (1851), is a response to criticism of Stub's work in Muskego. The other two letters contain detailed data about the La Crosse, Wisconsin, area as to topography, congregations (especially Coon Prairie), parsonages, roads, distances, living conditions, schools, sects, salaries, and transportation facilities.

840.   STUB, HANS GERHARD (1849–1931). PAPERS, 1881–1931. 20 items. P 372.
Speeches, articles, and lectures of a Lutheran clergyman.

841.   STUB, JACOB AAL OTTESEN (1877–1944). LETTER, 1936. Typescript, 9 pages. P 373.
Letter by a Lutheran clergyman to Johan Arnd Aasgaard, president of the Evangelical Lutheran Church, regarding unionism within the church.

842.   SVANØE, ATLE (1869–1958). CHURCH, n.d. Pamphlet, 74 pages. P 556.
Laegmandsvirksomheten i luthersk lys, an article discussing the place and value of laymen's activity in the church.

843.   *SVARTEBOKA*, 1859. 3 items. P 374.
Booklets that present some of the black arts and their prevalence in Norway.

844.   SVERDRUP, LEIF J. (1898–1976). BIOGRAPHY, 1956. 4 items. P 375.
Biographical material on a Norwegian-born major general in the United States Army Engineers and member of the firm Sverdrup & Parcel, Inc., engineers and architects.

845.   SWENDSEID, CLARENCE. FAMILY HISTORY, ca. 1950. Typescript, 61 pages. P 376.
"The Men from Telemark," the story of Rolleiv Svendseid and his family, who migrated in 1867 from Telemark, Norway, settling first in Fillmore County, Minnesota, and then in 1883 at Nelson, North Dakota. Among the topics treated are politics, church, higher education, agriculture and financial depressions.

846. SWENSON, MAGNUS (1854–1936). PAPERS, 1927–1938. 10 items. P 377.
Articles, clippings, and biographical material recounting Swenson's contributions as a chemical engineer.

847. SYFTESTAD, PAUL OLESON (1816–1902) and SYFTESTAD, PAUL P. (1859–1940). BOND, 1882. P 378.
Copy of document reminiscent of the Norwegian *kaar brev*, drawn up in Dane County, Wisconsin, stipulating conditions under which the father conveyed his farm to his son.

848. SYNODICAL CONFERENCE CONVENTION, 1872. DOCTRINE, 1873. Pamphlet, 51 pages. P 556.
Om Retfærdiggjørelsen, an exposition of the doctrine of justification, translated from the report of the Synodical Conference convention of 1872.

849. SYSE, SOPHIA STUEGAARDEN (1866–1947). PAPERS, 1853–ca. 1930. 10 items. P 379.
Emigration documents and letters concerning the Anders Stuegaarden family.

850. SYTTENDE MAI. PAPERS, 1933. 7 items. P 700.
Correspondence and clippings relating to a *Syttende Mai* festival held in Moscow, Iowa county, Wisconsin (May, 1933), commemorating the 1873 celebration when Ole Bull and Rasmus B. Anderson appeared on the program together with Syver Holland who sang his *Heimtraa* folk ballad.

851. TANK, NILS OTTO (1800–1864). BIOGRAPHY. Typescript, 20 pages. P 454.
Biography of a Norwegian-born philanthropist and churchman, Green Bay, Wisconsin, by Nels C. Lerdahl, Madison, Wisconsin. Subjects treated are heritage, church, motives for emigration, marriage, Moravian community at Green Bay, and Tank Cottage, the oldest dwelling in Wisconsin. Other items on Tank are included.

852. THE TEACHERS' ASSOCIATION OF THE NORWEGIAN SYNOD. RECORDS, 1890–1902. 1 volume. P 381.
Minutes of an organization founded in 1890. Among the topics discussed were bilingualism, introduction of new courses, methods of instruction, athletics, discipline, and social life.

853. TEIGEN, KNUT MARTIN (1854–1914). SCRAPBOOK. 1 volume. P 902.
Clippings of articles by and about a Minneapolis physician, author, and poet, whose interests included religion and politics. Dr. Teigen wrote for newspapers and medical journals.

854. TEMPERANCE MOVEMENT. PAPERS, 1841–1962. 3 boxes. P 594.
Articles, reports, songs, stories, and pamphlets concerning the temperance movement among Norwegian Americans. There are reports from organizations in Alberta, Canada, Minnesota, North Dakota, South Dakota, and Wisconsin, and articles by Waldemar Ager, Adolph Bredesen, Carl E. Carlson, Theodor H. Dahl, Knut Gjerset, Paul M. Glasoe, and Gjermund Hoyme.

855. TESLOW, ANDERS N. (1828–1908). DIARY, 1866–1908. 1 volume, typescript, 93 pages. P 869.
"An account of the Life of Anders N. Teslow, A Diary," a translation of the diary of a Norwegian-born merchant and farmer, who came with his wife and family to Winneshiek County, Iowa, in 1862. In 1865 he moved to a farm in Freeborn County, Minnesota, where he lived the rest of his life. The diary begins with reminiscences of his life in Norway, his marriage and the journey to America, and continues with the record of his experiences in Minnesota.
The account was translated by Dr. Gunnar Malmin, and edited by Valborg Teslow Fyneboe and Carl Fyneboe.

856. TESLOW, RICHARD (b. ca. 1872). PAPERS, 1875–1955. 11 items and 2 volumes. P 603.
Papers and scrapbooks of a farmer of Hayward, Minnesota, including a farm auction bill (1902).

857. TEXAS, BROWNSBORO. CLIPPINGS, 1976. 5 items. P 870.
Clippings and programs concerning the erection of an historical marker for the Brownsboro Norwegian Lutheran Cemetery, land for which was donated by Ole Reierson who came to Texas from Norway in 1839. Also passenger list of the ship "Alisto" which arrived at New Orleans (June 9, 1845); it includes the names of ten Norwegians, among them Ole Reierson.

858. TEXAS LUTHERAN COLLEGE. PAPERS, 1928–1945. 3 items. P 529.
Catalogues and brochures of a junior college and academy at Seguin, Texas, with which Clifton Jr. College later merged.

859. THOMPSON, CHRISTIAN S. (1876–1963). SCRAPBOOK, 1890–1897. P 393.
Contains pictures, programs, and clippings from Thompson's student days at St. Olaf College and Luther College as well as from the Mount Horeb Academy.

860. THOMPSON, ELLING (1859–1922). LETTERS, 1904–1921. 14 items. P 455.
Letters written by a Wiota, Wisconsin, farmer to a friend in Norway describing farm activity, topography, recreation, travel, and politics, and expressing appreciation of both America and Norway.

861. THOMPSON, HENRY (1891–1968). CLIPPINGS, ca. 1920–1934. 3
      items. P 383.
Newspaper articles concerning the history of the Koshkonong Lutheran parish in eastern Dane County, Wisconsin. Thompson was a
minister in that parish.

862. THOMPSON, J. JØRGEN (1881–1963). PAPERS, 1896–1963. 13
      boxes and 1 volume. P 595.
Articles, clippings, correspondence, pamphlets, and records of a
Wisconsin-born St. Olaf College administrator and teacher. The papers
concern campus life, public relations, counseling, courses of study,
student and teacher recruitment, funds solicitation, band and choir tours,
and Norwegian-American culture. Manuscripts include: "Rølvaag som
lærer," "Min konfirmations dag" (1938), and minutes of the Board of
the Norwegian Conference of the Evangelical Lutheran Church.
      Thompson was president of Spokane College (1917–1920); dean of
men at St. Olaf college (1923–1942); secretary of NAHA (1931–1958);
president of the National Association of Deans and Advisers of Men
(1940–1941). For a list of correspondents, see description file in NAHA
Archives.

863. THOMPSON, JOHN A. ("SNOWSHOE") (1827–1876). CLIPPING,
      1977. P 903.
"A Man to Match the Mountains," by Marjorie Wagner, is the story
of a Norwegian-born emigrant who became a legendary hero of the
West.

864. THOMPSON, JULIA. AUTOGRAPH ALBUM, 1881–1892. 1 item.
      P 382.
Autographs to Julia Thompson, Scandinavia, Wisconsin, written by
persons in the same area.

865. THOMPSON, M. BURNETTE. THESIS, 1939. 1 item. Typescript,
      160 pages. P 384.
"The Significance of the St. Olaf Lutheran Choir in American Choral
Music," MA degree, Eastman School of Music, University of Roches-
ter. The study includes chapters on the history of the choir, a biography
of F. Melius Christiansen, the ideals and influence of the Choir, and a
list of Christiansen's compositions.

866. THOMSEN, T. G. (b. 1864). PAPERS, 1934–1950. 8 items. P 385.
Correspondence and articles (typescript, 32 pages) of a Norwegian-
born farmer at McGrath, Minnesota. The articles consist of anecdotal
accounts of land claims, Indian neighbors, transportation, housing,
forest fire, live stock, drought, wild life, and schools during pioneer
days in Aitkin County.

867. THORSHOV (THORSHAUG), OLAF (1883–1928). LETTER, 1901. 1
      item. P 701.

A letter written from Willmar, Minnesota, by a Norwegian-American architect.

868. THRANE, MARCUS (1817–1890). PAPERS, 1870–1965. 4 items and 3 volumes. P 456.
Material by and about the father of the labor movement in Norway, author, journalist and satirist. Thrane emigrated from Norway to the United States in 1863.

"The Wisconsin Bible," a translation of *Wisconsin Biblen* (1881), by Linsie Caroline Krook (typescript, 53 pages). "Holden," a translation of an unpublished satirical three-act play with the same title, by Henrietta Naeseth (typescript, 67 pages). "Autobiographical Reminiscences" translated by Vasilia Thrane Struck (typescript, 16 pages, 1917). *Dagslyset*, a monthly journal edited and published by Thrane in Chicago. The issues run from 1870 to 1873. "Ernst Skarstedt and Marcus Thrane," by Sigvald Stoylen (typescript, 12 pages). Assorted clippings and articles.

869. THUN, ARLYS EDMAN. PAPERS, 1977. 2 items. Typescript. P 918.
A poem, "The World of the Vikings," and an article, "The Red River Valley of the North" (8 pages), written by a former resident of the Red River Valley area.

870. THYE, EDWARD J. (1896–1969). PAPERS, 1945–1958. 94 items. P 386.
Newsletters, speeches, press releases, clippings, and letters of a Minnesota farmer and a United States senator (1947–1961). Thye's parents were born in Norway.

871. THYKESEN, ANNA (1879–1964). PAPERS, 1903–1934. 6 items. P 445.
Papers of a teacher of Norwegian at St. Olaf College: a Bjørnstjerne Bjørnson letter and a scrapbook of clippings dealing largely with Bjørnson and the 100th anniversary celebration of his birth; a scrapbook on O. E. Rølvaag and other writers (1931–1956); a scrapbook of clippings on the reorganization problem in the Norwegian Lutheran Church of America in the early 1930's.

872. TINGELSTAD, OSCAR A. (1882–1953). PAPERS, 1899–1953. 23 boxes. P 596.
Correspondence, records, articles, reports, and account books of a Lutheran clergyman, educator and author.

Dr. Tingelstad was professor of psychology and education and registrar (1909–1928) and professor of philosophy and Bible (1944–1953) at Luther College, and president of Pacific Lutheran College (1928–1943).

Personal as well as professional correspondence runs throughout the collection and provides information on family affairs and on educational and professional careers of friends and colleagues. He defended the classical course of study in the colleges he served and in the main took a conservative stance on religious doctrine. Topics discussed are theory of evolution, liberal theology, rationalism in the church, curriculum development, church mergers, student recruitment, building programs and problems related to financing private colleges. In brief, his correspondence treats issues and problems prominent in college and church affairs during the first half of the twentieth century.

Manuscripts by Tingelstad: "The Historic Position of Lutheranism" (1927), "Registration Procedure and Preparation of Class Lists" (1927), "Academic Freedom and Tenure" (1939), "Brought up a Lutheran — But" (ca. 1945), "Thy Word is Truth" (1948), and "How Do Our Colleges Measure up to Present Day Educational Standards" (1948).

Meticulously kept, the account books contain detailed records of all correspondence and all personal financial transactions for the years indicated. For a list of correspondents, see description catalogue in NAHA Archives.

873. TJERNAGEL, NEHEMIAS (b. 1868). PAPERS, 1890's–1955. 64 items and 16 volumes. P 448.

Articles, clippings, and pamphlets of an Iowa farmer, author, and musician dealing with the history of Norwegian Americans in the Story City area. Among the papers are a list of Tjernagel's musical compositions and writings; a Story City, Randall, Roland community bibliography; stories by Tjernagel clipped from *The Story City Herald* about early pioneers, and from other journals containing articles by Tjernagel and others on pioneer churches, prairie fires, agriculture, foods and water supply, homes, peddlers, horse thieves, music, disease, and the 1855 settlement.

874. TØLLEFSEN, RØNNING. LETTER, 1863. 1 item. P 435.

Copy of a letter written at Eau Claire, Wisconsin, to parents and relatives. The letter makes reference to the Civil War and to the Indian uprising in Minnesota and discourages emigration.

875. TOFTEZON, ZACHARIAS M. (1821–1901). PAPERS, 1806–1939, n.d. 163 items. P 457.

Correspondence and legal papers of, and biographical information on a Norwegian who immigrated in 1847 and came to Washington in 1850.

Toftezon was probably the first white man in the Stanwood area. His mother, sister, and brother came later. A Toftezon memorial stone was erected in 1939.

The bulk of the collection consists of letters written in Norway, Washington, and Door and Oconto counties, Wisconsin, by and to members of the Toftezon family, and deal with church, crops, health, and weather.

876. TOLLEFSON, ANDREW (b. ca. 1866). CORRESPONDENCE, 1881–
1906. 80 items. P 458.
Correspondence of a Norwegian-born teacher and sheep rancher written mostly from Montana, Minnesota, and Wisconsin dealing with
health, rural schools, politics, and economic conditions on farm and
ranch. There are letters concerning St. Olaf College, Augsburg College,
Concordia College, Augustana Academy, and Scandinavia Academy.
Tollefson was a student at St. Olaf College (1890–1893).

877. TOLLEFSON, THOR C. (b. 1901). ARTICLE, 1953. 1 item. Type-
script, 7 pages. P 387.
"Norsk bidrag til Amerikansk liv," a translation by Gus O. Solum,
Seattle, Washington, of an address appearing in the *Congressional
Record* (May 15, 1953). Discusses the history, growth, and contribution
of Norwegians to American culture. Tollefson was a congressman from
Tacoma.

878. TOLLEY (TOLLEFSRUD), CLARENCE H. BIOGRAPHY, 1959. 17
pages. P 388.
Biography of Fingar Enger, a bonanza farmer in the Goose River
area, North Dakota. Clipped from *North Dakota History* vol. 26, no. 3.

879. TORBENSON, MARY SYVERSON (MRS. OSCAR) (b. 1880). LOCAL
HISTORY, 1965. Typescript, 11 pages. P 389.
Historical sketch of pioneer life in Moore Township, Ransom
County, North Dakota, by a native of the area.

880. TORGERSON, TORGER A. (1838–1906). PAPERS, 1837–1936. 118
items. P 390.
Papers of a Norwegian-born Lutheran clergyman at Lake Mills, Iowa
(1865–1906): letters of transfer, baptismal certificates, histories of congregations he served, an article on slavery, and a typescript copy of a
biography of Torgerson's wife, Dina Anderson (Kvelve), by Erling
Ylvisaker.

881. TORKELSON, IVER (d. 1902). LETTERS, 1863–1878. 2 items.
P 459.
Copies of letters of Norwegian-born Jackson County, Wisconsin,
farmer, county official, and Civil War veteran.

882. TORRES, LUIS. ORAL HISTORY, 1975–1976. 1 volume, 266
pages. P 831.
Conversations with the Recent Past, ed. by Luis Torres, reproduced
from typescript into book form. The articles are by Luther College
students who interviewed residents in the area concerning their lives and
experiences.

883. TORRISON, OSULD (1825–1892). PAPERS, 1924–1930. 7 items.
P 392.

Clippings and correspondence concerning a Norwegian-born Manitowoc, Wisconsin, merchant and his family.

884. TORVIK, INGVALD. LECTURES, 1950. 2 items. Typescript, 14
pages. P 449.
"The Language Situation in Norway" and "Seventeenth of May
Thoughts " by a visiting professor at St. Olaf College.

885. TOSDAL, HARRY RUDOLPH (b. 1889). BIOGRAPHY, n.d. 1 item.
Typescript, 2 pages. P 450.
Biographical notes concerning a professor in the Harvard Graduate
School of Business Administration.

TRACTS, See Special Collections, No. 948.

886. TROCKSTAD, AXEL P. (1879–1955). BIOGRAPHY, 1915. 5 pages.
P 451.
A biographical sketch of Martin Ulvestad, author of *Nordmændene i
Amerika* and other books. Trockstad was a journalist.

887. TRONNES, ELLING. PAPERS. 5 items. P 904.
Biographical information about Elling Tronnes, a portrait painter,
who emigrated from Norway in 1893.

888. TURLI, IRENE (b. 1926). NOVEL. Typescript, 133 pages. P 452.
Unpublished manuscript of "The Three Red Hills," a novel treating
the western prairie during the decade following 1912. Hunger for land is
the central theme.

889. TUVE FAMILY. FAMILY HISTORY, 1977. 1 volume, typescript, 63
pages. P 842.
"Families of the Five Tuve-Tuff-Tew Brothers " by George L. Tuve,
Cleveland, Ohio. Also, biographical information (clippings, news releases, etc.) concerning the descendents of this immigrant family.

890. TVILLINGBYERNE NORSK LITERÆRE FORENING. CONSTITUTION,
n.d. 1 item. P 702.
Constitution of a Minneapolis-St. Paul literary society.

891. TYSTAD, SØREN A. (b. 1849). LOCAL HISTORY, 1924. 8 handwritten pages. P 453.
A history of the Norwegian settlement in Miner County, South
Dakota (1880–1924), prepared for the Nordfjordlag convention at Howard, South Dakota (1924), by Tystad, one of the first settlers. It gives
names of pioneers; comments on the 1880 snowstorm, prairie fires, and
farming; and discusses religious life in the settlement.

892. UELAND, BRENDA. BIOGRAPHY, 1967. Typescript, 501 pages.
P 108.
"Clara Ueland of Minnesota" by her daughter, Brenda, covers the

years 1830 to 1927; includes letters by members of her family; and discusses such topics as war, woman suffrage, child discipline, League of Women Voters, religion, education, politics, and manners.

893.   ULVESTAD, MARTIN (1865–1942). CORRESPONDENCE, 1933– 1936. 14 items. P 394.
Correspondence of a Norwegian-American author regarding his books.

894.   UNSTAD, LYDER L. (1895–1959). PAPERS, 1928–1937. 1 box and 2 volumes. P 660.
Paper of a Norwegian-born college teacher and press correspondent. The scrapbooks contain clippings from Norwegian-American newspapers pertaining to such subjects as current literature, the Norwegian language controversy, technocracy, Marxism, Thorstein Veblen, and Marcus Thrane.

895.   UPPER MIDWEST HISTORY CONFERENCE. PAPERS, 1947. 5 items. Typescript, 25 pages. P 395.
Four papers, including one by Carlton C. Qualey entitled "Upper Midwest Centennials." Introduction by Theodore C. Blegen.

896.   VALDER COLLEGE. CATALOGUES, 1908–1917. 7 items. P 530.
Catalogues of a business and teacher training institution founded in 1899 in Decorah, Iowa, by Charles H. Valder.

897.   VALLEY GROVE LUTHERAN CONGREGATION, NERSTRAND, MINNESOTA. RECORDS, 1868–1920. 4 volumes. P 396.
Minutes of the congregation (1868–1890, 1893–1916) including some discussions on doctrine, property, and programs; treasurer's account book (1860–1881); and a history (1855–1920) of the congregation by O. H. Stenbakken which gives names of first settlers and itinerant preachers, and dates of significant events.

898.   VALLON, JULIA SANDO. BIOGRAPHY, 1937. Typescript, 5 pages. P 735.
Copy of an article which first appeared in *Grand Forks Herald* (January 24, 1937) about scouting for land in Red River Valley, North Dakota, by her father, Halvor Lars Sando.

899.   VANGEN, CHRISTINA. DIARY, 1892. 1 item. P 246.
Diary of a St. Olaf College student from Cannon Falls, Minnesota: housing, social life, study and classes.

900.   VEBLEN, ANDREW A. (1848–1932). PAPERS, 1902–1964. 3 boxes. P 598.
The papers consist mostly of manuscript material (data, research notes, genealogical information) for Veblen's *The Valdris Book* (1920), and of World War I military service records of natives of Valdres,

Norway. Among the papers are Simle and Ruste genealogies; a family sketch written in the Valdres dialect by Sam Thompson; a description of the journey from Valdres to Whalen, Minnesota, by E. A. Hjelde; letters from Nils Brandt, Juul Dieserud, Nils Flaten, J. C. M. Hanson, and Ole Juul; and a memorial statement by Dr. Laur. Larsen about G. O. Rustad, supervisor of construction operations of the first Luther College building.

Veblen was a professor of physics; first president of the Valdres *bygdelag* and first editor of its magazine, and first president of the Common Council of the *bygdelags*.

901. VIGENSTAD, PAUL THORSTENSEN (1839–1925). PAPERS, 1860–1962. 8 items. P 397.
Recommendations and biographical sketches of a Norwegian-born teacher and farmer of Ottertail County, Minnesota.

902. VOLSTEAD, ANDREW J. (1860–1947). ARTICLE. 1 item. P 871.
Copy of an article describing Congressman Volstead's interest in farmers' cooperatives and the 1922 Capper-Volstead Act.

903. WÆRENSKJOLD, ELISE TVEDE (1815–1895). LETTERS, 1851–1866. 2 items. P 435.
Copies of letters, one published in *Morgenblad* (June 17, 1852) and the second in *Addressebladet* (February 20, 1867). The first letter was written in response to T. Andreas Gjestvang's request for information regarding Texas to counteract the dark picture painted by Captain A. Tolmer in his series of letters which appeared in *Hamars Budstikke* (1850–1851). In the second letter Mrs. Wærenskjold gives a detailed account of the murder of her husband, Wilhelm.

904. WALDELAND, MARTIN E. (1876–1933). PAPERS, 1931–1933. 1 box. P 599.
Short stories, articles, poems, and correspondence of a Lutheran clergyman. Waldeland served in Iowa parishes, was the chairman of his synod's publicity and transportation bureaus, and the author of short stories.

905. WALDELAND, PAUL. RECORD BOOK, 1931–1933. 1 item. P 680.
Account book of a St. Olaf college student.

906. WALDORF LUTHERAN COLLEGE. PAPERS, 1904–1964. 3 boxes. P 535.
Catalogues, brochures, bulletins, journals, and reports of a Lutheran academy founded in 1903 (a junior college in 1920), located in Forest City, Iowa.

907. WALOE, OLE C. (1872–1952). PAPERS, 1897–1953. 17 items. P 398.
Letters, certificates, and medals of a Norwegian-born army colonel.

Waloe immigrated to Wisconsin ca. 1891; served in the United States Army in Cuba and the Philippines (1896–1924).

908. WASHINGTON, GEORGE (1732–1799). GENEALOGY, 1932–1963. 10 items. P 399.
Clippings and pamphlets concerning the George Washington genealogy.

909. WASHINGTON BENEVOLENT SOCIETIES. PAPERS, n.d. 3 items. P 643.
Historical sketches in manuscript of the Ebenezer Old Folks' Home and the Martha and Mary Orphan Home at Poulsbo and the Josephine Sunset Home at Stanwood.

910. WEFALD, KNUD (1869–1936). ADDRESSES, 1925, 1933. 2 items. P 400.
Two addresses by a Norwegian-born lumberman, poet, congressman, and Minnesota railroad and warehouse commissioner.

911. WESTPHAEL, MICHAEL. LAND PATENT, 1889. 1 item. P 402.
A Homestead Certificate issued to a resident at Watertown, South Dakota.

912. WICK, BARTHINIUS L. (1864–1947). PAPERS, 1904–1947. 14 items. P 403.
Mainly articles of a Norwegian-born Cedar Rapids, Iowa, attorney, philanthropist, and history instructor at the University of Iowa: "Pioneer Traits," "The Pioneer Memorial Association of Norway (Iowa)" and a biography of Nicolai Ibsen, brother of the dramatist, who was a resident of Emmet County, Iowa.

913. WIDEN, GUDRUN. NOVELS. 2 volumes, typescript. P 757.
Two unpublished novels entitled "Varden" (Cairn), a story written in Norwegian and laid in Norway (223 pages); and "Why Don't They Go Home," the story of an immigrant girl in Brooklyn, New York (234 pages).

914. WIESE, MARKUS FREDRIK (b. 1842). CHURCH HISTORY, 1915. Pamphlet, 63 pages. P 556.
Nogle bidrag til retledning og forsvar is a discussion of points of conflict among several Norwegian Lutheran synods previous to the merger in 1917.

915. WIGELAND, ANDREW E. AND G. NORMAN. REPORT, 1975. P 836.
"The Andrew E. and G. Norman Wigeland Professorship in Norwegian Studies, University of Chicago, 1975," a report covering the history of the establishment of the Wigeland Professorship.

916. WIGERS, A. NOVEL, 1909. 1 volume. 482 manuscript pages.

An unpublished story with a religious theme entitled "De to rekrutter" by a resident of Tacoma, Washington.

917. WILD RICE CHILDREN'S HOME. REPORTS, 1920–1931. 2 items.
P 637.
Information about an institution founded at Twin Valley, Minnesota, in 1899.

918. WILLMAR LUTHERAN BIBLE SCHOOL. PAPERS, 1921–1923. 7 items. P 531.
Catalogues and correspondence.

919. WILLMAR SEMINARY. PAPERS, 1882–1965. 2 boxes. P 536.
Articles, correspondence, catalogues, record books, reports, photographs, programs, and scrapbook concerning a Lutheran secondary school at Willmar, Minnesota (1893–1919).

920. WISCONSIN, BLACK EARTH, FOND DU LACK, AND MADISON. LETTERS, 1851–1866. 7 items. P 435.
Copies of letters by anonymous writers that appeared in *Adressebladet, Christiania-posten*, and *Morgenbladet*: description of Madison, procedures to use in dealing with immigration agents, life in Pleasant Springs Township, land and tax systems and Americanization, Yankee respect for honorable work, the Westward movement, politics, the common school controversy, and the slavery question.

921. WISCONSIN, GREEN COUNTY, TOWN OF YORK. SCHOOL RECORDS, 1891–1939. 70 items and 9 volumes. P 661.
Petitions, teachers' contracts, teachers' reports, school census reports, and financial records of School District No. 3 in Town of York. Ninety-eight per cent of the residents of the district were of Norwegian background.

922. WISCONSIN, STATE OF. CONSTITUTIONS, 1846, 1848. 2 items.
P 405.
Copies of the constitution written in Norwegian. The names Henry Nubson and Evend Aanundsen Hiattvedt appear on the title page.

923. WISCONSIN, VIROQUA. REMINISCENCES, 1912. 1 item. 101 manuscript pages. P 703.
"En gammel Setlers Histori Skreved da jeg var 68 Aar" by one known only as N. N. Treating life in the Viroqua area, the topics discussed include prices, crops, land, machinery, live stock, logging, wages, buildings, fire insurance, Farmer Trading Association (farmers store); temperance movement; district school; disease and medical service, congregation, and synodical controversies. The author immigrated in 1869.

924. WITTENBERG, WISCONSIN, SCHOOLS. PAPERS, 1889–1923. 10
     items. P 532.
Catalogue, correspondence, and reports concerning three schools:
Norwegian-English Normal School (1887–1890), Wittenberg Academy
(1901–1913), and Indian School (ca. 1916–ca. 1920).

925. WOLD, CHRISTIAN. LETTER, 1846. 1 item. P 435.
Copy of a letter written in Buffalo, New York, and published in
Morgenbladet (April 7, 1846). Wold offers criticism of J. R. Reiersen's
book on America, questioning the sincerity of his praise and suggests
that emigrants be cautious in their dealings with immigration personnel.

926. WOLDEN, P. P. (1844–1908). CORRESPONDENCE, 1861–1877.
     74 bound letters. P 406.
Letters by clergymen and laymen in Norway, Minnesota, Wisconsin,
and Iowa to Wolden regarding private religious problems with an occa-
sional reference to the relationships between the Augustana and Conference synods and their schools. Wolden, who immigrated in 1866, was
an itinerant Norwegian school teacher.

927. WOMEN'S MISSIONARY FEDERATION. PAPERS, 1911–1957. 33
     items. P 556.
Articles, constitutions, handbooks, and reports containing history of
the women's organization of the Norwegian Lutheran Church.

928. WORKERS LYCEUM, CHICAGO. ANNIVERSARY, 1928. P 816.
Tenth anniversary booklet giving the history of a worker's organization in Chicago, earlier known as Branch nr. 1, Karl Marx, associated
with the American Socialist Party.

929. WORLD WAR I. ROSTER, 1918. 1 item. P 408.
Roster of World War I veterans in the Duluth, Minnesota area.

930. WORLD WAR II. PAPERS, 1940–1954. 38 items. P 409.
Pamphlets and clippings concerning Norwegian Americans on active
duty in World War II, including St. Olaf College graduates and students.

931. WRAAMAN'S ACADEMY. CATALOGUE, 1890. 1 item. P 533.
Catalogue of a private high school in Minneapolis (1890–1897) operated by Wilhelm W. Wraamann.

932. WRIGHT, ANDREW (1835–1917). PAPERS, 1857–1921. 17 items
     and 1 volume. P 604.
Legal papers, correspondence, anecdotes, poems, articles, and scrapbook of a Norwegian-born Lutheran clergyman.

933. YGDRASIL LITERARY SOCIETY OF MADISON (1896). HISTORY,
     1971. Booklet, 49 pages. P 906.
Ygdrasil, 1896–1971, a souvenir record for the 75th anniversary of

the society in Madison, Wisconsin, written by Olaf A. Hougen. The contents cover lists of members, a brief history, the constitution and by-laws, together with lists of officers, speakers, programs and papers by Ygdrasil members.

934. YTTERBOE, HALVOR T. (1857–1904). PAPERS, 1861–1942. 7 boxes. P 600.

Correspondence, St. Olaf College papers and treasury reports, reminiscences, certificates, and family historical data of a member of the St. Olaf College faculty (1882–1904). The papers deal largely with St. Olaf College and are concerned with student registration, course work, athletics, health, and social life; faculty appointments, salaries, academic and social life; reports on the school activities; solicitation campaigns for students and funds; construction and furnishing of Ytterboe Hall; and the relation of the College to the Church.

935. ZAHL, THEODOR BUGGE. PAPERS, 1891–1921. 6 items. P 410.

Correspondence and a poem regarding Norway's relations with England, France, and Germany.

SPECIAL COLLECTIONS

936. ANNIVERSARIES. PAMPHLETS, 1900–1943. 18 items. P 21.
Birth, death, ordination, wedding.

937. ARTICLES: PAMPHLETS AND REPRINTS. 6 boxes. P 436.

Articles by Norwegian Americans in the field of language, literature, mathematics, natural sciences, and social sciences. For a list of authors, see description catalogue in the NAHA Archives.

938. ARTIFACTS. 6 cases.

Organizational seals, plaques, banners, flags, tapestries, wall hangings, awards, gavels, book ends, anniversary greetings, and other memorabilia. For inventory, see description catalogue in NAHA Archives.

939. BIOGRAPHICAL FILE, 1914–1978. Estimated 125,000 items. 104 drawers (208 linear feet) and 77 volumes.

The file was begun in 1914 by Andrew A. Rowberg (1887–1969), a Northfield, Minnesota, journalist. He gleaned Norwegian-American newspapers and a number printed in the English language for articles giving information on Norwegian Americans be they feature stories, obituaries, or articles treating weddings, wedding and birth anniversaries, promotions, honors, tributes, Norway visits, etc. Some entries predate 1914, but only in a fragmentary manner.

The shorter articles are mounted on 3×5 cards, and the longer articles are found in scrapbooks. Reference cards indicate volume and page number. Each entry cites name of newspaper and date of publication.

The file also provides references to biographical information found in Norwegian-American periodicals.

Because many have their names mentioned in a newspaper for the first time when they die, a large portion of the file entries are obituaries. These obituaries vary greatly in the data they provide, but many include information on geographic origin in Norway; dates of birth, marriage, and emigration; names of parents, sisters, brothers and children; location of settlement, occupation and church affiliation. The file has proved valuable to those seeking initial leads in developing a family history or tree as well as a general reference source. The file has been maintained after Rowberg's death in 1969, but not with his thoroughness.

940.   CALENDARS, 1900–1950. 63 items. 1 box. P 648.
Commercial, church, and school calendars.

941.   CATALOGUES, 1877–1967. 4 boxes. P 616.
Book catalogues (143) issued by 22 different Scandinavian-American publishing firms and bookstores.

942.   CLIPPING FILE, ca. 1900–1952. 136 boxes.
Initially the clipping file of *Minneapolis Tidende* (1886–1935), but includes clippings from other newspapers and journals, including some printed in Norway. A card index provides references to box and envelope number. Carl G. O. Hansen, editor of *Minneapolis Tidende* (1923–1935), continued to maintain the file into the early 1950's.

943.   CUTS COLLECTION. 12 boxes. P 1003.
Cuts for illustrations in a variety of publications, but mostly for books published by the Norwegian-American Historical Association.

944.   IN MEMORIAM. PAMPHLETS, 1873–1959. 75 items. P 183.
Memorial statements written on the occasion of death. For names, see NAHA description catalogue.

945.   MUSIC: CHORUS, SOLO, SONG AND HYMN. 10 boxes. P 558.
Vocal music, mostly religious, mainly by Norwegian-American and Norwegian composers. For list of composers, see description catalogue in NAHA archives.

946.   PAMPHLETS, 1839–1958. 12 boxes. P 576.
Pamphlets consisting of articles, brochures, constitutions, lectures, poems, reports, sermons, stories and plays on religious and secular subjects. For inventory, see catalogue description in NAHA Archives.

947.   PHOTOGRAPHS. 13 boxes and 3 cases. P 655.
A collection of photographs, topically classified: churches, parsonages, hospitals, schools, colleges, and seminaries; interiors of homes, stores, offices and business firms; farm, rural, and street scenes; group pictures of confirmation classes, student bodies, reunions, bygdelag

meetings, college faculties, conventions, weddings, funerals, and church congregations; and photographs depicting dress, pioneer homes, threshing crews, saw mills, dairies, leisure activities, country schools, etc. For a detailed inventory, see description catalogue in the NAHA Archives.

948. TRACTS, 1866–1945, n.d. 447 items in 2 boxes. P 597.
Tracts on religious subjects in English and Norwegian published by various groups, including the Norwegian Evangelical Lutheran Church in America.

Index

Camp Little Norway Association, papers, 119

Camp Nidaros, Ottertail Lake (Minn.), papers, 120

Camrose Lutheran College, papers, 121

Canada, 40, 103, 119, 121, 366, 427, 636

Cannon Falls (Minn.), 327, 899

Canton (S.D.), 45, 221, 302

Canuteson, Richard, papers, 122

Capper-Volstead Act, 902

Carlsen, Clarence J., thesis, 123; 173

Carlson, Carl E., 854

Carlton County (Minn.), 50

Carmel Highlands Norwegian Lodge (Calif.), papers, 124

Carthage College, 410

Casberg, Selma S., genealogy, 125

Caspari, Th., 698

Catalogues, 941

Central Wisconsin College, papers, 126

Cerro Gordo County (Ia.), 404

Certificate, 127

Charney, Seth D., biography, 128

Chicago, 73, 670, 720; A Century of Progress, 288, 670, 726; church, 179; homes and hospitals, 499, 670; journalism, 147, 317, 407, 411; organizations, 207, 317, 403, 407, 578, 584, 593, 595, 596, 615, 670, 685

Chicago Lutheran Bible School, papers, 129

Chicago Norwegian Technical Society, papers, 130

Christian the Seventh, legal documents, 131

Christiania (Norway), 109, 206, 670, 680. See also Oslo.

Christiansen, F. Melius, papers, 132, 307, 472, 865

Christopher, Ole C., papers, 133

Church, doctrine and controversey, 24, 141, 189, 198, 211, 253, 273, 311, 369, 410, 418, 445, 497, 715, 771, 848, 872; education, 497; for deaf and blind, 186; Hauge, 173; history, 64, 77, 161, 164, 179, 308, 404, 497, 501; merger, 691, 715, 726, 771; name change, 258; records, 590; schools, 134. See also academies, clergy, colleges, and congregations.

Civil War, Andersonville Prison, 331, 825; diary, 376; Hans C. Heg, 328; hospital life, 263; letters, 2, 32, 189, 243, 466, 471, 747; Navy, 41; Norwegians in Confederate Army, 135; references to, 57, 636, 874; veterans, 566, 665

Claire City (S.D.), 571

Clausen, Clarence A., 314

Clausen, Claus L., papers, 136; 162, 402, 456, 652, 771, 837

Clausen, Marvin, speech, 137

Cleng Peerson Memorial Institute, archives, 138

Clergymen, papers, 93, 253, 277, 304, 316, 352, 363, 379, 398, 410, 447, 475, 522, 523, 526, 528, 575, 682, 711, 715, 840, 904, 932; in education, 87, 86, 434, 726, 771; memoirs, biographies, and diaries, 97, 577, 749, 784, 804, 837; letters, reports, articles, 161, 372, 384, 839, 841; Unitarian, 401; Methodist, 421

Clifton (Tex.), 139

Clifton Junior College, catalogues, 139

Clipping File, 942

Clubs, 525, 614; Norweg. (San Fran.), 184, (Chicago), 615, 670; arts, 580; ski, 584; social, 695; womens, 580, 612

The Coeur d'Alene Homes, journals, 140

Colleges, business, 3, 146, 537, 706, 737, 896; Danish, 42; Lutheran, 43, 46, 68, 69, 121, 142, 143, 237, 257, 408, 491, 534, 603, 672, 674, 675, 696, 817, 858, 906; teachers', 146, 537, 896; Swedish, 602; history, 82

Colloquium at Madison (Wis.), pamphlet, 141

Columbia Lutheran College, papers, 142

Concordia College, papers, 143; 876; Language Camps, 144

Congregations, 145

Consulate, Norwegian, 67

Coon Prairie (Wis.), 332, 374, 375, 839

Coon Valley (Wis.), 107, 528, 748

Copenhagen (Denmark), 670

Cottonwood (Minn.), 134, 158, 646

Cramer, August, 715

Crookston (Minn.), 146

Crookston College, catalogues, 146

Cuts Collection, 943

Daae, Austen, clippings, 147
Dagslyset, 868
Dahl, Borghild, papers, 148; 697, 698
Dahl, Dorthea, papers, 149
Dahl, Jens M., 218
Dahl (Øksendahl), Nels T., autobiography, 150
Dahl, Theo. H., 711, 854
Dahl, Valborg, 150
Dahlby, Anne (Mrs. Ole), papers, 151
Dahle, Aanund, 399
Dahle, Isak, 576
Dahle, John, journals, 152; 378
Dakota Lutheran High School, paper, 153
Dallas Norsk Evangelisk Luthersk Kirkegaard, records, 154
Dane County (Wis.), 208, 274, 262, 263, 399, 419, 830
Danielson, John, 331
Danish Norwegian Adventist, 385
Darwinian Theory of Evolution, 108
Daughters of Norway Lodge, papers, 155
Davidson, James O., 168
Decorah (Ia.), 5, 262, 270, 288, 306, 779, 782
Decorah Institute, journals, 156
Decorah-Posten, 36, 53, 698
Deed, 157
Deen, Tilla R. Dahl, reminiscences, 158
Deerfield (Wis.), 85
De Kalb (Ill.), 325
Detroit (Mich.), 439
Devils Lake (N.D.), 1
Dewitt, Ruth, local history, 159
Diaries (selected), 2, 7, 160, 285, 370, 439, 466, 484, 644, 645, 662, 680, 711, 728, 783, 804, 855, 899
Dieserud, Juul, 578, 698, 754, 900
Dietrichson, Gustav F., letters, 161; 402
Dietrichson, Johannes W. C., papers, 162; 197, 402, 456, 741
Dodge County (Wis.), 743
Dørring, Carl, papers, 163
Dommernaes, Lauritz P., 697
Door County (Wis.), 115, 875
Dovre Menighed, Osnabrock, N.D., record book, 164
Drama, 291, 426, 671, 720, 834

Drammen (Norway), 439
Draxten, Nina, 205
Drewsen, Viggo, biography, 165
Dreyer, Peder, 711
Duckstad, Paul A., article, 166
Duffner, Russel, article, 167
Dundas, J. C., 384, 636
Dus, N. F., 583
Duus, O. F., 189

Eagle Bend (Minn.), 640
Eagle Lake (Minn.), 70
Eau Claire (Wis.), 12, 492
Ebenezer Home (Minneapolis), 705
Eckers, H. A., 12, 692
Eckholth, Torgeir T., article, 168
Edgerton (Wis.), 726
Education, 845, 852
Educators, 436, 467, 553, 585, 653, 705, 710, 728; languages and literature, 51, 56, 174, 225, 280, 319, 429, 472, 664, 732, 779, 810; engineering, 114; history, 246, 458; chemistry, 248, 667; administrators, 86, 310, 346, 347, 434, 542, 688, 726, 739, 872; physics, 267, 342, 900; religion, 103, 290, 330, 418; library, 208; agriculture, 489, 653
Egeberg, Hans O., papers, 169
Egge, Albert E., 225
Eggen, Beret, 729
Eggen, Thore, 711
Egilsrud, Helen, 732
Eide, Arthur H., papers, 170
Eide, Lars B., letter, 171
Eide, Randolph, papers, 172
Eielsen, Elling, papers, 173; 123, 162, 456, 569, 733
Eielsen Seminary (Lisbon Seminary), papers, 482
Eikeland, Peter J., papers, 174; 698, 711
Einerson (Tjøn), John, papers, 175
Einuung, H. H., 735
Eittreim, Knud G., papers, 176
Ekrem family, 177
Ekroll, Øystein, family history, 177
Elholm, Augustus C. G., papers, 178
Ellefsen, Edward M., church history, 179
Ellestad, Gilbert B., papers, 180
Ellestad, Nils J., 189, 711, 715, 771
Ellickson, Lars, 740
Ellingsen, John, papers, 181

Ellingson family, 177
Ellington Prairie, Winnebago Co. (Ia.), 218
Ellsworth, Susie C., 732
Emigrant roster, 809
Emigranten, article, 182
Emigration, analysis, 433; appeal for, 530; documents, 4, 7, 9, 33, 128, 175, 281, 334, 512, 642, 849; causes and effects, 547; opposition to, 110, 162, 197, 229, 275, 413; radio programs, 483; report, 485
Endressen, Guri, 183
Enestvedt, Ole O., papers, 183
Enger, Fingar, 878
Enger, Ralph, papers, 184
Engineers, 35, 41, 80, 114, 130, 169, 199, 214, 242, 303, 335, 448, 656, 658, 785, 844, 846
Enockson, Marie J., reminiscences, 185
Ephphath Missions, papers, 186
Ephraim (Wis.), 359
Episcopal Church, 694
Erickson, John T., papers, 187
Erickson, Rolf H., 268, 665
Erickson, Thomas, copybook, 188
Eriksen, Ingebret, papers, 189
Erikson, Alfred O., 189
Ernstsen, Oline, reminiscences, 191
Erpestad, Emil, 46
Erskine (Minn.), 417
Ethnic Studies, papers, 192; 704
Evangelical Free Church, reports, 193
Evanson, Evan I., papers, 194
Evanston (Ill.), 195, 805
Evanston Bible School, catalogues, 195
Evensen, Anders, letter, 196
Evensen, Lars, report, 197
Evenson (Evans), Benedick, article, 198
Everett (Wash.), 68, 142
Evinrude, Ole, biography, 199
Evjen, John O., 12

Faerevaag, Lars, autograph album, 200
Fairmont (Minn.), 331
Fairview Hospital, papers, 201
Fairytale, 100
Falkberget, Johan, journal, 202; 354, 698
Family Histories and Genealogies, 203; 2
Fargo (N.D.), 3, 235
Faribault (Minn.), 186, 517

Farming, see agriculture and frontier life
Farseth, Elisa Pl, 587
Farseth, Olaus C., notebook, 204
Farseth, Pauline, clippings, 205
Fedde, Elizabeth, memoirs, 206; 500, 627
Federation of Norwegian Women's Societies (Chicago), records, 207
Felland, Ole G., papers, 208; 225
Fenstad, Trondby, 529
Fergus Falls (Minn.), 209, 495, 647
Fertile (Ia.), 218
Fetvedt, Anund O., letters, 209
Fifteenth Wisconsin (regiment), 135, 825
Fillmore County (Minn.), 134, 260, 262, 366, 845
Finley (N.D.), 87
Finmark Misjonsforening (Minneapolis), records, 210
Finseth, Knut, 2
Fjeld, John N., 399
Fjelde, Rolf, 697
Fjeldsaa, Ruth, 12
Fjellbu, Arne, 726
Fjelstad, Rolf K., doctrine, 211
Flaaten, O. K., 135
Fladager, Mons H., correspondence, 212
Flaten, Nils, 900
Fleischer, Frederick, clipping, 213
Fleischer, Wilhelm, lecture, 214
Flekkefjordlaget, records, 215
Fletre, Lars, papers, 216
Floan, Peter O., reminiscences, 217
Flugum, Niels C. and Ole. N., 218
Folk Arts Foundation of America, papers, 219
Folkedahl, Beulah, papers, 220
Folkedahl, Knudt, papers, 221
Folkestad, Sigurd, 12, 115
Folklore, 291, 647
Foreign Language Information Service, Norwegian Bureau, reports, 222
Forshaug, Jens H., travel report, 223
Fort Rice (Dakota Territory), 397
Foss, Hans A., papers, 224; 479
Fossland, Gyda and Sam, 766
Fossum, Andrew, papers, 225
Fossum, Robert, 241
Fostveit, Knut, poems, 226
Four Mile Prairie (Tex.), 795
Fox River Valley (Ill.), 227, 720

Hougen, Olaf A., 933
Hougstad, Hans C., papers, 370
Hougstad, Martha H., reminiscences, 371
Houkom, Anders, reports, 372
Houkom, John A., 375
Houkom, Nellie S. J., local history, 373
Houkom, Olaf S., letters, 374
Houkom, Svennung O., correspondence, 375
Hovde, O. M., 376
Hovden, George J., Civil War diary, 376
Hovland, Peder, papers, 377
Hoyem, Nell M., dissertation, 378
Hoyme, Christopher T., 398
Hoyme, Gjermund, papers, 379; 2, 373, 398, 711, 715, 854
Hudson's Bay Co., 348
Humboldt College, papers, 380
Humphrey, Hubert H., papers, 381
Hurdal (Minn.), 644
Huron (S.D.), 298, 438
Huseby, Olaf, biography, 382; 225
Huset, Aalaug Aaker, papers, 383
Hustvedt, Halvor B., articles, 384
Hustvedt, S. B., 636
Hutchinson Theological Seminary, papers, 385
Hvamstad, Per, papers, 386
"Hvem er hvem blandt norsk-amerikanerne," 350
Hydle, Odmund, novel, 387
Hytta, Christian L., letter, 388

Ibsen, Henrik, 174, 389, 390
Ibsen, Johan A., letter, 389
Ibsen, Nikolai, clippings, 390; 912
Idun Edda Foreningen, records, 391
Illinois, 683
Illinois, Benevolent Societies, papers, 392
Illinois State University, papers, 393
Independent Realty Company, papers, 394
Indians (Am.), 239, 183, 397, 469, 476, 874
Ingerson, Carl A., 692
Ingvoldstad, Orlando, 227
In Memoriam, pamphlets, 944
Iowa, 88, 97, 636, 683, 713

Iowa Benevolent Societies, pamphlets, 395
Iowa County, (Wis.), 361
Insurance, 496, 629, 787
Inventors, 6, 35, 199, 242, 267, 335, 488, 516, 755, 765
Iverslie, P. P., 115, 771
Iverson, O. B., articles, 396
Iverson, Sigrid, 829

Jåstad, Iver J., 116
Jacobsen, Niels, letter, 397
Jacobson, Abraham, papers, 398
Jacobson, Anna, 309
Jacobson, Christopher, 349
Jacobson, Clara, papers, 399
Jæger, Luth, papers, 400
Jahr, Torstein, 636
Jakobsen, Jakob, 698
Janesville (Wis.), 292
Jansen, Anne E., 702
Janson, Kristofer, papers, 401; 107, 400, 497, 586, 647, 697, 771, 830
Jansonists, 567
Jayne, Dr. D., 606
Jefferson Prairie (Wis.), 11
Jefferson Prairie, (and other congregations), ministerial record book, 402
Jensen, Birgith, papers, 403
Jensen, Carl C. A., articles, 404
Jensen, Hanna B., papers, 405
Jensen, Magny Landstad, clippings, 406
Jensenius, Bertram, papers, 407
Jensvold, Gulbrand, 399
Jessie James, 570
Jewel (Ia.), 408
Jewel Lutheran College, papers, 408; 705
Joergenson, Gustav B., papers, 409
Johannesen, (Stølsvig), Johs, (Johnson, J. J.), papers, 410
John Anderson Publishing Company, papers, 411; 296
Johnsen, Ole, letter, 412
Johnsøn, Peter, article, 413
Johnson, (Aasen), Andrew, papers, 415
Johnson, Alfred B., letter, 414
Johnson, Arne O., 698
Johnson, Clyde, article, 416
Johnson, Derwood, 135
Johnson, Emil, papers, 417
Johnson, Erik K., doctrine, 418

Larsen, Magnus, letters, 459
Larson family, 177
Larson, Agnes M., correspondence, 460; 419
Larson, C. W., address, 461 .
Larson, Christian, biography, 462
Larson, Clifford, biography, 463
Larson, Ever, papers, 464
Larson, L. O., 309
Larson, Laurence M., 246, 462
Larson, Lauris, papers, 465
Larson, Lewis A., papers, 466
La Salle County, (Ill.), 480, 636
La Salle, Robert, 359
Lauritsen, Wesley, 186
Lawrence, Audrey, 205
Lawrence, Carl G., papers, 467
Lawson, Victor, 411
Lee, Agnes G., 260
Lee, Berge O., 471
Lee, Ingmar A., Jr., 472
Lee, Johannes J. Sr., poems, 468
Lee, Lars, letter, 469
Lee, Ludvig H., letters, 470
Lee, Nels A., papers, 471
Lee, Olav, papers, 472
Le Grand (Ia.), 820
Leif Erickson, papers, 190, 272, 613, 716, 636; monument assoc., 96, 190; memorial proposal, 473
Leland (Ill.), 318
Leland, Mabel J., 238
Leland, Ragnvald, scrapbooks, 474; 238
Lenker, John N., papers, 475
Lenske, Gerhard, 711
Lerdahl, Nels, C., 851
Levang, Ola M., 513
Libak, Hans and Helene, 327
Liberg, O. P., letter, 476
Liberty Prairie (Wis.), 116; church, 85
Lieberg, P. O., papers, 477
Lien, Petra, 102
Lillehei, Lars, 12
Lima, Martha and Ole, 509
Lincoln, Abraham, 398
Lindbaek, Lise, 810
Lindberg, Duane R., papers, 478
Lindelie, Andreas, H., reminiscences, 479
Lipschutz, Wendy, student paper, 480
Lisbon (Ill.), 482, 713

Lisbon (N.D.), 327
Lisbon General Store, account books, 481
Lisbon Seminary (Eilsen Seminary), papers, 482
Literary societies, 37, 732
"Little Synod," 24
Ljone, Oddmund, radio scripts, 483
Loe, Hans, N., papers, 484
Løiten, Hedemark (Norway), 247
Løvenskjold, Adam, report, 485
Loftfjeld, Gabriel, 537
Logging, 32, 540, 644, 923; camps, 396
Lokke, Carl L., papers, 486
Lokken Ole J., scrapbook, 487
Lommen, Andrew O. and Ole T., 398
Long Prairie (Wis.), parish, 402
Los Angeles (Calif.), 803
Loss, Henrik V. Z., papers, 488
Lovoll, Odd S., 594
Lund, Lars, 711
Lundby, Theressa, 574
Lundy, Gabriel, biography, 489
Lundeberg, K. O., 733
Luther Academy, papers, 490
Luther College, papers, 491; 859
Luther Hospital and Training School, papers, 492
Luther Inn., papers, 493
Luther League, 103
Luther Valley (Wis.), 161, 485, 545
Lutheran Bible Institute, catalogue, 494
Lutheran Bible School, papers, 495
Lutheran Brotherhood Insurance Company, correspondence, 496
Lutheran Church, papers, 497
Lutheran Church in America, articles, 498
Lutheran Deaconess Home and Hospital, Chicago, papers, 499; Minneapolis 500
Lutheran Historical Conference, newsletter, 501
Lutheran Ladies' Seminary, papers, 502
Lutheran Missionary Training School, papers, 503
Lutheran Normal School (Minn.), papers, 504; (S.D.), 505
Lutheran Publishing House, papers, 506
Lutheran Student Assoc., 770
Lutheran Synods, 780

Norwegian Old People's Home Society of Chicago, papers, 632
Norwegian Picture Postcards, 633
Norwegian settlements, 485, 620
Norwegian Singing Societies, papers, 634; 293
Norwegian Students' America Chorus, 635
Norwegian Synod, 451
Norwegians in the United States, scrapbooks, 636
Nubson, Henry, 922
Nygaard family, 177
Nygaard, Kaare K., papers, 637
Nygard, Berit Veblen, 59

Oak Grove Seminary, papers, 638
Oconomowoc (Wis.), 97
Oconto County, (Wis.), 875
Odegaard, M.R., 697
Odegaarden family, 791
Odin Lyceum Bureau, Inc., papers, 639
Odland, Gunder T., diary, 640
Odland, Lisa, poems, 641
Odland, Thomas, papers, 642
Øihaugen, Ole T., letter, 643
Østerud, Ole O., papers, 644
Østervold Congregation, 87
Østrem, Ole O., reminiscences, 645
Oftedahl, Maria, reminiscences, 646
Oftedal, Sven, 181
Oftelie, Torkel, papers, 647; 12, 115, 246, 726, 733
Ohme, Thor, autobiography, 648
Oien, John G., clippings, 649
Olav, Crown Prince, 231
Olesen, John Y., history, 650
Oleson, Soren, local history, 651
Olsen, Emily Veblen, papers, 652
Olsen, Johan, 652
Olsen, John W., autobiography, 653
Olsen, Michael L., student papers, 655
Olsen, M. M., family history, 654
Olsen, Niels H. F., papers, 656
Olsen, Nils A., catalog, 657
Olsen, Olaf, papers, 658
Olsen, Sigurd, 652
Olson, Eleanora, monologue, 659
Olson, Floyd B., clippings, 660
Olson, Gilbert, reminiscences, 661
Olson (Langrud), Hans, diary, 662

Olson, Jacob, papers, 663
Olson, Julius E., papers, 664; 698, 726
Olson, Ludwig E., biography, 665
Olson, Paul A., papers, 666
Olson, Reier, bond, 723
Omland, Gunnulf J., 402
Onsager, Lars, clipping, 667
Onson, Samuel C., 665
Onstad, Andrew, papers, 668
Onstad, Ole O., 566
Oral history, 882
Ore, Øystein, articles, 669
Orfield, Didrick J., 697
Osland, Birger, papers, 670; 246, 430, 726
Oslo (Norway), 658
Oslo Luth. Church, Texas, 546
Ostenso, Martha, 356
Ostrander (Minn.), 109, 644
Ottawa (Ill.), 33
Ottertail County (Minn.), 209
Ottertail Lake (Minn.), 120
Ottesen, J. A., 771
Ousdal, Asbjørn P., papers, 671
Outlook College, papers, 672
Owatonna (Minn.), 298
Owen, John 23
Oyen, E. J., 726

Pacific Coast Norwegian Singers Assoc., papers, 673
Pacific Lutheran University, papers, 674
Pamphlets, 946
Parkland (Wash.), 310, 674
Park Region Luther College, papers, 675
Parsonages, 399, 754
Pasadena (Calif.), 477
Passavant, W. A., 711
Passenger list, 857
Pastoral Conference, 1884, minutes, 676
Paulsen, Gunder, reminiscences, 677
Paust, Benjamin A., papers, 678
Pedersen, Carl O., papers, 679
Pedersen, Jens C., papers, 680
Pederson, Maren P., biography, 681
Pederson (Sabø), Paul, papers, 682
Peerson, Cleng, papers, 683; 162, 663
Perley (Minn.), 465
Person, Mrs. Nels U., letters, 684
Petersen, Berthe C., papers, 685
Petersen, Franklin, papers, 686; 663, 698

Rice Lake (Wis.), 32
Richards, Richard O., 438
Rippy, Nels A., letter, 725
Ristad, Ditlef G., papers, 726; 12, 246, 697, 733
Ritter, Mattie W., papers, 727
Roalquam, Halvard, papers, 728; 771
Roan, Carl M., family narrative, 729
Roch a Cree Luth. Church, 346
Rock Prairie (Wis.), 524
Rock Run (Ill.), parish, 402
Rockstad, Andres, papers, 730
Roe, Herman, papers, 731
Rølvaag, Ole Edvart, papers, 732; 115, 319, 321, 325, 394, 430, 513, 620, 636, 698, 726, 793, 871
Rølvaag, Jenny (Mrs. O. E.), 12, 733
Rønning, Nils N., papers, 733
Rørvik, Åsmund, 806
Rogstad, Berger and Anna, 355
Roinestad, Soren C., article, 739; 697
Roland (Ia.), 873
Rollag, Austin K., papers, 735
Rollag, Grace, reminiscences, 736
Ronnei Business College, report, 737
Rood, Paul, papers, 738
Roosevelt, Theodore, 261
Root, Elihu, 261
Rorem, Edward, biography, 739
Rosdail (Ill.), 740
Rosdail, Ove, letters, 740
Roseland, J. C., 636
Rosendahl, Peter J., 53
Rosholt (Wis.), 285, 741
Rosholt, Malcolm, papers, 741; 285
Rossing, Lars A., papers, 742
Rosvald (Solveson), Halvor, papers, 743
Roswell, Engebret S., 743
Rove, Olaf I., 328, 744
Rowberg, Andrew A., scrapbooks, 745
Rude, Ole, correspondence, 746
Rulland, Knud O., correspondence, 747
Rundahl (Roundal), Ole, papers, 748
Rushford (Minn.), 71
Rustad, G. O., 900
Ruste (genealogy), 900
Ruste, Erick Olsen, papers, 749
Ruud, Martin B., article, 750; 618
Rye, Haldor O., 717
Rygg, Andreas N., papers, 751; 236, 698, 726

Rynning, Jens, articles, 752
Rynning, Ole, papers, 753; 752

Sacred Heart (Minn.), 63
Sacred Heart News, 182
Særvold, Ola Johann, papers, 754
Sæter Lodge, Sons of Norway, 283
Sageng, Halvor O., brochures, 755
St. Ansgar (Ia.), 756
St. Ansgar Seminary, papers, 756; 436; congregation, 652
St. Olaf College, papers, 757; 279, 346, 436, 542, 705, 711, 712, 715, 732, 771, 804, 859, 862, 876, 899, 930, 934; choir, 865
St. Paul (Minn.), 96, 295, 327, 331, 446, 619
St. Peter (Minn.), 644
St. Petersburg (Fla.), 298
St. Stephen Luth. Church (N.D.), 554
San Francisco (Calif.), 184, 734, 828
San Pedro (Calif.), 47
Sandaker, Arvid, speech, 758
Sandbeck, Oscar P., papers, 759
Sando, Halvor Lars, 898
Sandsvær (Norway), 809
Santa Barbara (Calif.), 42
Santa Fe (N.M.), 740
Sargent County (N.D.), 640
Sather, Anfin O., 17
Saugen, Ivar, 386
Saugstad, Christian T., lecture, 760; 761
Saugstad, Jesse E., biography, 761
Sawyer (Wis.), 661
Saxe, Ludwig, 698
Scandinavia (Wis.), 189, 313, 864
"Scandinavian and American Culture," 819
Scandinavian Lutheran Seamen's Mission, papers, 762
Scandinavian settlements, 687
Scandinavian Sisters of America, newsletter, 763
Scanpresence II Conference, papers, 764
Schaefer, Frederic, correspondence, 765
Schefstad, Jermia, biography, 766
Schenectady (N.Y.), 751
Schern Family, letters, 767
Schevenius, Carl, travel, 768
Schibstad, Torjus, 383
Schilling, W. F., reminiscences, 769